The Raging Hearth

The Raging Hearth

Spirit in the
Household of God

Nancy M. Victorin-Vangerud

Chalice Press.
St. Louis, Missouri

Biblical quotations, unless otherwise noted, are from the *New Revised Standard Version Bible*, copyright 1989, Division of Christian Education of the National Council of the Churches of Christ in the United States of America. Used by permission. All rights reserved.

The prayer by Catherine J. Foote is reproduced from *Survivor Prayers*, © 1994 Catherine J. Foote. Used by permission of Westminster John Knox Press.

Cover Art: Detail of doves drinking in basin, Byzantine mosaic, ca. 425 A.D., Mausoleum of Galla Placidia, Ravenna, Italy. Photograph courtesy of Ken Laurence.
Cover Design: Michael Foley
Art Direction: Michael Domínguez
Interior Design: Wynn Younker

This book is printed on acid-free, recycled paper.

Visit Chalice Press on the World Wide Web at
www.chalicepress.com

10 9 8 7 6 5 4 3 2 1   00 01 02 03

Library of Congress Cataloging–in–Publication Data

Victorin-Vangerud, Nancy M.
   The raging hearth : spirit in the household of God / by Nancy M. Victorin-Vangerud.
     p. cm.
  ISBN 0-8272-3221-7
  1. Holy Spirit. 2. Feminist theology. 3. Family–Religious aspects–Christianity.
I. Title.
  BT121.2.V53   2000   00–008134
  231'.3–dc21   C1P

Printed in the United States of America

For those who walked through fire

When I look at human history, freedom will never be given freely. It's the same with women's rights. If you go out of the church, do you think that society is not patriarchal? There's no way out. The church is also our home, so we have every right to transform our home.

Chung Hyun Kyung

Contents

Preface

Recently, I returned to Perth, Western Australia, with a special memento from a family Christmas visit to Texas. My mother had found a small, glass paperweight I made for my parents as a child. Between the glass and the felt backing was a black and white picture of me—a grinning five year old with short brown hair, wool cap, and buttoned coat—standing in front of my home-town Methodist church's building marquee. The words on the board an-nounced the youth worship service and the theme, "Spirit of God, Descend Upon My Heart." Now, since my current academic research focuses on the relation of theology, family, church, and Spirit, this picture startled me! We may travel great journeys in our lives, but often we come to find ourselves deeply connected to the places and times of our past.

The Raging Hearth is a book about God the Spirit, or pneumatology. *Pneuma* is the Greek word for spirit. In its root meaning, *pneuma* presents a "moving-air metaphor" associated with images of wind, breath, fire, voice, and life.[1] In academic circles of Christian theology, pneumatology means the study of the Spirit, more precisely the third member of the Trinity, the Holy Spirit. In the latter years of the twentieth century, contemporary theology has undertaken a turn to the Spirit. This book offers a feminist analysis of the functioning of Spirit-language in Christian theology by wondering, How does the Spirit func-tion in the divine family, the Trinity?

But first and foremost, *The Raging Hearth* is about human families. In the latter decades of the twentieth century, family has become a contested issue. Changes in family structure from the statistical norms of the 1950s raise seri-ous concerns for the future of human societies. Employment opportunities for women, re-defined gender roles, children's rights, cultural pluralism, and the experiences of lesbians and gays have contributed to the controversy sur-rounding family values. Who defines family, and what are the values needed by families today? Family reformers return to the "traditional" family, while family transformers celebrate the new potential of nontraditional models. Argued from a feminist maternal standpoint, this book affirms mutuality as a

---

[1]Steven G. Smith, *The Concept of the Spiritual: An Essay in First Philosophy* (Philadelphia: Temple University Press, 1988), 9–10, 44.

necessary value of families not only for future family formation, but for theological construction as well.

Some people will say this book is too angry; others will say it is not angry enough. Some critics will conclude that my analysis of family relations dangerously undermines family life; others will argue it doesn't go far enough in re-figuring family relations justly. Some readers will suggest my pneumatological implications distort a Christian understanding of Jesus, church, and Trinity; others will say the implications need to extend much further. This book is based on an expansion of my Ph.D. dissertation, *From Economies of Domination to Economies of Recognition: A Feminist Pneumatology.*[2] It stitches one small patch of the quilt, to use Sallie McFague's image. Or, drawing on Spirit-images, this book speaks one voice among others seeking recognition; it offers one more stick of kindling for the fire of social transformation. My hope is that it will spark much more.

When I was a child, the last thing I ever dreamed I would grow up to be was a theologian, and I'm sure I would not have been able to pronounce, let alone comprehend, the word *pneumatology*! But here I am now, teaching a graduate seminar on "Turning to the Spirit in Contemporary Theology" as a white, North American woman in a Western Australian university. The Spirit blows freely, and my children, husband, and I have found our new home in Perth to be a rich, beautiful, and gifted place.

But growing up in the Methodist Church of white, suburban New Jersey during the 1960s and 1970s, I cannot remember a specific awareness of God as Spirit. Certainly the congregation was a warm-hearted mob, busy with being a nurturing community of potlucks and programs, but the focus was always on the second person of the Trinity, Jesus the Son. Language about God the Spirit was tacked on to the ends of prayers, doxologies, and benedictions almost as an afterthought, a ritualistic formality. While I now understand that the language of "Holy Ghost" has been, and continues to be, a vital part of other Christian traditions, and even streams of Methodism, as a child this language seemed irrelevant and even strange to me.

Christocentric Protestantism carried me through an active youth ministry as a teen, an evangelical awakening in young adulthood, and a conversion to the discipleship of social justice as a graduate student at Scarritt College, and later at Vanderbilt Divinity School, both in Nashville, Tennessee. When I first seriously contemplated Ph.D. work, I proposed a study of the burgeoning field of feminist and womanist christologies. The writings of Rita Nakashima Brock, Chung Hyun Kyung, Mary Daly, Elisabeth Schüssler Fiorenza, Jacquelyn Grant, Carter Heyward, Mercy Amba Oduyoye, Rosemary Radford Ruether, Letty Russell, and others had raised vital challenges for the person and work of Jesus Christ. At the time, the figure of Christ presented the crucial key for liberating and transforming Christian traditions.

---

[2]Nancy M. Victorin-Vangerud, "From Economies of Domination to Economies of Recognition: A Feminist Pneumatology" (Ph.D. diss., Vanderbilt University, 1996).

But in my own research, I felt that I had come to a roadblock. Feminist christology seemed to reach not so much a dead end, but a point of needing connection or depth within a larger theological matrix. Re-imagining the figure of Christ, even as a communal symbol, was important, but still not sufficient in moving beyond modern autonomous notions of selfhood to an intersubjective paradigm. "How do we image human wholeness?" was the question fueling feminist christology's vision. To answer this question, I decided that any conception of "life in Christ" would benefit from a renewed relationship with biblical, historical, and contemporary voices of "life in the Spirit." Human wholeness, or salvation, could only be imagined and sought within a paradigm of right relationship, interdependence, and cosmic breadth. From my perspective, the language of Christ and church needed larger framing within the language of Spirit and life. Spirit signified the shared breath, the shared struggle for life in all its abundance (Jn. 10:10).

Several events came together, instigating a shift in my dissertation focus from christology to pneumatology. In 1991, Chung Hyun Kyung set fire to the World Council of Churches at the Seventh Assembly gathering in Canberra, Australia. The pneumatological theme for the assembly proved an ecumenical first, "Come Holy Spirit—Renew the Whole Creation." While I did not attend the Seventh Assembly, the study guides, journal articles, media coverage, and videotapes provided a creative and evocative body of material for exploring pneumatological themes. I realized that Pentecostal and charismatic traditions, while contributing valuable legacies, were not the only Christian traditions with vital witnesses to God the Spirit. Life in the Spirit of God constitutes a polyvocal life in which diversity may be valued, even encouraged, for vocations of entering more deeply into the Triune fellowship of compassion and justice.

While the Seventh Assembly sparked my imagination and passion, the academic influences of my teachers at Vanderbilt further contributed to the shift from christology to pneumatology. Sallie McFague's metaphorical theology prompted questions about the role of Spirit in various models of God. Feminist theology was examining the function of Father and Son language in patriarchal models of God—why not now explore the function of Spirit-language? Peter Hodgson's critical retrieval of Hegel as a theologian of Spirit introduced me to the concept of mutual recognition (*Anerkennung*), which is further explored in the work of philosophers Robert R. Williams and Charles Taylor, but is also used by feminist psychoanalyst Jessica Benjamin. Recognition refers to the dialogical, even conflictual, constitution of self and other in relations of respect, dignity, and value. For me, recognition became the hermeneutical key for a feminist pneumatology.

But the outpouring of research concerning the Spirit in the last ten years inspired me as well. Certainly earlier in this century, Paul Tillich and Karl Rahner wrote substantial works with a pneumatological character. But recently, José Comblin, Gordon Fee, Colin Gunton, Peter Hodgson, Elizabeth Johnson, Sallie McFague, Anselm Min, Jürgen Moltmann, Geiko Mühler-Fahrenholz,

Krister Stendahl, Michael Welker, Mark I. Wallace, and many others (beyond the scope of my limited study) have been crucial in shaping, through a variety of perspectives, a pneumatological landscape for theology. But many more voices representing the rich legacies of Christian traditions and the many social/cultural contexts of Christian faith are needed today. Through *The Raging Hearth*, I make my own contribution, one located within the (wide) standpoint of feminist theology.

But turning to the Spirit has also come from a personal transformation. In 1991, my first son, Aaron, was born, and Will was born in 1997. Becoming a mother brought the context of raising children to the fore of my feminist theological awareness. But as Bonnie Miller-McLemore argues, family life provides a vantage point from which to engage not only contemporary culture, but feminism as well. A feminist *maternal* perspective provides theology with new eyes. Yet family life can be a struggle even for adults committed to new forms of mutuality. I found that criticism of the male-headship model in family life had to extend to the relational qualities embodied in the patriarchal family, no matter the sex of the parent caring for children. The new struggles of motherhood implicated my own tendencies toward the relational dynamics of unilateral power, blind trust, and controlling authority. Commitment to mutual recognition raised the question of how seriously I take my children as "others" to whom I am accountable, responsible, and respondable. Were they not others requiring respect, proper trust, and dignity in their differences from me? Feminist democratic values meet their match in relations with children, which I hope can embody mutuality as the *telos*. Sarah Ruddick's theory of maternal thinking, Alice Miller's concept of poisonous pedagogy, and Jessica Benjamin's use of recognition in family relations underwrite my feminist maternal analysis of patriarchal family relations.

The journey as a feminist theologian and parent brought me to the point of wondering about the relationship in theology between models of the Spirit and models of family life. Rita Nakashima Brock claims that "patriarchal family relationships are the bricks of the patriarch's theological house of worship."[3] She joins Sallie McFague in analyzing the male-headed family of unilateral power as one of the formative models for Christian theological language and communal practice. Thus, the first part of a feminist analysis traces the way language of God the Spirit functions within patriarchal churches and theologies. But then the second part of a feminist analysis is a re-constructive move that privileges nonpatriarchal models of family life. This is not to say that family should remain the *primary* model for theological construction. In fact, I argue family models retain grave limitations. Yet if nonpatriarchal norms are valued in family relationships, will different understandings or roles of the Spirit come to light? Will there be pneumatological "fruit" for our families, congregations, communities, and world?

---

[3]Rita Nakashima Brock, *Journeys By Heart: A Christology of Erotic Power* (New York: Crossroad, 1988), 4.

In *The Raging Hearth*, I propose that an analogy exists between the distortion or lack of recognition in the patriarchal family and the distortion or lack of recognition in Christian theologies and communities taking the patriarchal family as their social norm. In theologies and communities that privilege the male-headship model of family, the language of Spirit functions to reduce (and even collapse) the space for recognition between self and other, thus reinforcing conformity, promoting homogeneity, and increasing fear of difference and conflict. The Spirit domesticates members of the "household of God" (Eph. 2:19) through what I term a *poisonous pneumatology* and orders the Many (members of the body) under the will of the One (the head). Thus, in this model, "unity" in the Spirit functions as a discourse of regulation, discipline, and oppression, creating persons of docility and usefulness. I hope the experiences of families struggling for new modes of mutuality challenge the normativity of the patriarchal family model and make positive contributions to theological construction. "We are one in the Spirit" need not mean we are all the same.

But while the ideas of my inquiry were forged within the generally personal and private context of parenthood, they had the opportunity for stoking within a very public and professional context. In 1993 I was appointed minister of education to a large, urban United Methodist church. I thought I would have plenty of time to both write my dissertation and lead an adult education ministry. Within two weeks of beginning my appointment, the lead pastor resigned amid allegations of sexual misconduct. Suddenly, all my thoughts about pneumatology, the abuse of power, and the struggle for recognition loomed larger than life within the body of my new "church family." The congregation entered a crisis and the processes for response became chaotic. In fact, new processes of justice, care, and healing had to be discovered in, through, and with the chaos. In the patriarchal model of Spirit, sexual misconduct victims would have been silenced and marginalized (and this did happen at first). Instead, the congregation struggled to discern and risk the empowerment of God's Spirit in the work of recognition for victims-turned-survivors, which eventually led to an examination and transformation of the whole congregational life. The support group for survivors and complainants, in which I participated as an advocate, experienced the Spirit, holy, as energy for life in the midst of life's most fragile, threatened, and raging moments. Looking back, I believe the Spirit energized a *We who are* in the midst of struggle.

Since this is a book on the Spirit (which seems such a weighty contradiction for a moving-air subject), I thought it important to testify to the story behind the text. The narrative leads to the following organization of theological analysis and re-construction: Chapter 1 introduces the subject of pneumatology through the dynamic presentation of Chung Hyun Kyung at the World Council of Churches' Seventh Assembly. What happened when a young Korean theologian speaking from a liberation perspective raised *her* challenging voice at the family "reunion" of churches? What embers sparked in the hearth of the ecumenical household? How was her call for mutual recognition heeded? What can we learn about pneumatology from the Seventh Assembly proceedings? Canberra's household controversy provides an incendiary case study for themes vital to the study of family and Spirit.

Chapter 2 shifts to contemporary theology's academic turn to God the Spirit. While offering a limited introduction, I focus on the primary pneumatological resources contributing to my own metaphorical analysis. I argue that the turn to the Spirit warrants neither the label of modern revival nor postmodern play, but actually signifies a liminal move toward a post-secular age of spirituality. In Christian circles, churches plan hopefully for the "third" millennium as a new Pentecost drawing the churches together and out into the rest of the world in new ways. Echoing across contemporary pneumatologies can be heard the shared concerns for liberation, life, and diversity-in-unity.

Chapters 3 and 4 form a parallel study on the controversial character of family life in contemporary North American society. Chapter 3 traces the arguments between family reformers and transformers in response to the family revolution of the second half of the twentieth century. While reformers return to the "traditional" family as the ideal, transformers show the historical roots of this family form in modern industrial capitalism. Nostalgia for the traditional (patriarchal) family further neglects and even mystifies the realities of paternal (and maternal) domination and abuse. Postmodern feminist families re-figure family life according to new family values of mutuality, equal regard, and diversity, offering new models for the common ground of concern for families emerging in society.

Chapter 4 examines the revolution in church life as viewed through the formative model of family. The household of God has also undergone challenges to its family values of male authority, clerical power, heterosexual normativity, and adult privilege. As with family nostalgia, church nostalgia for a glorious institutional past hides the realities of domination and abuse. Church transformers seek new models of ecclesiastical life based on new church values of mutuality, equal regard, and diversity. By viewing chapters 3 and 4 together, we can see how new models of family life contribute to new models of church life and vice versa. The parallel analysis shows the transformative potential of mutual recognition in households of families and churches.

Taking a deeper look at the dynamics of patriarchal family values, chapter 5 offers a feminist maternal meditation on the significance of recognition. Since the new values of mutuality, equal regard, and diversity comprise part of the work of recognition, the patriarchal family may be assessed as a relational system in which mutual recognition breaks down. The relation of self and other twists so that the other serves only to reflect the distorted subjectivity of the head. Through poisonous pedagogy, family members learn conformist ways of relating that minimize or avoid conflict. The particular embodiment or otherness of family members becomes, in effect, domesticated and subordinated. Movement toward mutual recognition thus entails the struggle of self-assertion, differentiation, and conflict. A feminist maternal standpoint reclaims this struggle as essential for just and free relations.

The feminist maternal hermeneutic of mutual recognition provides the investigative framework in chapter 6 for examining how Spirit-language and family models functioned in early Christian communities and theologies. From the beginning, tension existed between Christian communities that on one hand continued to retain ancient Mediterranean family values (though they may have modified them to a degree) and on the other hand embraced transformed models of household order. Chapter 6 analyzes the shift in Spirit-language as Aristotelian household codes became normative for communal life, casting the work of the Spirit in terms of order and regulation. From a feminist maternal standpoint, this move had a domesticating effect on gifted household members. I argue that once patriarchal norms were reinforced within families and churches, poisonous pneumatologies came to function within early church theologies.

Chapter 7 jumps from the ancient Mediterranean world to our contemporary day for a more detailed presentation of contemporary theology's turn to the Spirit. I present the recent pneumatological work of three primary figures–Jürgen Moltmann, Michael Welker, and Colin Gunton. Their varied perspectives make valuable contributions toward new social models of diversity-in-unity, but a feminist maternal hermeneutic of mutual recognition highlights obstacles in the pneumatologies with poisonous potential. Each theologian associates God the Spirit with a privileged norm of Jesus' personhood–his self-surrender, self-withdrawal, and self-giving sacrifice–which from the perspective of survivors diminishes possibilities for healing, wholeness, and reconciliation. A richer, more complex portrait of Jesus' personhood discloses the self-commitment, self-assertion, and self-care of Jesus in the midst of struggle for God's kin-dom. A feminist maternal standpoint refines and strengthens contemporary pneumatological options by questioning sacrificial obstacles, which ultimately undermine the powerful vision of diversity in the Spirit.

But what about women's pneumatologies? During previous decades, women have been exploring spirituality, but now the turn to the Spirit infuses women with new energy for new theological directions. In chapter 8 I claim that while women's systematic or constructive efforts regarding the Spirit have begun, much of women's contextual work, following Mary Daly's radical challenge, has been focused on christology–with good reason. I suggest a trajectory in the development of women's contextual christologies from first re-figuring the subjectivity of Jesus; to second, re-figuring the subjectivity of Christ; to then third, re-figuring an intersubjective Christa/Community. But the move to relational, intersubjective models actually offers a fourth creative option involving the shift from women's contextual christologies to women's contextual pneumatologies. Women's concerns for spirituality now find hopeful possibilities in a deeper connection with models of the Spirit.

In chapter 9 I present a feminist maternal pneumatology of mutual recognition based on the values of postmodern feminist families. Building a new hearth for family life, the values of mutuality, proper trust, and self-assertion likewise build a new hearth for the household of God, the church. But today's hearth of mutual recognition finds resonance in the biblical narrative of the

Gentile Pentecost (Acts 10–11:15), where the Gentiles' inclusion in God's household of dignity creates conflict and the renegotiation of identity for the "elder" household members. Through the cunning of diversity, the Spirit energizes communal life inclusive of others whose differences are not diminished or marginalized in the struggle. Yet today, in living toward the ideal of mutual recognition in families and churches, we revisit household fears to discover new fruits of the Spirit necessary for initiating and sustaining the struggle. Mutual recognition as dignified diversity challenges models of social headship not only in families and churches, but in Trinitarian theology as well.

Many thanks need to be passed around. First, I am thankful for the family I was born into and the family into which I married. Both continue to nurture and challenge me as part of the ongoing generational flow of life. I celebrate my children, Aaron and Will, definitely the greatest teachers of mutual recognition, and my husband and partner, Bob. There never seems to be enough time for all the bike rides, bush walks, and beach swims we enjoy so much.

Besides Sallie McFague and Peter Hodgson, I am also thankful for my other Vanderbilt teachers over the years–Don Beisswenger, David Buttrick, Edward Farley, Jack Forstman, John Lachs, Charles Scott, Fernando Segovia, Eugene TeSelle, Mary Ann Tolbert, and Peggy Way. Lloyd Lewis also deserves a note of thanks for friendship and encouragement. I am grateful to Vanderbilt University for granting me the Harold Stirling Vanderbilt Scholarship for my years of Ph.D. study. But then I also want to thank my "mates" of the Graduate Department of Religion–Joyce Arnold, Eleazar Fernandez, Mark Justad, Anne McWilliams, Darby Ray, Laurel Schneider, and Holly Toensing.

Friends over the years have been generous–Alix Evans, Nancy and Larry Hendry, Phil and Cathy Cralle Jones, and Paul and Mary Tuttle. Betty Schilling continues to share her great sense of humor, perspective, and compassion. Thanks also to Sallie Gibson Holmes, with whom I continue to share the journey–inward and outward.

I am grateful to Murdoch University, the Uniting Church Synod of Western Australia, and my colleagues Bill Loader and Sue Boorer for inviting me to teach and learn, speak and listen to what nonindigenous Australians are coming to know (and Aboriginal Australians have always known) in the land of the Spirit. Students and new friends have graciously extended their hospitality, tolerated my pronunciations, and shared their deep sense of place.

Two symposiums have given me the opportunity to participate with other scholars of pneumatology. Thank you to Bradford Hinze and Lyle Dabney of Marquette University, who organized the 1998 event "Advent of the Spirit: Orientations in Pneumatology." Thank you also to Hilary Regan and the Australian Theological Forum for inviting me this year to Canberra for "The Task of Theology Today: Tracking the Spirit in Tradition and Contemporary Thought." The conversations and challenges shared with symposium participants have been invaluable.

I want to extend a special thanks to Jon L. Berquist of Chalice Press for his encouragement and support through the various extended stages of writing this manuscript. I am grateful for his collaboration, skill, and insight that recognized the strengths within my work.

Last, I want to thank Val Webb—artist, theologian, friend, and colleague—who invited me to coteach with her for four excellent years the "Theology for the '90s" class in Rochester, Minnesota. To that small community of inquiring spirits and those special persons of the clergy sexual misconduct support group, I am sincerely grateful for their wisdom, courage, and companionship through the crucible of recognition. May this book honor our common vision in the Spirit of God.

Nancy Victorin-Vangerud
September 1999

CHAPTER 1

An Incendiary Household

Sisters and brothers—Arise.

Arise and lift your hearts

Arise and lift your eyes

Arise and lift your voices.

The living God,

the living, moving Spirit of God

has called us together—

in witness

in celebration

in struggle.

Reach out towards each other,

for our God reaches out towards us!

Let us worship God![1]

Come, Holy Spirit!

The following case study introduces pneumatology as a subject of new theological interest and sets forth the thematic relationship of household, family, and Spirit.[2] The case study involves specific events of the World Council of Churches' Seventh Assembly, held in Canberra, Australia, in 1991. While the WCC is formally understood as a fellowship of churches, informally, family metaphors are used to express the unity or interrelations of Christian churches. For example, in his "Report of the General Secretary to the Seventh Assembly," Emilio Castro referred several times to the WCC as an "ecumenical family."[3] But the analogy of family and church is not new. Biblical writers

---

[1]World Council of Churches, *In Spirit and in Truth: Prayers to the Holy Spirit* (Geneva: World Council of Churches, 1991), 4.

[2]*A New Dictionary of Christian Theology*, ed. Alan Richardson and John Bowden (London: SCM Press, 1983) defines pneumatology as "derived from Greek *pneuma*, spirit: the branch of theology which deals with the doctrine of the (Holy) Spirit" (451).

[3]Emilio Castro, "Report of the General Secretary," *Signs of the Spirit: Official Report of the Seventh Assembly*, ed. Michael Kinnamon (Geneva: WCC Publications, 1991), 161–65.

employed a variety of family images, including children and heirs (Gal. 4:5–7), brethren (1 Thess. 4:1), and household of God (Eph. 2:19), to characterize Christian communal life. Thus, when ecumenists use family or household analogies, they draw on a deep legacy within Christian tradition.[4]

So what happened in Canberra when the ecumenical family experienced a household crisis in theological dialogue? Chung Hyun Kyung's dramatic presentation on the Seventh Assembly theme, "Come Holy Spirit–Renew the Whole Creation," provides a rich context for examining the proposal that models of family influence both theological language and church practice. The first section of this chapter places the ecumenical household study in a global context. Throughout what Martin Luther King, Jr., called the "great world house," the groans and cries of struggling people have made claims upon the global house rules.[5] Will humanity embrace a revolution of values, recognizing our differences not as sources of threat, but of enrichment? In the second section, I turn to the context of Christianity and argue that theologies of struggle and liberation, which have arisen from the groans and cries of the world, mark a new Pentecost in the life of Christian churches. The later sections of the chapter trace the impact of Chung Hyun Kyung's address, as she brought the world's groans and cries directly into the family gathering of churches. Will acknowledging diversity within the ecumenical household threaten or strengthen Christian unity in the Spirit of God?

The Great World House

Leaf through advertisements in major magazines or newspapers and one central image stands out–our world as a vast blue-green globe. In glossy ads for everything from travel to computers to coffee, our world is portrayed as one great global village bustling with unique experiences and the latest goods. The sky-view perspective gives the impression that we stand poised on the edge of a new millennium without the limits of time and space. National borders give way to cosmopolitan identities. Talk of globalization creates an optimistic air of power and plentitude. Now the world is our marketplace, and we have access at a fingertip!

But underneath the glossy images lies another story–in fact, many stories, a world of other stories–and as Charles Villa-Vicencio writes, "We need to tell one another stories."[6] From various parts of the village come stories of disease, hunger, poverty, and violence. Other villagers tell of loneliness, spiritual malaise, and lives with little hope or meaning. Burdened with so much debt, some villagers claim that total remittance remains the only way forward. Deforestation, ocean warming, species loss, and pollution constitute

---

[4]Lesslie Newbigin, *The Household of God: Lectures on the Nature of the Church* (London: SCM Press, 1957).

[5]Martin Luther King, Jr., *Where Do We Go From Here: Chaos or Community?* (Boston: Beacon Press, 1967), 167.

[6]Charles Villa-Vicencio, "Telling One Another Stories," in *The Reconciliation of Peoples: Challenge to the Churches*, ed. Gregory Baum and Harold Wells (Maryknoll, N.Y.: Orbis Books, 1997), 31.

precarious times for the village's habitat. From one end to the other, neighbors threaten neighbors with land mines, machetes, and nuclear weapons. War conscripts armies of children and creates refugee tent cities on the edges of the village. Great disparities in wealth and other resources afflict the village, but much of the disparity lies concealed and forgotten in day-to-day struggles. If the world is a global village, certainly cries of anguish and rage echo among the homefires.

Yet contemporary authors use the image of a "sacred balance" to describe the intricate relatedness of life on our blue-green planet.[7] Others talk of the world as a living, sacred being, or *Gaia*.[8] These images call attention to our world as a holistic dwelling place. In 1967, Martin Luther King, Jr., used the image of a world house to address the interdependent yet estranged relations of humanity. From the heat of the civil rights struggle, King wrote:

> This is the great new problem of [human] kind. We have inherited a large house, a great "world house" in which we have to live together—black and white, Easterner and Westerner, Gentile and Jew, Catholic and Protestant, Moslem and Hindu—because we can never again live apart, must learn somehow to live with each other in peace.[9]

King envisioned a global revolution of values inspiring human beings to live together peacefully. The differences between people of culture and race, religion and nationality must change from being perceived as sources of antagonism to sources of richness and dignity. If estrangement among household members continued, King warned, future generations would annihilate each other.[10]

King's image of the great world house continues to speak to us today; likewise his grave warning. With the stakes of social, political, economic, and ecological estrangement rising higher with each passing year, humanity requires a revolution of values. While his words depict a global human family, King's values of other-preservation, other-concern, and the interdependency of all life lead in the direction of incorporating an environmental ethic into the world house.[11] Thus, the image of the great world house encompasses the ecological sensibilities that we have today. By drawing on King's global household image, a variety of meanings can be gathered together from the heart of the Jewish and Christian traditions.[12] In Greek the word for household is

---

[7]For example, see Albert Gore, *Earth in Balance: Ecology and the Human Spirit* (Boston: Houghton Mifflin, 1992); and David Suzuki, *The Sacred Balance of Life: Rediscovering Our Place in Nature* (St. Leonards, New South Wales: Allen & Unwin, 1997).

[8]For example, see James E. Lovelock, *The Ages of Gaia: A Biography of Our Living Earth* (Oxford: Oxford University Press, 1988); and Rosemary Radford Ruether, *Gaia & God: An Ecofeminist Theology of Earth Healing* (San Francisco: HarperSanFrancisco, 1992).

[9]King, Jr., 167.

[10]Ibid., 186–91.

[11]Garth Baker-Fletcher, *Somebodyness: Martin Luther King, Jr., and the Theory of Dignity* (Minneapolis: Fortress Press, 1993), 170–71.

[12]On the rich associations of this concept, see M. Douglas Meeks, *God the Economist: The Doctrine of God and Political Economy* (Minneapolis: Fortress Press, 1989), 2–13.

oikos. Related to *oikos* is *oikonomia*, meaning household management or economy, and *oikonomos*, or steward. The Greek term *oikoumene* refers to the whole inhabited world and thus shows its connections with our term *ecology*. But in Christian ecumenical circles, *oikoumene* connotes God's worldly habitation with all creation. We can remember the psalmist's words, "O LORD, how manifold are your works! In wisdom you have made them all; the earth is full of your creatures" (Ps. 104:24).

The image of Earth as a great world house calls us to account for our past and present household participation. Do the global household rules contribute toward a peaceable world house or, as Don Messer wonders, to "world havoc"?[13] What are the living conditions for members of the world house? How are food, water, air, and other household goods shared? Who is recognized within the household? Who is not? What kind of householder is God? How do we characterize the *oikonomia tou theou,* God's economy of life in the world? Do our theologies help or hinder us in living together in God's household? What new theological vision do we need? Eleazar Fernandez claims that "when theology itself has become instrumental in the subjugation of the people, theology is one area where struggle has to be waged."[14] King's voice is one of many who challenge not only modern ideologies of progress, but Christian complicity with global household management that recognizes some householders to the exclusion of the dignity of others.

Images of the blue-green house from miles above (the penthouse view?) may appeal to the idea that our house is in order and all is well. It is a pleasing, beautiful view and in profound moments may inspire us to attend to our world in new ways. But a view of the house from below, on the ground, tells other stories. All is not well within the great world house. Groans and cries can be heard from the homefires of Jasper, Kosovo, Laramie, Jakarta, Johannesburg, and many other villages.[15] Household members raise their voices in calling attention to their marginalized presence and challenging the global house rules. Will the household groans be heard? For King, the choice was clear: "Together we must learn to live as brothers [and sisters] or together we will be forced to perish as fools."[16]

A New Pentecost

The title of this book, *The Raging Hearth: Spirit in the Household of God,* plays with the image of fire as a metaphor for the Spirit. In nearly all cultures,

---

[13]Don Messer, *A Conspiracy of Goodness: Contemporary Images of Christian Mission* (Nashville: Abingdon Press, 1992), 45–66.

[14]Eleazar S. Fernandez, *Toward a Theology of Struggle* (Maryknoll, N.Y.: Orbis Books, 1994), 32.

[15]In Jasper, Texas, James Byrd, Jr., was murdered by white racists. In Kosovo, ethnic Albanians have been found slaughtered in mass graves. In Laramie, Wyoming, gay student Matthew Shepard was murdered. In Jakarta, students protest the privileges and abuses of the political and economic oligarchy. From Johannesburg come stories of suffering told through South Africa's Truth and Reconciliation Commission.

[16]King, Jr., 171.

the survival of the family, clan, or community depends on fire for cooking, warmth, protection, communal gathering, ritual, and craft.[17] Some groups carefully protect coals from one day's activities to the next. For other people, a large brick hearth provides the focal point for household activity. In yet other cultures, people gather around a sleek fireplace, even though the household activities of cooking and cleaning are carried out in an electric or gas kitchen. Symbolizing energy or transformation, fire represents creative and destructive forces, both necessary for life. Thus, fire is instilled with sacred meaning and divine power.[18] For example, ancient Greek culture venerated Hestia, goddess of the household hearth.[19] Throughout religious history, the divine empowerment of life has been imaged as fire burning in the hearth.

In the New Testament, fire and the household hearth connect with images of breath and wind to narrate the genesis of the universal Christian church. As God brought forth the living earth creature from the dust of the ground with God's creative, energizing breath (Gen. 2:7), so God breathed reviving energy upon the ashen coals of the Jesus movement. The biblical account in Acts 2:1–4 reads:

> When the day of Pentecost had come, they were all together in one place. And suddenly from heaven there came a sound like the rush of a violent wind, and it filled the entire house where they were sitting. Divided tongues, as of fire, appeared among them…All of them were filled with the Holy Spirit and began to speak in other languages, as the Spirit gave them ability.

On Pentecost Sunday, Christian communities around the world celebrate the global church's incendiary ignition point. The most prominent Pentecost symbol is the flame, the fiery energy of God's Spirit, who empowered the vulnerable, fragmented body of believers with voices for God's ongoing ministries. Pentecost's pageantry evokes images of the many-membered body of Christ, the new *oikos,* or household of spiritual diversity-in-unity.[20] But Pentecost's fire was no gentle burn. The "empowering presence" of God the Spirit turned ashen coals into a raging hearth that transformed the entire household.[21]

Today, the fiery Spirit of God continues energizing new communities within the ecumenical church fellowship. Pentecostal churches and charismatic movements make spiritual contributions through their traditions'

---

[17]Carl-Martin Edsman, "Fire," in *The Encyclopedia of Religion,* vol. 5, ed. Mircea Eliade (New York: Macmillan, 1987), 340–46.

[18]E. M. Good, "Fire," in *The Interpreter's Dictionary of the Bible,* ed. George Arthur Buttrick, vol. 2 (Nashville: Abingdon Press, 1962), 268–69.

[19]Carolyn Osiek, "The Family in Early Christianity," *Catholic Biblical Quarterly* 58 (1996): 14.

[20]Peter C. Hodgson, *Winds of the Spirit: A Constructive Theology* (Louisville, Ky.: Westminster John Knox Press, 1994), 295–99.

[21]Gordon Fee, *God's Empowering Presence: The Holy Spirit in the Letters of Paul* (Peabody, Mass.: Hendrickson, 1994), 8, 229.

experiences of baptism in the Spirit, glossolalia, healing, and gifts of the Spirit.[22] Representing vital dimensions of ecumenical mission, these churches and movements claim nearly 500 million members worldwide and add 19 million members a year.[23] Many cries and groans of suffering household members have found recognition and hope within Pentecostal and charismatic communities.

But Pentecostal churches and charismatic movements are not the only Christian communities manifesting "energies of the Spirit" in God's economy.[24] Fueling theologies of struggle and liberation, the stories "from below" or from "the underside of history" currently challenge the house rules of Christian traditions and globalized societies.[25] These challenges emerge in the Spirit from the "groans of creation" (Rom. 8:22), suffering inequitable human systems in what José Miguez Bonino describes as "an *oikoumene* of domination."[26] Recognizing a common householder status for all people, theologies of struggle and liberation address social, political, cultural, economic, and personal

---

[22]Recent resources include Jürgen Moltmann and Karl-Josef Kuschel, "Pentecostal Movements as an Ecumenical Challenge," *Concilium* no. 3 (London: SCM Press, 1996); Nigel Scotland, *Charismatics and the Next Millennium: Do They Have a Future?* (London: Hodder & Stoughton, 1995); Jean-Jacques Suurmond, *Word and Spirit at Play: Towards a Charismatic Theology* (London: SCM Press, 1994); Eldin Villafáne, *The Liberating Spirit: Toward an Hispanic American Pentecostal Social Ethic* (Lanham, Md.: University Press of America, 1992); and Keith Warrington, *Pentecostal Perspectives* (Carlisle, U.K.: Paternoster Press, 1998).

[23]Walter J. Hollenweger, *Pentecostalism: Origins and Developments Worldwide* (Peabody, Mass.: Hendrickson Publishing, 1997), 1.

[24]Krister Stendahl uses the Orthodox image "energies of the Spirit" in characterizing God the Spirit as the energizing source of all of life. See his Seventh Assembly resource, *Energy for Life: Reflections on the Theme "Come Holy Spirit, Renew the Whole Creation"* (Geneva: World Council of Churches, 1990).

[25]I am linking together theologies of struggle and liberation, though both have different bearings. From his context of struggle in the Philippines, Fernandez makes a distinction between theologies of liberation and theologies of struggle. The latter are rooted in the struggle of people *for* liberation; thus, the focus is on the immediacy of the struggle: "Liberation is still the direction of the theology of struggle, but the focus of the theology of struggle is on the struggle" (*Toward a Theology of Struggle*, 23). Classically, liberation theology had its genesis in Latin American Catholicism, yet the movement connects with other struggles for liberation such as black theology, womanist theology, feminist theology, and ecotheology. See Gustavo Gutiérrez, *A Theology of Liberation: History, Politics and Salvation*, trans. and ed. Sister Caridad Inda and John Eagleson (Maryknoll, N.Y.: Orbis Books, 1973); Rebecca S. Chopp, *The Praxis of Suffering: An Interpretation of Liberation and Political Theologies* (Maryknoll, N.Y.: Orbis Books, 1986); Leonardo Boff and Clodovis Boff, *Introducing Liberation Theology* (Maryknoll, N.Y.: Orbis Books, 1993); James H. Cone, *A Black Theology of Liberation* (Philadelphia: J. B. Lippincott, 1970); Delores S. Williams, *Sisters in the Wilderness: The Challenge of Womanist God-Talk* (Maryknoll, N.Y.: Orbis Books, 1993); Rosemary Radford Ruether, *Sexism and God-Talk: Toward a Feminist Theology* (Boston: Beacon Press, 1983); and Charles Birch, William Eakin, and Jay B. McDaniel, eds., *Liberating Life: Contemporary Approaches to Ecological Theology* (Maryknoll, N.Y.: Orbis Books, 1990). While acknowledging the contextual differences between theologies of struggle and liberation, I draw on them collectively, as in Susan Brooks Thistlethwaite and Mary Potter Engel, eds., *Lift Every Voice: Constructing Christian Theologies from the Underside* (San Francisco: HarperSanFrancisco, 1990). Together they call attention to the multifaceted, interrelated oppressions, inequities, and structural sins of historical life.

[26]In Thomas Wieser, ed., *Whither Ecumenism? A Dialogue in the Transit Lounge of the Ecumenical Movement* (Geneva: World Council of Churches, 1986), 29–30, quoted by Konrad Raiser, *Ecumenism in Transition: A Paradigm Shift in the Ecumenical Movement?* (Geneva: World Council of Churches, 1991), 63–64.

renovations necessary for the great world house.[27] The groans and cries of suffering household members seek "total deliverance," including liberation beyond a strictly religious or private realm.[28] Chung Hyun Kyung's presentation at the Seventh Assembly made clear that movements within Christian traditions from the perspective of struggle and liberation are also movements of the Spirit. The Canberra case study presents theologies of struggle and liberation as a new Pentecost not only for Christian traditions, but for the great world house as well. The raging hearth within the ecumenical household burns not only for inner renewal, but with fiery tongues for worldly transformation.

Canberra–The Seventh Assembly

Contemporary theologies of the Spirit stand indebted to the 1991 World Council of Churches' Seventh Assembly in Canberra, Australia. While God the Spirit was the subject of twentieth-century theological works prior to the 1990s, the preparations surrounding the Seventh Assembly theme, "Come Holy Spirit–Renew the Whole Creation," provided a focused opportunity for pneumatological study.[29] But the Assembly provided an additional creative, yet controversial, spark for theology's turn to the Spirit. Amid Korean *minjung* and Australian Aboriginal dancers, Korean theologian Chung Hyun Kyung presented an incendiary interpretation of the theme that challenged the unity of the ecumenical family.[30] While some Assembly delegates viewed Canberra as a breakdown, others deemed the Assembly a breakthrough, a theological turning point for discerning the person and work of God the Spirit today.[31]

---

[27]José Comblin, *Called for Freedom: The Changing Context of Liberation Theology* (Maryknoll, N.Y.: Orbis Books, 1998).

[28]Fernandez, 41.

[29]Seventh Assembly materials include: *Come Holy Spirit, Renew the Whole Creation: Six Bible Studies* (Geneva: World Council of Churches, 1989); *Let the Spirit Speak to the Churches: A Guide for the Study of the Theme and the Issues* (Geneva: World Council of Churches, 1990); and *The World Council of Churches Seventh Assembly 1991: Resources for Sections–The Theme, Sub-themes and Issues* (Geneva: World Council of Churches, 1990).

[30]The choice of Canberra as the site for the Seventh Assembly carried important implications for the Spirit theme. Australia may have received its Western name through the initial efforts of Pedro Ferdinandez de Quiros, a Portuguese explorer in the service of Spain. After a pilgrimage to Rome, Quiros believed he had been called by God to bring the true faith to God's adopted children in "the great south land." When he reached the New Hebrides in 1605, he thought he had reached his destination and named the land *Australia del Espiritu Santo*, the "South Land of the Holy Spirit." But as Denis Edwards reflects on the irony of the situation, "Quiros never did arrive in the great south land and never met its inhabitants. But his name for this country was perfectly apt. Australia was, and is the South Land of the Holy Spirit. Quiros had no way of knowing that the people of the south land had lived there for up to 50,000 years. He imagined them living in the darkness of unbelief. He could not have understood that, although they had never heard the good news of salvation in Jesus, they had learned to listen to the Spirit of God moving across the land of Australia" (98). See his chapter, "Sin and Salvation in the South Land of the Holy Spirit," in *Discovering an Australian Theology*, ed. Peter Malone (Homebush, New South Wales: St. Paul Publications, 1988), 89–102.

[31]Larry Rasmussen and Joseph Bush, Jr., "Breakdown or Breakthrough?" *Ecumenical Review* 44 (July 1992): 285.

The following case study highlights theological contributions and issues arising from the Seventh Assembly relevant to the association of Spirit and family household. In light of Canberra, it is important to note that four of the six previous assemblies bore christological themes.[32] The Seventh Assembly theme, "Come Holy Spirit–Renew the Whole Creation," was chosen as a prayer in 1987, according to Emilio Castro, "under the full sway of the Cold War, the threat of nuclear catastrophe, [and] a prevailing mood of powerlessness. The invocation of the Holy Spirit was conceived as an affirmation in God's resources to lead us into the unknown and uncertain future."[33] But in the years leading up to 1991, dramatic sociopolitical changes in Europe and the former Soviet Union presented a changed context for the prayerful utterance of the theme. Still, ending the Cold War did not diminish the cries of suffering, despair, poverty, and oppression. Military struggle shifted anew to the Persian Gulf War. Thus, despite the changing world situation, "Come Holy Spirit" maintained a relevant plea for the churches.

The Seventh Assembly sought to renew the ecumenical movement through challenging parochial horizons of the churches' mission with an inclusive, worldwide vision.[34] Krister Stendahl celebrated the new scope of Canberra's *oikoumene* in his preassembly guide:

> We all know that the word [*oikoumene*] means "the inhabited world" and the theme of the Seventh Assembly urges us to recognize the whole *oikoumene* as we recognize the whole creation. It would be both arrogant and silly to claim the word *oikoumene* for ourselves. We share our world with people of many living faiths and many who claim to have none–all created in the image of God and thereby our sisters and brothers in the family of common humanity. For this wider ecumenism the Spirit gives both mandate and energy.[35]

The wider ecumenism of God's Spirit inspired member churches to celebrate the WCC's diverse constituencies and movements. Orthodox churches viewed the theme as an opportunity to affirm a richer, Trinitarian perspective in contrast to the West's "Christomonism."[36] Pentecostal churches heard in the Spirit theme an invitation for their participation from "ecclesiastical

---

[32]Albert C. Outler, "Pneumatology as an Ecumenical Frontier," *Ecumenical Review* 41 (July 1989): 363. The sites, dates, and themes of the previous assemblies are as follows: Amsterdam, 1948: Man's Disorder and God's Design; Evanston, 1954: Christ, the Hope of the World; New Delhi, 1961: Jesus Christ, the Light of the World; Uppsala, 1968: Behold, I Make All Things New; Nairobi, 1975: Jesus Christ Frees and Unites; and Vancouver, 1983: Jesus Christ, the Life of the World.

[33]Castro, "Report of the General Secretary," 150.

[34]The *Ecumenical Review* devoted three full issues to preassembly reflections: 41 (July 1989); 42 (April 1990); and 42 (July-October 1990). For a comprehensive view of preassembly process, assembly events, and evaluation, see Michael E. Putney, "Come Holy Spirit, Renew the Whole Creation: Seventh Assembly of the World Council of Churches," *Theological Studies* 52 (1991): 607–35.

[35]Stendahl, 49.

[36]Aram Keshishian, "The Assembly Theme: More Orthodox Perspectives," *Ecumenical Review* 42 (July-October 1990): 197–206.

peripheries."[37] Women's movements, claiming their own marginalized gifts, planned to raise their voices on issues of empowerment, survival, and "the community of women and men."[38] The WCC's concerns for cultural diversity, religious pluralism, and "dialogue with people of other living faiths" found greater emphasis through the focus on the Spirit and the *oikoumene*.[39] The Seventh Assembly theme further provided space for advocates of programs involved with social change, liberation, and justice.[40] Finally, the theme provided an ecological context for reflection on the churches' mission and faith.[41] The global horizon of God's household provided hope for an ecumenical diversity-in-unity.

But Chung Hyun Kyung's presentation tested the bonds of family relations and ecumenical unity. Chung was one of two major presenters on the theme. The first presentation was a lecture prepared by His Beatitude Parthenios III, the Greek Orthodox patriarch of Alexandria and all Africa. Unfortunately, the Persian Gulf War kept Parthenios from attending, so Grand Protopresbyter George Tsetis read the address instead. The Patriarch's lecture emphasized the mystery of the Trinity's inner relations and the Spirit's significance in sanctifying and transforming the cosmos toward unity with the Trinity.[42] Thus, while the Spirit is present in creation as the "Giver of Life" (Constantinopolitan Creed) and is concerned about whatever divides and enslaves people, the Spirit brings about the visible unity of humankind in and through the church's liturgy and sacraments. The Christian church serves as the focal point of unity for all creation, and fostering that unity is the primary purpose of ecumenical relations.

Fire Dancing

Chung's presentation directly followed Parthenios' lecture, and even though there were several corresponding theological concerns (e.g., for liberation and transformation of God's creation), Chung's dramatic style and use of visual arts provided a stunning contrast.[43] The presentation opened

---

[37]Henry I. Lederle, "The Spirit of Unity: A Discomforting Comforter," *Ecumenical Review* 42 (July-October 1990): 279–87.

[38]Barbara Stephens and Jocelyn Armstrong, "Thoughts on Reconciliation: Contributed by a Women's Group," *Ecumenical Review* 42 (July-October 1990): 264–67.

[39]Stanley Samartha, "The Holy Spirit and People of Other Faiths," *Ecumenical Review* 42 (July-October 1990): 250–63; and Justin S. Ukpong, "Pluralism and the Problem of the Discernment of Spirits," *Ecumenical Review* 41 (July 1989): 416–25.

[40]P. Mohan Larbeer, "The Spirit of Truth and Dalit Liberation," *Ecumenical Review* 42 (July-October 1990): 229–36; and M. M. Thomas, "The Holy Spirit and the Spirituality for Political Struggles," *Ecumenical Review* 42 (July-October 1990): 216–24.

[41]Jay McDaniel, "Where is the Holy Spirit Anyway? Response to a Sceptic Environmentalist," *Ecumenical Review* 42 (April 1990): 162–74; and Lukas Vischer, "Giver of Life–Sustain Your Creation!" *Ecumenical Review* 42 (April 1990): 143–49.

[42]Parthenios, "The Holy Spirit," in *Signs of the Spirit*, 28–37.

[43]For the full text, see Chung Hyun Kyung, "Come Holy Spirit–Renew the Whole Creation," in *Signs of the Spirit*, 37–47. Chung's address can also be found in "Welcome the Spirit; Hear Her Cries," *Christianity and Crisis* (July 15, 1991): 220–23. My narrative of Chung's presentation is based on the video "WCC Seventh Assembly Address by Professor Chung Hyun Kyung" (Nashville: Ecufilm, 1991).

with a lone Australian Aboriginal man dancing on stage accompanied by an Australian Aboriginal musician playing the didgeridoo. After several minutes, Chung and sixteen young Korean dancers, musicians, and banner-bearers emerged from the back of the auditorium, chanting and rhythmically moving through the audience to join the dancers on stage. Several dancers placed large candles, incense burners, and a flame pot in the center of the stage.

When the drumming and dancing finished, Chung greeted the delegates and invited them to remove their shoes out of respect for the holy ground of indigenous Australian people. She continued, "Let us listen to the cries of creation and the cries of the Spirit within it!" Chung then produced a list and read the names of martyred or murdered people throughout history. She called for the spirits of Uriah, Jepthath's daughter, male babies killed by Herod's soldiers, victims of the Crusades and witch trials, indigenous peoples, Holocaust victims, people killed by nuclear bombs and tests, freedom fighters, and the recent dead in the Persian Gulf War. Across the stage were projected artistic images illustrating her list. Invoking these names, Chung also included the spirits of the Amazon rain forest, earth, air, and water crying out under human exploitation. Finally, she called for the spirit of "our brother Jesus, the Liberator, tortured and killed on the cross." Chung then burned the list in Korean shamanistic style, fanning the ashes upward over the audience. The music and dancing solemnly began again, with the performers gradually moving back into the stage's darkness.

Left alone at center stage, Chung provided the theological reflection that informed her Spirit-ritual. Drawing from *minjung* spirituality of the Korean indigenous religion, Chung claimed that the angry, grieving, and justice-seeking *Han*-spirits of the suffering beings were agents through whom the Holy Spirit was speaking her compassion and wisdom for life. Chung poignantly challenged the Assembly participants, "Without hearing the cries of these spirits, we cannot hear the voice of the Holy Spirit." The spirits were calling for recognition and *metanoia* from the churches, which have too easily forgotten the God of compassion who weeps with the spirits. Chung contrasted the "unholy spirit of Babel," which drives greedy humans toward division, acquisitiveness, and economic oppression, with the "Holy Spirit of Pentecost," the source of God's "political economy of life," which empowers humans for "creating, liberating, and sustaining life in its most concrete, tangible and mundane forms." In contrast to the Babel spirit's dominating power, the Holy Spirit's political economy of life is inspired by the power of mutuality and interdependence.

Chung claimed that the Spirit's call to *metanoia* presented three specific changes in human orientation. (Remember King's call for a revolution in values.) First, the turn from anthropocentrism to "life-centrism" involves understanding the human species as part of nature, which as a whole is sacred. Aligning herself with the perspective of the marginalized, Chung suggested rereading the Christian scriptures from the perspective of birds, trees, and mountains, the ones now most despised by the Babel spirit. The second change involves turning from the "habit of dualism" to the "habit of interconnection." Dualism results in the loss of empathy for other beings, who have been objectified and turned into enemies, and thus are easily extinguished. The habit of interconnection breaks through the walls of dualistic thinking so that *ki,* the life-energy in Asian spirituality, flows and renews life for the whole. The third change involves turning from exploitation and war in the "culture of death" to the Spirit's "culture of life." In the latter, compassion and the ability to suffer with others create a new social orientation inclusive of "the least of these" (Mt. 25:40–45). Chung wove together these three changes necessary for the Spirit's political economy of life through the image of the *bodhisattva* Kwan In, goddess of compassion and wisdom. Drawn from popular women's religion in East Asia, Kwan In stands on Nirvana's shore healing all forms of life and, as "a feminine image of the Christ," empowers them to join her. In closing, Chung made the following appeal to the delegates:

> Dear sisters and brothers, with the energy of the Holy Spirit let us tear apart all walls of division and the "culture of death" which separate us. And let us participate in the Holy Spirit's political economy of life, fighting for our life on this earth in solidarity with all living beings, and building communities for justice, peace, and the integrity of creation. Wild wind of the Holy Spirit, blow to us. Let us welcome her, letting ourselves go in her wild rhythm of life. Come Holy Spirit, Renew the Whole Creation. Amen![44]

Suddenly, the chanting Korean dancers and Australian Aborigines returned to the stage. From the ends of billowing sheets of white cloth, an Australian Aboriginal male dancer and a Korean female dancer slowly moved toward one another, culminating in a joyous embrace. Then they saluted Assembly delegates and observers, many of whom began rising to their feet, clapping and shouting in affirmation. Chung and the dancers gradually moved off the stage the way they came, down through the audience and out the back doors.

A Holy Moment?

In general, responses to Chung's presentation followed two directions. As one Assembly delegate remarked, immediately after the performers finished, "there was passionate applause, but there was also passionate silence."[45] For some participants the presentation was "a holy moment," for others it was "the most egregious event of the meeting."[46] Denominational news reports

---

[44]Chung, "Come Holy Spirit," 46.

[45]Leonid Kishkovsky, "Ecumenical Journey: Authentic Dialogue," *Christianity and Crisis* (July 15, 1991): 228.

[46]Roy Sano, "'Holy Moments' at Canberra," *Christianity and Crisis* (July 15, 1991): 227; and Carl A. Volz, "Reflections on Lossky (and Canberra)," *Cross Currents* 42 (Spring 1993): 141.

cited observers' and delegates' immediate charges of syncretism, paganism, and apostasy.[47] Orthodox delegates prepared a formal response in which they raised concerns about the "limits of diversity" and the vocation of the ecumenical movement for church unity, rather than "the wider unity of humanity and creation."[48] They claimed Chung's presentation lacked the "central affirmations" of the "apostolic faith" and too closely associated the Holy Spirit with particular historical movements.[49]

Evangelical delegates prepared a formal response as well. First, they affirmed the need for the gospel's contextualization. But then they called attention to the WCC's "theological deficit," which evidenced "insufficient clarity regarding the relationship between the confession of the Lord Jesus Christ as God and Savior according to Scripture, the person and work of the Holy Spirit, and legitimate concerns which are part of the WCC agenda."[50] Unfortunately, the Seventh Assembly closed without opportunities for discussing the Orthodox and Evangelical reflections. Thus, as Konrad Raiser pointed out, the Seventh Assembly delegates did not even have "a common understanding of the problem."[51]

As noted earlier, delegates to the Seventh Assembly arrived in Canberra with the passionate hope for ecumenical inclusion and theological renewal. One of the mandates for the Seventh Assembly from the 1983 Sixth Assembly in Vancouver was for the Seventh Assembly to articulate "a vital and coherent theology."[52] But by the end of the Seventh Assembly, the passionate hope had changed to passionate debate. Reflections by delegates on Canberra showed concern with doctrinal boundaries and used the concepts of "legitimating, limiting pluralism" and "discerning the spirits."[53] One side of the debate stressed returning to the "apostolic faith of the church and the Trinitarian nature of God."[54] The other side affirmed Chung's theology as an "ecumenical theology of liberation" through "a dialogue of cultures."[55] Raiser claimed that Canberra's hermeneutical impasse was situated between the WCC's Commission on Faith and Order and the Commission on World Mission and

---

[47]Edgar R. Trexler, "Down and Out Down Under?: WCC Ponders Direction of Ecumenism," *The Lutheran* (April 3, 1991): 23–41; and Stephen L. Swecker, "WCC Hits Flashpoint on 'Syncretism,'" *The United Methodist Reporter* (February 22, 1991): 3.

[48]"Reflections of Orthodox Participants," in *Signs of the Spirit*, 279–80.

[49]Nicholas Lossky, "Reflection on Canberra," *Cross Currents* 32 (Spring 1993): 140–41. Also, "Reflections of Orthodox Participants," in *Signs of the Spirit*, 281–82.

[50]"A Letter to Churches and Christians Worldwide from Participants Who Share Evangelical Perspectives," in *Signs of the Spirit*, 283.

[51]Konrad Raiser, "Beyond Tradition and Context: In Search of an Ecumenical Framework of Hermeneutics," *International Review of Mission* 80 (July-October 1991): 347.

[52]Ibid.

[53]John Deschner, "Legitimating, Limiting, Pluralism," *Christianity and Crisis* (July 15, 1991): 230; and Samuel Solivan, "Which Spirit? What Creation?" *Christianity and Crisis* (July 15, 1991): 224.

[54]Emmanuel Clapsis, "What Does the Spirit Say to the Churches?" *International Review of Mission* 80 (July-October 1991): 327–29.

[55]K. C. Abraham, "Syncretism Is Not the Issue," *International Review of Mission* 80 (July-October 1991): 340.

Evangelism, representing a tension between a hermeneutic of tradition and a contextual hermeneutic respectively. The controversy

> dramatically revealed the lack of clarity in the ecumenical move-
> ment about the criteria for hermeneutics, i.e., *the process of mutual
> communication, understanding and recognition*...What is at stake is not
> only the understanding of the Holy Spirit, but also *the ways of doing
> theology* in the ecumenical movement, even the very basis of the WCC
> itself, and its function of *sustaining the search for the unity* of the church.[56]

Raiser's analysis acknowledges the diversity of theological perspectives in the WCC and supports the continuing dialogue on how unity may be understood within the ecumenical movement. But more importantly, he further challenges ecumenists and churches to struggle with reviewing *the conditions* that may make continuing dialogue even possible. According to Raiser, mutual communication, understanding, and recognition are fundamental to the process.

Was Canberra a holy moment for the ecumenical family? The answer boils down to whether one interprets Chung's presentation as creative inculturation or dangerous syncretism. For delegates and observers of the former opinion, Chung's presentation articulated a passionate and compassionate vision of the Spirit of God. A celebratory life of diversity-in-unity in the face of grave threats, Chung's fire dancing creatively grounded a cultural exchange between Korean and Australian indigenous spiritualities and Christian traditions. Many delegates and observers experienced Chung's vision as the creative expansion of Christian contextuality necessary for a suffering, multicultural, and interreligious world.[57]

For Assembly participants who concluded that the presentation was dangerously syncretistic, the dance of fire provoked concern, offense, and even outrage. Chung went too far beyond Christian boundaries by including elements foreign to Christian traditions, and she left behind too many definitive Christian elements. But the WCC had encountered theological differences between delegates and churches in the past. Discussions about the apostolic faith, Triune identification, and the absoluteness of Jesus as Savior were long-running subjects of assemblies past and present. Chung's presentation evoked more. Following the Seventh Assembly, Chung was harassed, had her phone tapped, and received death threats that forced her to move from her campus housing at Ewha University.[58] This is not to suggest that concerned Assembly participants were responsible. But in the conflict of ecumenical vision at the Seventh Assembly, more than theology seemed to be at stake.

---

[56]Raiser, "Beyond Tradition and Context," 347. Emphasis added.

[57]Mary Evelyn Tucker, "Expanding Contexts, Breaking Boundaries: The Challenge of Chung Hyun Kyung," *Cross Currents* 42 (Summer 1992): 236–43.

[58]Chung Hyun Kyung, "Survival-Syncretist," *The Christian Century* (March 11, 1992): 272.

Family Unity

The controversy regarding Chung's presentation takes on greater meaning when the metaphor of ecumenical family or household is more closely examined. As stated earlier, though the WCC is formally referred to as a fellowship of churches, ecumenists draw on domestic, family metaphors to express the unity of Christian churches. In his report to the Seventh Assembly and in reflections after Canberra, former General Secretary Emilio Castro referred to "the ecumenical family," "confessional families," "the Christian family," and "the family of the WCC."[59] The analogy of church and family becomes compounded through the ecumenical correlation of *oikos* (household or home), *oikoumene* (the earth as dwelling place), and *oikonomia* (household management or economy). Following the Seventh Assembly, Castro suggested that the unity of the ecumenical family is grounded in the fatherhood of God: "When we pray 'Our Father who art in heaven,' we cannot conceive this Father as the tribal head of one particular group of human beings. This prayer taught by Jesus affirms the *family nature* of humanity's relation to its Creator."[60] Thus, examining the analogy between family unity and church unity sheds light on the Seventh Assembly's proceedings.

Does the Canberra controversy about Spirit, culture, authority, and tradition reveal a family conflict within the ecumenical household? Parthenios' lecture recognized a gap between generations in the household when he called for "fraternal cooperation" between the "ancient" and "more recent and younger churches."[61] Emmanuel Clapsis also drew on generational imagery to explain the Seventh Assembly events: "At the assembly, the 'younger' churches challenged the theological supremacy of the 'older churches.'"[62] In addition to the generational conflict, Lee Jae-Won called attention to Chung's gender status in the household: "The Canberra Assembly was a historic event. The most striking external sign is that a young woman theologian from the Third World was a keynote speaker."[63] Through the analogy of family and church, Chung's presentation may be interpreted as a generational challenge to the household power, knowledge, experience, and tradition of elder churches.

The family controversy became even more complicated as additional household management concerns emerged: southern nations challenged northern nations, impoverished nations challenged wealthier ones, and churches of non-European cultures challenged churches of European cultures. Mary Evelyn Tucker reflects that Chung's presentation "signalled the emergence of Asian peoples within a vast Western-centered bureaucratic religious structure.

---

[59]Castro, "Report of the General Secretary," 161, 165; and *A Passion for Unity: Essays on Ecumenical Hopes and Challenges* (Geneva: World Council of Churches, 1992), 2, 7, 43.

[60]Castro, *A Passion for Unity*, 40. Emphasis added.

[61]Parthenios, 35.

[62]Clapsis, 328.

[63]Lee Jae-Won, "Spirit and Practice: A Radical Understanding," *Christianity and Crisis* (July 15, 1991): 226.

This is especially significant when one realizes that the majority of Christians today are no longer in the West but in Latin America, Africa and Asia."[64] The cultural complexity of ecumenical Christianity made the charge of syncretism acute. As a result, Asian and African delegates raised the issue of early Christianity's own contextualization process. Kwok Pui-Lan remarked, "Such attempts were considered legitimate, and nobody condemned them as syncretism. But when Christians from Third World countries tried to relate the Gospel to their religious and cultural contexts, they were accused of mixing different religions together."[65] From across the nations, delegates looked forward to the Seventh Assembly as a great homecoming. But like many homecomings, the close gathering of kin became a divided and stormy celebration. The younger, contextual household members had become more fully differentiated during the years after Vancouver. They came to Canberra with a collective presence seeking recognition and a transformed ecumenical agenda.

Are contextual theologies—theologies of struggle and liberation—the unruly disruptions of young household members (children?) in need of direction and apostolic restraint, or are they new "tongues as of fire" (Acts 2:1–4) for our time? Changing metaphors, do they represent the new "fruit of the Spirit" (Gal. 5:22) and thus the "new wine" (Mt. 9:17) empowering the future of the churches? Chung remarked during a special session of the Seventh Assembly that liberation theologies were "the new paradigm, the new wine that you can't put in your wineskins. Yes, we are dangerous, but it is through such danger that the Holy Spirit can renew the church."[66] Echoing Chung, James Bretzke suggests that in *minjung* theology, "finding one's voice is the first hallmark" for Koreans who have broken out of the mold of Western theological approaches.[67] Challenging voices can be taken seriously, or they can be squelched, discounted, and forced back into more acceptable, proper subjects of the household. Labels of heresy for Chung (and contextual others) or patronizing evaluations that she return to the apostolic faith discount her voice and shut down communication. In a household of established authority, subordinate household members who challenge the acceptable order become labelled as subversive, and reconstituting the order requires the imposition of discipline. Members who assert their own identities and differentiate themselves threaten family unity, when unity is understood as oneness or uniformity. A family analysis suggests that Chung's challenge to the ideal of monovocal unity called into question the house rules of the ecumenical household. For the future, what kind of family will the ecumenical family be—one in which diversity is recognized or assimilated? How do theologies of the Spirit contribute to either liberating or assimilating processes? As new tongues of fire, theologies of struggle and liberation resist assimilation and burn toward

---

[64]Tucker, 236.

[65]Kwok Pui-Lan, "Gospel and Culture," *Christianity and Crisis* (July 15, 1991): 223.

[66]Reported in Trexler, 23.

[67]James T. Bretzke, "Cracking the Code: Minjung Theology as an Expression of the Holy Spirit in Korea," *Pacifica* 10 (October 1997): 319–30.

transforming not only the ecumenical household, but the global household as well.

Ecumenical Growing Pains

Looking back on the Seventh Assembly controversy from the vantage point of the 1998 Eighth Assembly in Harare, Chung remarked in an interview that she holds no regrets.[68] An observer to the Eighth Assembly, Chung led an indigenous Korean healing service immediately before as part of the concluding celebration of the Ecumenical Decade of Churches in Solidarity with Women. Chung reflected on the decade in light of the Canberra controversy: "When I look at human history, freedom will never be given freely. It's the same with women's rights. If you go out of the church, do you think that society is not patriarchal? There's no way out. The church is also *our home, so we have every right to transform our home.*"[69]

Drawing on the ecumenical household image, Chung addressed the ongoing controversy between tradition and context: "It's like growing pains. We cannot pretend we will be one family in Christ. No, it seems like a big dysfunctional family. In order to overcome the dysfunction, everything needs to become open as when women talk about their experiences of violence."[70] In an open environment, the ecumenical family needs to face its struggles, legacies of hurt, and profound differences of theological perspective. Chung advised, "As a church we really have to listen and experience our differences enough so we can really appreciate them. Without hearing these experiences enough, we make a very superficial bridge, which can fall down at any time."[71] A new ecumenical process needs to be risked in which differences can emerge honestly, even if it means that divisions and separations come about "until we have another need to come together."[72] Chung's remarks continue pointing toward a new economy, a new understanding of household management for the Christian churches.

Chung's Seventh Assembly presentation brought forth publicly the great differences between delegates regarding the character of ecumenical unity. She presses the questions, How can the churches concern themselves with a basis of unity that does not take into consideration the historical estrangement of beings within the great world house? Can Christians share together in spiritual communion separate from the social, political, cultural, and economic legacies we bear? How can ecumenical householders view cultural differences as sources of gospel enrichment instead of presuming a gospel neutral toward cultures and histories? The events of the Seventh Assembly presented the opportunity for recognizing future ecumenical relations not *in*

---

[68]Stephen Brown, "Korean Controversial Feminist Theologian has 'No Regrets,'" *Ecumenical News International* 24 (December 17, 1998): 17/8.

[69]Ibid., 17. Emphasis added.

[70]Ibid., 18.

[71]Ibid.

[72]Ibid.

spite of diversity, but *because of* the differences in cultures and theologies. Not a family breakdown but a breakthrough, Canberra offered a new understanding of unity by recognizing diversity in the Spirit of God.

Canberra's legacy remains vital to the turn to the Spirit in contemporary theology. Parthenios' and Chung's presentations, along with the other reflections generated out of the Assembly, provide a breadth and depth of theological inspiration. One central affirmation is the cosmological scope of God the Spirit. Through the metaphors highlighted in the four Assembly sub-themes—Spirit as Sustainer, Liberator, Reconciler, and Sanctifier—the Spirit's triune personhood is reclaimed from diminishing models of divine bi-unity or mono-unity and related to the whole of creation. Canberra irrevocably interpreted the Spirit as the "Giver of Life" (in keeping with the apostolic, Constantinopolitan tradition) within the Spirit's "political economy of life" and thus included the themes of struggle for liberation and dignity in God's great world house.

Other central questions arise from Canberra for constructive pneumatology. What understandings of human spirit and God the Spirit emerge from our biblical and theological traditions? How is God as Spirit related to human experience and historical movements? How does christology relate to pneumatology? What is the character of Triune relations? What understandings and experiences of the Spirit have been neglected? How do contextualization and globalization reorient our pneumatological work? The questions raised and discussed throughout the Seventh Assembly continue fueling new research and practice.

The Seventh Assembly's greatest legacy, though, can be found in its greatest controversy. Chung's contextual presentation became a flash point signifying that models of ecumenical unity can no longer be understood as unification, assimilation, or conformity. Not just new members to be assimilated into the dominant theological discourse on classical controversies of Christian traditions, contextual theologies of struggle and liberation represent a new Pentecost with multivocal tongues of fire. Chung and her dancing partners raised their voices as an "insurrection of subjugated knowledges" calling into question the foundations of church unity.[73] Some may interpret the incendiary controversy at Canberra as a "woman question" or a younger church problem, but Canberra was first and foremost a "Church question."[74] The Seventh Assembly's events poignantly challenged ecumenical models of

---

[73]Melanie May, *Bonds of Unity: Women, Theology and the World-Wide Church* (Atlanta: Scholars Press, 1989), 5. In her analysis of the World Council of Churches' "Community of Women and Men in the Church Study" and its implications for the Commission on Faith and Order's view of unity, May draws on Foucault's understanding of "subjugated knowledges." May presents the World Council of Churches' study as an "'insurrection' against the unifying discourse of much twentieth-century theology, including much North American feminist theology." I am considering Chung's presentation in a similar light.

[74]Ibid., 17. May quotes Kathleen Bliss, chair of the Commission on the Life and Work of Women in the Church (World Council of Churches), who wrote in her 1952 book *The Service and Status of Women in the Church* (London: SCM Press, 1952) that "this is not a women's question, it is a Church question" (13–14).

unity not only to recognize and receive diversity, but to celebrate and even encourage diversity for the sake of God's abundant life (Jn. 10:10). Contemporary theologies of the Spirit learned from Canberra the need for re-imagining ecumenical unity as diversity-in-unity. They stand indebted to Chung Hyun Kyung's fiery testimony and the willingness of others to struggle together with her in the Spirit.

This chapter has presented a case study to introduce contemporary issues of pneumatology. The World Council of Churches' Seventh Assembly in Canberra turned to the Spirit with its theme, "Come Holy Spirit–Renew the Whole Creation." But instead of a hopeful celebration of ecumenical unity, the events of the Assembly revealed a household controversy. In the ecumenical family, challenging voices have been raised for recognition and full participation toward an inclusive household of mutuality. Theologies of struggle and liberation, voiced through Chung Hyun Kyung's presentation, provide a new Pentecost for the churches in their witness to God's abundant life of grace. They burn in the hearth of the ecumenical household and testify to life in the Spirit through the rich diversity and dignity of all household members.

CHAPTER 2

Turning to the Spirit in Contemporary Theology

"Forgetfulness of the Spirit" gave way to a positive obsession with the Spirit. But if we look critically at the actual results, we are bound to conclude that in sober fact, although light has been thrown on a whole number of individual aspects, a new paradigm in pneumatology has not yet emerged.[1]

The Renewal of Pneumatology

The 1991 World Council of Churches' Seventh Assembly theme, "Come Holy Spirit, Renew the Whole Creation," signified a turn to the Spirit in the life of Christian churches. The Seventh Assembly in Canberra provided an opportunity for the ecumenical fellowship of churches to articulate and share in one another's witness to life in God's Spirit. But through the course of events, delegates and churches realized they did not hold in common a unified understanding or experience of the Spirit. Thus, recognizing the diversity of gifts emerged as a primary outcome of Canberra's incendiary discussions on unity in the Spirit. While the proceedings of the Seventh Assembly proved challenging and controversial, today churches continue framing their ecumenical hopes of renewal and unity through the language of Spirit. The third Person of the Trinity remains a primary focus for ecumenical witness and participation.

Indebted to the Seventh Assembly, *academic* Christian theology has also taken a turn to the Spirit. In the last decade of the twentieth century, the third Person of the Trinity has taken center stage, no longer forgotten as the "Cinderella" of Western theology.[2] José Comblin addresses the current renewal of pneumatology:

---

[1]Jürgen Moltmann, *The Spirit of Life: A Universal Affirmation* (Minneapolis: Fortress Press, 1992), 1.

[2]Ibid. Moltmann may be alluding to Frederick Dale Bruner and William Hordern's image of the Spirit as a shy Cinderella. In *The Holy Spirit—Shy Member of the Trinity* (Minneapolis: Augsburg, 1984), Bruner and Hordern challenge pneumato-centric characterizations of Christian faith that focus on a "second baptism" or "full gospel" as the fulfillment of the kingdom. Through the metaphor of shyness, they re-subordinate the Spirit to Christ, since "the Holy Spirit does not mind being Cinderella outside the ballroom if the Prince is being honored inside his Kingdom" (16).

Present-day experience of the Holy Spirit...has become a major factor in the life of the Christian churches, to an extent totally unforesee-able even twenty-five years ago. No one then would have predicted that the end of the twentieth century would see the Holy Spirit once again in the forefront of Christian concern. Nor could anyone have foreseen that experience of the Spirit would have become the basis for a renewed theology.[3]

As introduced in this chapter, the third Person of the Trinity has become a new focus of biblical, historical, and systematic theological study. Sympo-siums like Marquette University's "The Advent of the Spirit" and the Austra-lian Theological Forum's "Tracking the Spirit in Tradition and Contemporary Thought" provide new opportunities for networking and research.[4] Courses in pneumatology have been added to university and seminary programs. An outpouring of books and articles presents a wide range of constructive pneumatological agendas.[5] Karl Barth's "dream" at the end of his life for a new theology beginning with the Spirit has become evident, but in directions very different than Barth may have imagined.[6] From Orthodox to Pentecos-tal, Protestant to Roman Catholic, liberation to evangelical, feminist to philo-sophical, Christian theologians around the world are renewing pneumatological inquiry. Critics may say that the diversity of perspectives represents a new Babel, but others claim the tradition of Pentecost instead.[7]

---

[3]José Comblin, *The Holy Spirit and Liberation* (Maryknoll, N.Y.: Orbis Books, 1989), 1.

[4]"The Advent of the Spirit: Orientations in Pneumatology" was held at Marquette Univer-sity in April 1998, coordinated by Bradford Hinze and D. Lyle Dabney. The Web address is www.theo.mu.edu/pneumatology/. In April 1999 the Australian Theological Forum presented a symposium titled "The Task of Theology Today: Tracking the Spirit in Tradition and Contempo-rary Thought." Information may be found on the ATF Web site, www.atf.org.au.

[5]Recent resources on the Spirit beyond the discussion of this book include: Allan Ander-son, *Moya: The Holy Spirit in an African Context* (Pretoria: University of South Africa, 1991); Joseph Bracken, *Society and Spirit: A Trinitarian Cosmology* (London: Associated University Presses, 1991); Miroslav Volf, *Work in the Spirit: Toward a Theology of Work* (New York: Oxford University Press, 1991); Thomas C. Oden, *Systematic Theology, Vol. 3: Life in the Spirit* (San Francisco: Harper and Row, 1992); Killian McDonnell and George T. Montague, *Christian Initiation and Baptism in the Holy Spirit: Evidence from the First Eight Centuries* (Collegeville, Minn.: Liturgical Press, 1991); Sinclair B. Ferguson, *The Holy Spirit: Contours of Christian Theology* (Downer's Grove, Ill.: InterVarsity, 1996); Caleb Oluremi Oladipo, *The Development of the Doctrine of the Holy Spirit in the Yoruba (African) Indigenous Movement* (New York: Peter Lang, 1996); Gary D. Badcock, *Light of Truth & Fire of Love: A Theology of the Holy Spirit* (Grand Rapids, Mich.: Eerdmans, 1997); John McIntyre, *The Shape of Pneumatology: Studies in the Doctrine of the Holy Spirit* (Edinburgh: T & T Clark, 1997); Rainbow Spirit Elders, *Rainbow Spirit Theology: Towards an Australian Aboriginal Theology* (San Francisco: HarperCollins, 1997); Duncan Reid, *Energies of the Spirit: Trinitarian Models in Eastern Orthodox and Western Theology* (Atlanta: Scholars Press, 1997); James D. G. Dunn, *The Christ and the Spirit,* vols. 1 and 2 (Grand Rapids, Mich.: Eerdmans, 1998); Amos Yong, "The Turn to Pneumatology in Christian Theology of Religions: Conduit or Detour?" *Journal of Ecu-menical Studies* 35, no. 3–4 (Summer-Fall 1998): 437–52.

[6]From Karl Barth, postscript to *Schleiermacher-Auswahl*, ed. H. Bolli (Munich, 1968), 310ff., as cited in Moltmann, *Life in the Spirit*, 1.

[7]Claude Geffré, Gustavo Gutiérrez, and Virgil Elizondo, eds., "Different Theologies, Common Responsibility: Babel or Pentecost?" *Concilium* 1, no. 171 (Edinburgh: T & T Clark, 1984), ix–xii. The editors write that between the extremes of "the totalitarianism of unity, or the Babel of disruption, there is nevertheless room for the mystery of Pentecost, as communion in diversity" (x).

This chapter situates the need for a feminist constructive project within a limited but general introduction to contemporary theology's turn to the Spirit. The chapter opens with the hopeful anticipation of churches for new ecumenical ventures fueled by the advent of the third millennium (by Western measure). New theologies of Spirit emerge contextually within this larger ecclesiastical horizon. Second, the turn to the Spirit in contemporary theology is set within discussions regarding postmodernity. Does the turn to the Spirit have affinity with modern or postmodern movements? I argue here that theologies of the Spirit represent a liminal position beyond the modern/postmodern impasse toward a time increasingly viewed as "post-secular."[8]

The third section introduces Spirit themes of liberation, life, and diversity from the works of selected contemporary pneumatologists. The exploration resists seeking one authentic theology of Spirit, but draws the theologies into a "field" of resonance and meaning.[9] The final part of the chapter situates the feminist analysis of Spirit models methodologically in the legacies of Sallie McFague's metaphorical theology and Jürgen Moltmann's social Trinitarian theology. The constructive efforts of *The Raging Hearth* aim toward a pneumatological model of mutual recognition that transforms political, church, and household monotheism. For an ecumenical millennium, many voices are needed in forming a new pneumatological paradigm. This chapter sets forth the inspiration for at least one of those voices.

Turning toward a New Millennium

Inspired by the advent of the third millennium, Christian churches prepare for a celebration of new ecumenical openness. Churches throughout the world seek ways to mark the ecumenical progress of this century and commit themselves to greater fellowship in the future. In 1994 the World Council of Churches' executive committee meeting in Bucharest noted:

> The emergence of the ecumenical movement during the last hundred years has brought about a qualitative change in the relationships between the Christian churches and a new understanding of the Christian calling in today's world. The end of the millennium is thus an invitation to the churches to be liberated from the burdens of the past and to move into the third millennium with a visible manifestation of unity. Any observance should therefore be oriented towards repentance and forgiveness, commemoration and liberation, thanksgiving and hope.[10]

Also in 1994, Pope John Paul II committed the Roman Catholic Church to celebrating the "Great Jubilee of the Year 2000" in his apostolic letter *Tertio*

---

[8]Phillip Blond, ed., *Post-Secular Philosophy: Between Philosophy and Theology* (London: Routledge, 1998).

[9]Michael Welker, *God the Spirit* (Minneapolis: Fortress Press, 1994), 22, 242–46.

[10]Minutes of the World Council of Churches' executive committee meeting in Bucharest, 1994, as cited by Konrad Raiser in "From Celebration to Commitment: A Proposal/Vision for the Year 2000," *Ecumenical Review* 49, no. 2 (April 1997): 204.

Millennio Adveniente. With a vision paralleling the hopes of the WCC, the pope affirmed that

> the approaching end of the second millennium demands of everyone an examination of conscience and the promotion of fitting ecumenical initiatives, so that we can celebrate the Great Jubilee if not completely united, at least much closer to overcoming the division of the second millennium.[11]

The WCC and the Roman Catholic Church anticipate the new millennium as a decisive threshold for ecumenical relations. Konrad Raiser, general secretary of the WCC, has further invited the main Christian faith streams—Roman Catholic, Protestant, Orthodox, and Pentecostal—to launch a process in the year 2000 toward a universal Christian council in keeping with the conciliar legacy of early church history.[12] The process would call forth new ecumenical relations beyond the existing structures of recognition (and lack of recognition).

But millennial enthusiasm moves beyond ecumenical reconciliation to incorporate a hope for new beginnings in what Martin Luther King, Jr., envisioned as the "great world house."[13] The 1998 Eighth Assembly of the World Council of Churches in Harare, Zimbabwe, marked not only the fiftieth year of assembly meetings, but also an opportunity for the churches to claim their unity with suffering people throughout the world. In preparation for the "jubilee" assembly, delegates studied the Hebrew Bible jubilee traditions and learned that ecumenical hope cannot be understood apart from solidarity with global needs.[14] Study guide author Sebastian Bakare explains,

> The biblical jubilee cannot be separated from the questions about appropriation and expropriation of resources. An ecumenical celebration under the theme of jubilee must be a moment of truth, when we put in order our relationship with each other and with God. It is a time to discover our identity as a redeemed people of God, a time to renew our faithfulness to the gospel, a time of reconciliation and of commitment to issues of peace and justice—including the issue of the unjust external debt which is threatening the peace and stability of so many countries today.[15]

---

[11] *Tertio Millennio Adveniente*, para. 34, as cited by Raiser, 203.

[12]"WCC Head Calls for Church Council," *The Christian Century* (May 20–27, 1998), 522.

[13]Martin Luther King, Jr., *Where Do We Go From Here: Chaos or Community?* (Boston: Beacon Press, 1967), 167.

[14]Hans Ucko, ed., *The Jubilee Challenge: Utopia or Possibility: Jewish and Christian Insights* (Geneva: World Council of Churches, 1997); Marlin VanElderen, *From Canberra to Harare: An Illustrated Account of the Life of the World Council of Churches 1991–1998* (Geneva: World Council of Churches, 1998), 28–29, 36–37; and Sebastian Bakare, *The Drumbeat of Life: Jubilee in an African Context* (Geneva: World Council of Churches, 1998), 30–34.

[15]Bakare, 33.

According to a growing consensus in the ecumenical community, the churches' ecclesiastical reconciliation must connect with a just and reconciled household management within the great world house. Alongside the work of liturgical and doctrinal encounter remains the work of reconciling Christian churches amid the political betrayals and social torments of the past and the structural sin of the present.[16] As Geiko Müller-Fahrenholz claims for the ecumenical movement, "The truth of the world is bound up with the truth about ourselves. It is indivisible."[17] Following Canberra and Harare, models of ecumenical unity in the Spirit of God incorporate a vision of diversity-in-unity for the whole inhabited Earth. Turning to the Spirit in contemporary theology must be viewed within this fiery vision of global transformation.

Beyond Postmodernity

Turning to the Spirit in contemporary theology may also be interpreted within the postmodern movements of academics. While it is difficult to define postmodernity or postmodernism, the terms generally characterize what Zygmunt Bauman calls a "state of mind...marked by a view of the human world as irreducibly and irrevocably pluralistic."[18] To the degree that plurality, multiculturalism, contextuality, and diversity characterize our postmodern age, contemporary theologies of the Spirit that also affirm these values may be understood as postmodern. But as seen in the ethical commitments of the ecumenical movement, Spirit theologies further support human communities of struggle and liberation in response to the rampant individualism, greedy neocolonialism, political tyranny, and monocultural globalization of our present (and future?). Thus, if postmodernism is defined as presenting "a life without truth, standards and ideals," then theology's turn to the Spirit clearly sits at odds with the postmodern state of mind.[19]

Theology's turn to the Spirit takes seriously the context of life in a "groaning" world (Rom. 8:22). Certainly more than groans compose the lives of beings in the great world house. But if the groans are not taken seriously, if they do not receive a central place in a pneumatological accounting, then, as Jon Sobrino warns, "We shall fail to grasp the fundamental element of our

---

[16]Commitment to church unity *and* combating racism undergirds the discernment processes of the Consultation on Church Union (COCU) churches. The nine member communions of COCU will be entering into a new relationship of mutual recognition early in 2002 named Churches Uniting in Christ. These churches include the United Methodist Church, Christian Church (Disciples of Christ), United Church of Christ, Presbyterian Church (USA), Episcopal Church, Christian Methodist Episcopal (CME) Church, African Methodist Episcopal (AME) Church, African Methodist Episcopal Zion (AMEZ) Church, and the International Council of Community Churches (United Methodist News Service, January 25, 1999); www.umc.org.umns.

[17]Geiko Müller-Fahrenholz, *God's Spirit: Transforming a World in Crisis* (New York: Continuum, 1995), 123.

[18]Zygmunt Bauman, *Intimations of Postmodernity* (London: Routledge, 1992), vii, 35. See also Daniel J. Adams, "Toward a Theological Understanding of Postmodernism," *Cross Currents* (Winter 1997–98): 518–30.

[19]Bauman, ix.

historical reality, and theology will be in serious danger of becoming unreal: of falling into a kind of docetism of reality–the docetism that, in any of its forms, has always been the greatest threat to theology."[20]

Joining in Sobrino's concern for victims, Gustavo Gutiérrez claims the groans of creation today come forth less from natural events than from the socially constructed oppressions of human civilization.[21] While the age of modernity is marked by the epistemological turn to the subject, theology's recent groans represent a turn to the *other,* the others from the "underside of history."[22] Thus, the privileged subjects of theological reflection have become those beings whose "faces" challenge the effacing and totalizing legacies of modernity. [23] Theologies based on the contexts of ethnicity, culture, race, sexuality, gender, or class represent the groaning struggles for more inclusive historical narratives, revalued identities, and new visions of human society. Critics like Bauman warn of "rampant tribalism" in "the new soft world of communities."[24] From his perspective, the "postmodern accolade of difference" may fan the flames of ethnocentrism, racism, and xenophobia, ending in "a series of soliloquies, with the speakers no more insisting on being heard, but refusing to listen into the bargain."[25] Yet Bauman too quickly jumps from the value of recognizing differences to the violence of fascism. Theologies of the Spirit acknowledge the risk of fragmentation when differences are recognized. But they also claim that unity without recognizing differences has already proven its violence. A new "tack" is needed for the winds of God's Spirit in our time.[26]

Thus, turning to the Spirit in Christian theology addresses not only the groans of global suffering, but also ways beyond suffering to the mutual recognition and dignity that are necessary for reconciliation. Movements such

---

[20]Jon Sobrino, "Theology from amidst the Victims," in *The Future of Theology: Essays in Honor of Jürgen Moltmann*, ed. Miroslav Volf, Carmen Krieg, and Thomas Kucharz (Grand Rapids, Mich.: Eerdmans, 1996), 164.

[21]Gustavo Gutiérrez, *A Theology of Liberation: History, Politics and Salvation*, trans. and ed. Sister Caridad Inda and John Eagleson (Maryknoll, N.Y.: Orbis Books, 1973), 172–73.

[22]See Gustavo Gutiérrez, *The Power of the Poor in History*, trans. Robert R. Barr (Maryknoll, N.Y.: Orbis Books, 1983); Rebecca S. Chopp, *The Praxis of Suffering: An Interpretation of Liberation and Political Theologies* (Maryknoll, N.Y.: Orbis Books, 1986); and Susan Brooks Thistlethwaite and Mary Potter Engel, eds., *Lift Every Voice: Constructing Christian Theologies from the Underside* (San Francisco: HarperSanFrancisco, 1990).

[23]Emmanuel Levinas, *Totality and Infinity: An Essay on Exteriority*, trans. Alphonso Lingis (Pittsburgh: Duquesne University, 1969).

[24]Zygmunt Bauman, *Postmodernity and its Discontents* (New York: New York University Press, 1997), 79–82.

[25]Ibid., 81.

[26]Peter C. Hodgson compares the contextualizing of theological thinking to sailing in *Winds of the Spirit: A Constructive Theology* (Louisville, Ky.: Westminster John Knox Press, 1994): "Theology is rather like sailing. It is in contact with powerful, fluid elements, symbolized by wind and water, over which it has little control and by which it is drawn and driven toward mysterious goals…On the open water sailing can be an exhilarating and joyous adventure but one filled with danger and disappointment. Truth, value, and beauty do not exist in the abstract but are created in the act of sailing through a symbiosis of ship and elemental forces" (3).

as the South African Truth and Reconciliation Commission, the German Protestant *Aktion Sühnzeichen Friedensdienste*, and the Vicariate of Solidarity in Chile pursue visions of redemptive justice and social wholeness.[27] In Australia, the Anglican, Roman Catholic, and Uniting Churches acknowledged their participation in the forced removal of Aboriginal children from their families in the nineteenth and twentieth centuries, yet now advocate reconciliation in a new multicultural vision of Australian society.[28] The groans of survival, which give voice to contextual theologies, have discovered a new "energy for life" in the power of God the Spirit.[29] To the degree that contemporary theologies of the Spirit fan the hopes for new social orders, then perhaps the turn to the Spirit stands more in the tradition of modernity than postmodernity.[30]

But Christian theology's turn to the Spirit warrants neither a modern nor postmodern characterization. Instead, the turn to the Spirit signifies a liminal period beyond the modern/postmodern impasse. Stephen Toulmin suggests that postmodernity is a world "that has not yet discovered how to define itself in terms of what is, but only in terms of what it has just-now-ceased to be."[31] Thus, postmodernity rejects the One, but in favor of what? Turning to the Spirit acknowledges that forms of homogeneous, assimilating universality no longer address with integrity the complex dimensions of human cultures as well as the rest of the world. We live in an ecological cosmos, from the (decreasing) biodiversity of our earth to the fiery relations of stars, atoms, and galaxies.[32] Turning to the Spirit affirms a relational ontology of diversity-in-unity, where an affirmation of the many plays a constitutive role in life's survival and flourishing. Thus, turning to the Spirit privileges the voices of others-at-risk and re-imagines inclusiveness at the heart of not only social process, but God's very identity.[33]

Turning to the Spirit further reclaims the centrality of mystery, wonder, and hope, not just in religious experience, but as the basis of all experience.

---

[27]Gregory Baum and Harold Wells, eds., *The Reconciliation of Peoples: Challenge to the Churches* (Maryknoll, N.Y.: Orbis Books, 1997), 16–42, 56–66, 144–57.

[28]Human Rights and Equal Opportunity Commission, *Bringing Them Home* (Sydney: Commonwealth of Australia, 1997), 276–93.

[29]Krister Stendahl, *Energy for Life: Reflections on the Theme "Come Holy Spirit, Renew the Whole Creation"* (Geneva: World Council of Churches, 1990).

[30]Bauman writes in *Postmodernity and Its Discontents*: "The end of modernity? Not necessarily. In another respect, after all, modernity is very much with us. It is with us in the form of the most defining of its defining traits: that of hope, the hope of making things better than they are—since they are, thus far, not good enough" (80).

[31]Stephen Toulmin, *The Return to Cosmology* (Berkeley: University of California Press, 1982), as quoted in Adams, "Toward a Theological Understanding of Postmodernism," 520.

[32]Charles Birch, *On Purpose* (Kensington: New South Wales University, 1990).

[33]Henry James Young correlates God and inclusivity in *Hope in Process: A Theology of Social Pluralism* (Minneapolis: Fortress Press, 1990): "In order for the idea of God to have liberating possibilities for victims of systematic oppression, God's nature must include the dynamic pluralistic dimensions of finite existence. We must forsake the theistic and supernaturalistic notions about God's detachment from the changing circumstances of finite existence. We must eradicate the bias that says there is something intrinsically inferior about the dynamic and pluralistic" (113).

The burden of self-creation on the certain and separative self of modernity has given way to more awe-filled understandings of life. Spirituality based on the freedom of the Spirit (Jn. 3:8) supports an openness to others, but also to the advent of God as Other. In an effort to deconstruct the metaphysics of presence in philosophy and Christian theologies, postmodern a/theologians foreclose the possibility of experiencing God.[34] But is not totalistic closure the very thing that deconstruction seeks to transgress in the first place?[35] In his work on deconstructing the death of God, Kevin Hart claims "deconstruction is not a wake after the death of God. It would be more fair to say it is a way of uncovering the gospel of the living God."[36] Turning to the Spirit in a liminal time recognizes the limitations of religious knowledge and experience yet provides the possibility for Jürgen Moltmann's pneumatological hope of "the experience of God in all things, and all things in God."[37] Reintroducing "life and nuance and movement" to the stagnating, closed orders of both modernity and postmodernity, we can view the turn to the Spirit in contemporary academic theology as signifying a turn to a postsecular age.[38] Pneumatology thus becomes a "first theology" for a new century.[39]

Contemporary Spirit Themes

In the years after Canberra, academic theologians have retrieved pneumatology with renewed vigor and creativity. Certainly, works on the Spirit prior to Canberra remain an important part of this century's pneumatological contribution, but the last ten years have brought a great

---

[34]See Mark C. Taylor, *Erring: A Postmodern A/theology* (Chicago: University of Chicago Press, 1984). Taylor writes, "Postmodernism opens with irrevocable loss and incurable fault. This wound is inflicted by the overwhelming awareness of death–a death that 'begins' with the death of God and 'ends' with the death of our selves…Death of God, Disappearance of Self, End of History, Closure of the Book. Our problem is how to count all of this not only as loss but as gain" (6, 17).

[35]In *The Prayers and Tears of Jacques Derrida: Religion without Religion* (Bloomington: Indiana University Press, 1997), John Caputo explores Derrida's concern that he has been misunderstood concerning the death of God. According to Caputo, Derrida's deconstruction of Western metaphysics does not necessarily mean the end of religion. Derrida's work represents a "religion without religion," in contrast to the totalizing foreclosure of religious experience by the Heideggarian "Church of Frieburg" (xxii).

[36]Kevin Hart, "Deconstructing the Death of God," *Zadok Perspectives* (Autumn 1998), 11.

[37]Moltmann, *The Spirit of Life*, 35–36.

[38]Douglas John Hall, *Thinking the Faith* (Minneapolis: Fortress Press, 1989), 104. Reflecting on the relation of Spirit and world, Hall writes: "The corrective to a theology which has neglected or dismissed the context by means of a rationalized and doctrinaire concentration on the second person of the Trinity is a theology which is goaded into engagement with its worldly reality by a fresh apprehension of the Holy Spirit. For the Spirit will not permit us to rest neither in the church nor in doctrinal formulations that know everything ahead of time. The Spirit will drive us, as it drove Jesus, to the wilderness of worldly temptation and the garden of worldly suffering" (105).

[39]D. Lyle Dabney, "Otherwise Engaged in the Spirit: A First Theology for a Twenty-first Century," in *The Future of Theology*, 154–63.

increase in research.[40] Some pneumatologies represent orientations within Pentecostal churches and charismatic renewal movements whose influence in ecumenical relations and contemporary theology should not be denigrated or written off as inauthentic or ancillary. But as we saw in the Seventh Assembly discussions, pneumatology presses beyond singular definitions within Pentecostal and charismatic orientations. Theologies of the Spirit reflect the wide breadth of Christian traditions, contexts, and faith orientations. While Pentecostal (or charismatic) and liberation pneumatologies share a renewal of Christian vitality, a global horizon of hope, and an experiential context of human dignity, great differences exist between their theologies.[41] This section sets a feminist perspective within the pneumatological field of a select group of contemporary theologians. Their positions incorporate three inspiring Spirit themes: liberation, life, and diversity.

The Spirit and Liberation

In his book *God the Spirit*, Michael Welker questions the tendency in Pentecostal and charismatic movements to concentrate on unusual, sensational, or inaccessible experiences as the truth of God's Spirit.[42] He challenges the assumption of a split between public secularity and private religious experience:

> Must not the liberating power of truth show itself in the fact that the insights of faith wrought by the Spirit could be carried over to faith within secularized cultures and postures of consciousness? Must not the liberating power of truth make recognizable in a way that is also

---

[40]A limited list of works on the Spirit from the second half of the twentieth century (prior to 1989) include: George S. Hendry, *The Holy Spirit in Christian Theology* (London: SCM Press, 1957); Lycurgus M. Starkey, Jr., *The Work of the Holy Spirit* (Nashville: Abingdon Press, 1962); Paul Tillich, *Systematic Theology, Vol. III: Life and the Spirit, History and the Kingdom of God* (Chicago: University of Chicago Press, 1963); Karl Rahner, *Spirit in the World* (New York: Herder and Herder, 1968); Frederick Dale Bruner, *A Theology of the Holy Spirit: The Pentecostal Experience and the New Testament Witness* (Grand Rapids, Mich.: Eerdmans, 1970); John V. Taylor, *The Go-Between God: The Holy Spirit and the Christian Mission* (Philadelphia: Fortress Press, 1972); Norman Pittenger, *The Holy Spirit* (Philadelphia: United Church Press, 1974); David Coffey, *Grace: The Gift of the Holy Spirit* (Manly, Australia: Catholic Institute of Sydney, 1979); Eduard Schweizer, *The Holy Spirit* (Minneapolis: Fortress Press, 1980); Daniel Day Williams, *The Spirit and the Forms of Love* (Lanham, Md.: University Press of America, 1981); Philip Rosato, *Spirit as Lord: The Pneumatology of Karl Barth* (Edinburgh: T & T Clark, 1982); Yves M. J. Congar, *I Believe in the Holy Spirit*, vols. 1–3 (New York: Seabury Press, 1983); Alasdair Heron, *The Holy Spirit* (Philadelphia: Westminster Press, 1983); Geoffrey Lampe, *God as Spirit* (London: SCM Press, 1983); and Donald Gelpi, *The Divine Mother: A Trinitarian Theology of the Holy Spirit* (Lanham, Md.: University Press of America, 1984). For an extensive bibliographical compilation, see Esther Dech Schandorff, *The Doctrine of the Holy Spirit: A Bibliography Showing its Chronological Development*, vols. 1–2, ATLA Bibliography Series no. 28 (Lanham, Md.: Scarecrow Press, 1995). Unfortunately, the resource does not include José Comblin's *The Holy Spirit and Liberation,* Jürgen Moltmann's *The Spirit of Life,* and Michael Welker's *God the Spirit,* which are vital works for contemporary pneumatology.

[41]I am indebted to conversations with Murdoch University student Elizabeth Way, whose comparative research in Pentecostal and liberation theologies encouraged me to see links between the two movements.

[42]Welker, 15.

accessible to this latter faith the dominant cultures' ruling powers of self-endangerment and self-destruction? Must not the liberating power of truth contribute to "driving out" these powers?[43]

Welker suggests that Christian faith today needs a more public, multi-directional understanding of the Spirit than that provided by the Pentecostal and charismatic movements, even though he doesn't exclude them from his vision. Instead, Welker advocates for liberation and feminist theologies as viable, authentic movements of God the Spirit. Based on a study of the biblical mercy laws and messianic promises, Welker claims that liberation and feminist movements embody, in all their diversity, the outpouring of the Spirit today on behalf of the weak, marginalized, and oppressed.[44] But these movements are not ends in themselves. In keeping with the mercy and messianic traditions, they "cultivate the expectation that those who are privileged will withdraw their own claims" and create with others communal spaces for just, righteous, and compassionate living.[45] God's Spirit is "poured out" from beyond human possibility "on all flesh" (Joel 2:28–32) for the universal spread of God's knowledge:

> The pouring out of the Spirit results not only in a universal capacity to participate in the life processes of the community, let alone that participation being limited to the processes of judicial and economic communication. Inasmuch as all—sons and daughters, old and young, male and female slaves—attain *prophetic knowledge through the Spirit, they are given the capacity to open with each other and for each other the reality and the future intended by God.*[46]

In Welker's interpretation of biblical traditions, the Spirit empowers movements of social justice that advocate right relations between people and struggle toward changing inequitable social structures.

---

[43]Ibid., 14–15.

[44]Ibid., 108–24. Welker studies the Holiness Code from Exodus 20–23 and the messianic texts of Isaiah 11:1–5, 9–10; 42:1–4, 6–8; and 61:1–11. These texts set forth God's particular partiality for the vulnerable, weak, and oppressed. The bearer of God's Spirit establishes justice, mercy, and knowledge of God and gives them universal extension. Welker writes, "The law remains a functional interconnection of ordinances *that serve the founding of justice, the routinization of mercy, and the cultivation of public, universally accessible relation with God,* where this relation is ordered in a way that people can come to expect. The promises that speak of the Spirit's resting hold out the prospect of a fulfilment of this law—a fulfilment whose effects extend beyond Israel" (111).

[45]Ibid., 18–19. On the association of liberation and feminist movements with pneumatology, Welker makes an important observation: "The messianic promises assign the name 'Spirit of God' to the power that both promises and realizes new community for poor and rich, strong and weak, people separated and alienated by economics, politics, racism and sexism. The publications of liberation theologies suggest that these theologies have not identified that power as their central motive force as decisively as was the case with the Charismatic Renewal Movement" (20). This project draws on Welker's observation to make a more explicit connection between pneumatology and feminist theology.

[46]Ibid., 150.

José Comblin and Anselm Min also connect movements for liberation with new theologies of the Spirit. Each theologian writes from a different context, but both locate the presence and experience of God's Spirit within the historical struggle for transformed societies. Comblin writes from the context of rural Brazil's basic Christian communities. Among the poor, the experience of God's Spirit creates "a new personhood" of people who together evidence the fruit of the Spirit—action, freedom, speech, community, and life.[47] In the face of violence and dehumanizing conditions, empowered communities of people experience dignity and joy in worship through their own prayers, leadership, and biblical interpretation. But the experience of the Spirit also relates to building schools, marching in the streets, forming workers associations, or risking martyrdom. God's Spirit enables the community to perceive a mission and initiate action, even at the cost of their own lives. Comblin explains the advent of a "liberation pneumatology":

> The experiences to which I am referring are experiences of an unexpected transformation. People feel themselves taken hold of by new strength that makes them do things they had never thought of doing. Individuals and communities that had been downhearted, lacking in dynamism, resigned to the endless struggle for survival, discover themselves to be protagonists of a history far greater than themselves.[48]

The new Pentecost of liberation movements is inspired by the experiences of life out of death, on behalf of the good of the community. Comblin acknowledges that while basic communities are not ideal or complete, the Spirit can still be experienced within the visible community of struggle. He summarizes his view: "The Spirit is known in the concrete activity of building a new world."[49]

Min joins Comblin's pneumatology of liberation, but from the context of middle-class life in an industrialized nation. For Min, the search of middle-class people for spirituality and transcendent meaning needs to be related to their social responsibilities. He suggests that "as beneficiaries and agents of the global economic process [middle-class people] also bear political responsibility for the oppression of the poor, exploitation of nature, and the general consequences of the globalizing process."[50] Min retrieves the classic Augustinian understanding of the Spirit as the mutual love between the Father and the Son, but enlarges the Spirit's fellowship to include the creation of a

---

[47]José Comblin, *The Holy Spirit and Liberation*, 19–33, 61–76. See also his *Retrieving the Human: A Christian Anthropology*, trans. Robert R. Barr (Maryknoll, N.Y.: Orbis Books, 1990).

[48]Comblin, *Holy Spirit and Liberation*, 20.

[49]Ibid., 4.

[50]Anselm Min, "The Holy Spirit as the Spirit of Solidarity of Others: Pneumatology in a Divided World," unpublished paper (Marquette University, April 1998). Used with permission. See also idem, "Renewing the Doctrine of the Spirit: A Prolegomenon," *Perspectives in Religious Studies* 19 (Summer 1992): 183–98; and "Dialectical Pluralism and Solidarity of Others," *Journal of the American Academy of Religion* 65, no. 3 (Fall 1997): 587–604.

"solidarity of Others" who together "create the common social conditions of life that will guarantee basic needs, justice and meaningful culture to every-one."[51] In a world divided between the privileged and the poor, the Holy Spirit, as the Spirit of solidarity, overcomes both middle-class nihilism and the suffering of people without access to resources and power. By the Spirit's resources and power, people from very different contexts meet across great divides and work together for a new world.

Welker, Comblin, and Min challenge individual, privatistic understand-ings of the Spirit and reframe pneumatology within a social world of inequity, violence, and human transformation. Echoing Chung's vision of the Spirit's political economy of life, these three theologians emphasize the institutional, political, and public dimensions of pneumatology, but not to the extent of denying personal dimensions.[52] By reading biblical texts with new eyes, Spirit eyes, they see that the person and work of God as Spirit must be interpreted within what Müller-Fahrenholz terms God's "ecodominical covenant."[53] God's habitation or dwelling place is creation, and thus, reflection on God's economy must include a divine-human partnership in building up and sustaining the global household. Müller-Fahrenholz reflects on his own liberating turn to the Spirit: "As I studied the biblical accounts, it soon became apparent that the Spirit is much more than the heart and soul of Pentecostal awakenings and sanctified living. It is the core-energy of creation itself."[54] The connection of Spirit and liberation within God's great world house brings the struggles for justice and freedom, community and covenant, to the heart of pneumatology.

---

[51]Min, "The Holy Spirit," 4.

[52]For the presentation on Chung, see chapter 1. Understanding liberation theologies as pneumatological need not imply a separation between the individual and society, or between personal conversion and social change. Liberation spirituality is at the heart of the liberation struggle, presented in Gustavo Gutiérrez's *We Drink From Our Own Wells: the Spiritual Journey of a People* (Maryknoll, N.Y.: Orbis Books, 1984). Interpreting the theme of liberation pneumatologically also need not pit liberation and Pentecostal movements against each other, since they are not mutually exclusive. In "The Response of Liberation Theology," in *Pentecostal Movements as an Ecumenical Challenge*, Virgil Elizondo claims that both Pentecostalism and theologies of liberation are about healing and deliverance, but have different emphases that need one another. He writes, "Liberation theology begins with a rational faith conviction that leads to progressive experiences of God, while Pentecostalism begins with the trans-rational and transformative experience of God—being slain—which gradually leads to a new rational understanding of person, society and world" (54–55). In *Pentecostalism: Origins and Developments Worldwide* (Peabody, Mass.: Hendrickson Publishing, 1997), Walter Hollenweger also points toward the integration of both personal and social transformation in Pentecostalism: "Which way will Pentecostalism go? Will it become a religion of the soul; will it celebrate one's own innermost being; or will it develop a passion for the kingdom of God in which the personal and the social are seen in their complementarity?" (397). Following Welker, Min, and Comblin, theologies of struggle and liberation can claim a pneumatological orientation as well as those renewal and independent movements typically re-ferred to in the twentieth century as "of the Spirit."

[53]Müller-Fahrenholz, *God's Spirit*, 108–12.

[54]Ibid., xii.

The Spirit and Life

By now we can see that the turn to the Spirit in contemporary theology has been energized by a recovery of neglected or undervalued biblical texts regarding Spirit language. While every reference to Spirit or spirit in the Hebrew Bible should not be read as a specific address to the third Person of the Trinity, a broad biblical study of Spirit talk and Spirit traditions enables contemporary theologians to articulate a multifaceted theology of God as Spirit.[55] Images of the Spirit as a "shy member" pale before the richness of the biblical texts, where God as Spirit is associated with much more than merely applying the work of Christ to the human soul and initiating and administering the Christian life.[56]

The most important move in contemporary pneumatology has been the recovery of the biblical association between Spirit and life. As heard in the Seventh Assembly resources, and Parthenios' and Chung's addresses, the cosmic breadth of the Spirit restores the relation of redemption and creation through the Constantinopolitan affirmation of the Spirit as the "Lord and Giver of Life."[57] Thus, the Spirit relates to finite, historical life as well as understandings of eternal life. But the relation of Spirit and life is strengthened through another connection. In his "unplanned" book, *The Spirit of Life,* Jürgen Moltmann returns to the Hebrew Bible tradition of God's *ruach* to reconnect redemption with creation and affirm the embodied, historical quality of spiritual life.[58] While the Greek term *pneuma,* the Latin *spiritus,* and the Germanic *Geist* may be interpreted as antithetical to body and matter, the Hebrew *ruach* refers to the embodied quality of beings and God. Interpreted through the images of breath, wind, storm, empowerment, and vitality, *ruach* "always means something living compared with something dead, something moving, over against what is rigid and petrified."[59] God's *ruach* is God's breath, which sustains all creatures, including Leviathan, according to the psalmist: "When you hide your face, they are dismayed; when you take away their breath, they die and return to their dust. When you send forth your spirit, they are created; and you renew the face of the ground" (Ps. 104:29–30).

Through the connection of Spirit and life, Moltmann presents a "holistic doctrine of God the Holy Spirit" that affirms a panentheistic model of God

---

[55]George Montague, *The Holy Spirit: The Growth of a Biblical Tradition* (New York: Paulist Press, 1976).

[56]Bruner and Hordern, 16. In *The Work of the Holy Spirit,* Starkey, like Bruner and Hordern, focuses on Christ's atoning death, which justifies the sinner before God. The Spirit then enables Christ's work to be appropriated by the believer through the gift of faith, the new birth, and perfection in grace (37).

[57]See chapter 1.

[58]Lyle Dabney recounts that Moltmann's *The Spirit of Life* was an unplanned volume in Moltmann's systematic works. See D. Lyle Dabney, "The Advent of the Spirit: The Turn to Pneumatology in the Theology of Jürgen Moltmann," *Asbury Theological Journal* 48 (1993): 81–107.

[59]Moltmann, *The Spirit of Life,* 41. For additional exegetical study, see "Pneuma, "in *Theological Dictionary of the New Testament,* ed. Gerhard Friedrich, trans. Geoffrey W. Bromiley, vol. 6 (Grand Rapids, Mich.: Eerdmans, 1968), 334–431.

and the world.[60] For Moltmann, modern epistemology reduces human experience and knowledge to an egocentric subject in a dead world of passive objects known and controlled as an extension of the ego. In this mechanistic universe, God becomes an expendable cause, a phantom, and human beings the autonomous, yet isolated, determiners of their reality. Moltmann passionately writes of the desolate erosion of life, sacrificed for the controllable verifiability of experience:

> The construction of the world according to the ideas of geometry means its complete loss of sensuousness and if "reason perceives only that which it brings forth itself according to its own design," as Kant says, then we are confronted with the critical question: is there any experience at all which is not projected experience of the self? If there is not experience of something other, which modifies the self, then there is really no experience at all. The self which knows no difference in itself, is to itself a matter of indifference. The ego which sees its own reflection in its projections and productions is merely bored in the hall of mirrors of its own self.[61]

In the irony of modernity's project, we find ourselves with a "brave new world" of narcissism, violence, a nonsustainable ecology, economic (ir)rationalism, and ultimately, the inability to behold dignity in any creature, including ourselves. Moltmann turns to the language of Spirit as a way beyond the reductionistic subject-object dualism founding modern knowledge toward the *intersubjectivity* of all knowledge and experience. Others, and particularly God as Other, become constitutive of human knowledge, experience, and faith. Life in the Spirit is a life of *immanental transcendence*, so God may be experienced in all things, and all things in God.[62] To breathe with God's breath means to turn from callous, death-filled ways of living and embrace God's praxis of the love of life:

> We then perceive the finite in the infinite, the temporal in the eternal, and the evanescent in what endures. We carry experiences of the world into the experience of God. "Reverence for life" is absorbed into reverence for God, and the veneration of nature becomes part of the adoration of God. We sense that in everything God is waiting for us.[63]

Through the biblical tradition of God's *ruach,* Moltmann attempts to overcome the epistemological dualism of modernity and the theological dualism separating creation and redemption. The Spirit of life is the living vitality of

---

[60]Moltmann, *The Spirit of Life,* 37. Panentheism claims that the world is in God, but the world does not exhaust God. God is both immanent in and transcendent to the world. Panentheism stands in contrast to theism, which maintains the distinction between world and God, and pantheism, which equates God and the world absolutely.

[61]Ibid., 30.

[62]Ibid., 35–36.

[63]Ibid., 36.

our present world in all its suffering and joy, as well as the living vitality of our hope in God's future.

With breath as his primary metaphor for constructing a theology of Spirit, Moltmann draws on other biblical and spiritual metaphors as well. He sets forth four categories for his holistic pneumatology.[64] The first category includes personal metaphors—the Spirit as Lord, Mother, and Judge. The second category offers formative metaphors, including the Spirit as energy, space, and Gestalt. Third, the movement metaphors address the Spirit as tempest, fire, and love. Fourth, he cites light, water, and fertility as the mystical metaphors for God's Spirit.

But while Moltmann draws on both personal and impersonal language to image God as Spirit, he concludes his book with the "streaming personhood" of the Spirit.[65] He anticipates his critics by saying that the diversity of language regarding the Spirit doesn't point to confusion or elusiveness; the metaphors express together a divine personhood that "comes into being with permeable frontiers…in life-giving relationships."[66] Thus, the personhood of God the Holy Spirit is "the loving, self-communicating, out-fanning and out-pouring presence of the eternal divine life of the triune God."[67] At first, Moltmann appears to define the Spirit as the sum of the triune relations, almost as if the Spirit represents a fourth mode within the Godhead. But Moltmann rejects individualistic understandings of personhood, advocating instead an intersubjective framework. As he notes, his Trinitarian pneumatology also calls for a redefinition of the personhood of the Son and the Father, but that must wait until another work![68] To summarize, Moltmann's pneumatology brings together fresh associations of Spirit and life, in particular, intersubjective human life.

Moltmann's focus on personal models of God the Spirit stands in contrast to Mark I. Wallace's project of connecting Spirit and life through impersonal models. Like Moltmann, Wallace incorporates a holistic view of life, but Wallace's focus in *Fragments of the Spirit* takes a decidedly environmental turn toward an "ecological pneumatology."[69] For Wallace, the relation of humans and nature has become so distorted that we live in danger of perpetrating ecocide against the planet. Reducing nature's wild and wondrous spaces to either real estate or managed resources, humans continue living in increasingly unsustainable ways, totally "unaware of the ties that bind us to the web of life that sustains all creation."[70] Like Moltmann and other contemporary pneumatologists, Wallace turns to biblical images of the Spirit as breath, wind,

---

[64]Ibid., 268–84.

[65]Ibid., 285.

[66]Ibid., 287.

[67]Ibid., 289.

[68]Ibid., 343.

[69]Mark I. Wallace, *Fragments of the Spirit: Nature, Violence, and the Renewal of Creation* (New York: Continuum, 1996), 134.

[70]Ibid., 135.

water, and fire to reclaim the Spirit's ecological identity. But Wallace takes a further step by suggesting that the Holy Spirit is a natural, living being who indwells and sustains all life-forms:

> The point is not that the Spirit is simply in nature as its interanimating force, as important as that is, but that the Spirit is a natural being who leads all creation into a peaceable relationship with itself…The Spirit is the unseen power who vivifies and sustains all living things, while the earth is the visible agent of the life that pulsates throughout creation.[71]

Wallace seeks a more radical panentheism than Moltmann, for while Wallace distinguishes the Spirit from creation, the two are so intimately related that the ecocide of life on Earth implies the deicide of the Spirit.[72] Utterly vulnerable, the Spirit lives at risk within Wallace's biocentric model.

Like Min, Wallace retrieves the Augustinian bond of love, the *vinculum caritatis,* but through his ecological hermeneutic, the bonds encompass all beings of the natural world.[73] Far from the sweet, gentle dove found in stained-glass windows or on Christian coffee mugs, the Spirit presents the "Green Face of God," a transgressive, brooding being whose work of "biotic reconciliation" dismantles the arrogant, artificial boundaries between humanity and nature.[74] Wallace draws from the medieval art series the Rothschild Canticles to reimagine the Spirit as a strong, large-taloned mountain raptor.[75] As God confronted Job out of the whirlwind, so the "wild bird that heals" confronts humans with their anthropocentricity and helps them embrace new vocations as humble pilgrims and sojourners, rather than as wardens and stewards.[76]

In contrast to Welker's, Min's, and Comblin's primary concern for *human* justice, Moltmann and Wallace extend the breath of God's Spirit to encompass the life of the whole creation. All five theologians share the concern for public, institutional transformation. But for Wallace and Moltmann, the Spirit's mission of righting unjust relations extends to the "greening" of human communities. Moltmann's holistic pneumatology rests on the eschatological trust in God's eternal life that pervades this life and draws creation forth. Yet Wallace's ecological pneumatology brings an urgency–a threat even–against the daily indifference of humankind that continually inflicts suffering on our planet and God. Both theologians, though, help us reclaim the biblical, earthy interrelatedness of life in the Spirit.

---

[71]Ibid., 136.
[72]Ibid., 143.
[73]Ibid., 138, 144–48.
[74]Ibid., 148–54.
[75]Ibid., 7.
[76]Ibid., 158–70.

The Spirit and Diversity

Turning to the Spirit enables theologians to take seriously contemporary concerns of pluralism. But rather than affirm positions of radical relativity (Bauman's rampant tribalism), theologians of the Spirit seek social orientations of diversity-in-unity. Colin Gunton and Michael Welker both turn to pneumatology as a way of affirming "the cunning of diversity,"[77] which means that through acknowledging differences between people, community may be more authetically constituted. But each theologian turns to the Spirit from a different starting point. Gunton faces the age of modernity and challenges its legacy of cultural homogeneity. Welker faces postmodernity and claims that cultural fragmentation remains its major problem. Through a renewal of pneumatology, both theologians work toward a social vision of diversity-in-unity.

Gunton claims that the philosophical, political, scientific, and economic interests of modernity created a legacy of Western cultural homogeneity, best symbolized by the image of a Coca-Cola sign in every village of the world.[78] He raises the following question: "Where might we find a theology of being which resists the pressures for homogeneity by giving due weight to the particular? A beginning can be found in a theology of the Spirit."[79] Gunton's turn to the Spirit picks up not only the Hebrew Bible *ruach* tradition of divine-human empowerment, but New Testament traditions featuring the Spirit freeing persons for God and for community. The Spirit brings God into relation with the world, and the world into relation with God, as in Romans 8:15–16: "When we cry, 'Abba! Father!' it is that very Spirit bearing witness with our spirit."[80] For Gunton, God's Spirit crosses boundaries by opening people and other beings to one another, yet without abolishing distinctiveness between beings. Instead of merging or assimilating others, as in homogeneity, the Spirit establishes others in their own true realities. Gunton exclaims, "We must put out of our minds the popular view that the Spirit was a homogeneous possession of Jesus, like a built-in soul-stuff. The Spirit is the one, the personal other, by whom Jesus is related to his Father and to those with whom he had to do."[81] Gunton's turn to the Spirit challenges structures and ideologies of homogenization that keep people and things from their particular purposes or vocations in praise of God.

---

[77]This phrase plays with Hegel's concept of "the cunning of reason" from his *Phenomenology of Spirit*, trans. A. V. Miller (New York: Oxford University Press, 1977), 33. According to Hegel, human understanding depends on the relation of self and other; reason is not abstract from the consciousness of self in and through others. The cunning of reason works as follows: What may at first seem like the loss of self in community is actually a gaining of self, because it is through the other that one gains recognition of oneself. Questions remain for Hegel about how *other* this other is in his pneumatology: Is the other not just a self-reflection? The phrase *the cunning of diversity* more fully discloses the acknowledgment of difference in relations.

[78]Colin E. Gunton, *The One, the Three and the Many: God, Creation and the Culture of Modernity* (Cambridge: Cambridge University Press, 1993), 180.

[79]Ibid., 181.

[80]Ibid., 182.

[81]Ibid.

Like Gunton, Michael Welker criticizes modern images of unity promoting homogeneity, but he addresses postmodernity and the social fragmentation within relationships, communities, and nations. From Welker's perspective, the destructive problems of our time include individualism, self-concern, and functional differentiation between multiple social subsystems (e.g., law, religion, economics, education, government, and family). Social fragmentation leads to a lack of coherence in our vision of the public good; thus, individuals and subsystems feel helpless and isolated in the face of threatening dangers. Resignation results, with individuals optimizing their own interests and preserving themselves at any cost.[82] In contrast to the "one world" of modernity, postmodernity's fragmentation leads to a narcissistic "my world" and mine alone.

Welker claims only the Spirit of God overcomes social fragmentation and the suffering that ensues. The miracle of Pentecost is not an extraordinary, inaccessible event, but the shared understanding across human differences of God's righteousness, mercy, and justice made public for the world.[83] For Welker, Pentecost unity offers an invigorating pluralism emerging through the diversity of participants to create a force field of public love: "The Spirit of God gives rise to a multi-place force field that is sensitive to differences. In this force-field, enjoyment of creaturely, invigorating differences can be cultivated while unjust, debilitating differences can be removed in love, mercy and gentleness."[84] While Welker encourages liberation and feminist movements, he avoids identifying the Spirit with any one person, movement, or social cause. Welker's pneumatology of "emergent change" supports complex social processes of multidirectional, nonhierarchical, and polyvocal transformation.[85] Through the Spirit's initiative and human participation, new forms of compassionate community rise out of the social ruptures. Because God's promises of justice, mercy, and knowledge of God extend to all people, the Spirit's diversity-in-unity transcends monocultural Christian models for new pluralistic communities.

The themes of liberation, life, and diversity shine through this sampling of contemporary theologians' perspectives on the Spirit. Differences exist between their projects, and in chapter 7 a more detailed analysis will be undertaken with the pneumatologies of Moltmann, Welker, and Gunton. But when taken together, their work points to the vital connection between Spirit and the right-relationship of self and other expressed throughout the political, ecological, economic, and social domains of life. According to Christian traditions, God the Spirit delivers, invigorates, and transforms unjust relations for full participation in a world of freedom and hope. Central to this transformation is the restoration and sustenance of difference in relationship—in other words, the cunning of diversity. The Spirit's solidarity of others or force field

---

[82]Welker, 28–40.
[83]Ibid., 233.
[84]Ibid., 22.
[85]Ibid., 39.

of mercy and justice creates unity not in spite of diversity, but in and through the dignified diversity of beings.

By lifting up the themes of liberation, life, and diversity in relation to God the Spirit, a feminist pneumatology of mutual recognition more closely examines the dynamics of the self-other relation. All three themes are necessary for interpreting the Spirit's presence and work as invigorating and empowering dignity. In chapters 7 and 9, a feminist pneumatology of mutual recognition enhances the Pentecost vision of diversity-in-unity by extending the Spirit's energy for life to the struggle for interpersonal differentiation in unjust structures or relations. Too often theologies of Spirit overlook, underestimate, or idealize the hard struggle for recognition and dignity. The concept of *mutual* recognition maintains the complex tension between self and other, with the corresponding need for assertion and response, without lapsing into either homogeneity or individualism. With this goal in mind, the final section of the chapter shifts from the thematic introduction to two specific starting points for a feminist analysis of Spirit in the household of God.

Models of the Spirit

Sallie McFague's metaphorical theology provides the first starting point for a feminist analysis of the function of Spirit language in models of God.[86] Throughout her writing, McFague explores the linguistic models and metaphors used by humans to understand God and God's relation to the world. McFague claims that while religious language has always risked idolatry, the paternal metaphor for God has become an intransigent patriarchal model:

> "God the father"…has become a model which serves as a grid or screen through which to see not only the nature of God but also our relationships to the divine and with one another. "Patriarchy" then is not just that most of the images of the deity in Western religion are masculine–king, father, husband, lord, master–but it is the Western *way of life:* it describes *patterns of governance* at national, ecclesiastical, business and family levels.[87]

McFague's exploration of the models of God as Mother, Lover, and Friend challenges the patterns of governance implicated in the models of God as Father, Master, and King.[88] The feminist analysis of Spirit in the following chapters follows a similar methodology, but from the perspective of the "family level" in our governing patterns. If the patriarchal family serves as the fundamental metaphor in the patriarchal model of God as Father, then how does the Spirit function within this model of God? If the Triune relations of Father, Son, and Spirit can be spoken of as an immanent family having an

---

[86]Sallie McFague, *Metaphorical Theology: Models of God in Religious Language* (Philadelphia: Fortress Press, 1982).
[87]Ibid., 9. Emphasis added.
[88]Sallie McFague, *Models of God: Theology for an Ecological, Nuclear Age* (Minneapolis: Fortress Press, 1987).

economy (*oikonomia*) of relations with the whole inhabited world (*oikoumene*), then how do models of human family relations contribute to our pneumatological understandings?[89] Do nonpatriarchal family models provide a new critical and constructive hermeneutic for reimagining God as Spirit within the Triune relations? While the pneumatological analysis begins on the level of family or household governance (*oikonomia*), the implications of mutual recognition bear social, economic, and political implications for the public household (*oikoumene*) as well.

In *Models of God*, McFague raised the possibility of reimagining God and God's relation to the world through the model of God as Spirit. But because of her theological agenda in privileging embodiment, McFague decided against this proposal at the time.[90] She acknowledged the non–gender-related, immanental character of Spirit language as well as the connection between Spirit and the inspired life of Jesus of Nazareth and his followers.[91] But for an ecological age, the model of Spirit unfortunately carried the heavy burdens of individualism and anthropocentrism. Definitely better than the metaphor of Holy Ghost, Spirit language sounded still "ethereal, shapeless and vacant"—in sum, too "bland."[92] McFague turned to the relations of parents, lovers, and friends to construct models of God that integrated God's transcendence with God's immanence, God's freedom with God's vulnerability, and God's inclusive love for the world with particular concerns of the marginalized.

But in her recent work *The Body of God*, McFague reassesses the model of God the Spirit.[93] She acknowledges indebtedness to Chung Hyun Kyung, who offered "one of the richest and most moving treatments of the Holy Spirit" in her Canberra address.[94] Now McFague rejects the disembodied, rationalistic interpretations of Spirit that influenced her in the past and returns to pneumatology as the basis for an embodied God. She constructs a panentheistic model of "the world as God's body" through the connection between body and breath (*ruach*), in contrast to body and mind (the latter associated with anthropocentric characterizations of God the Spirit). McFague then sets forth this analogy: God is related to the world as spirit is to the body. The connection of Spirit and breath challenges strong versions of the anthropic

---

[89]Drawing on Trinitarian family analogies of Greek theologians such as Gregory of Nazianzen, Methodius, and Ephraim, Leonardo Boff writes in *Trinity and Society* (Maryknoll, N.Y.: Orbis Books, 1988): "The Three together form the family of God, within which everything is bound up in the same circle of life, just as in a human family. This analogy is powerfully evocative, being based on the most natural of human experiences, one that has been raised to a sacrament in the Christian faith: married life. There is no need to introduce sexual differences into the analogy; it is enough to consider the personal differences that make up the plurality in unity of every family" (106). But what happens when the engendered differences of the family (as patriarchal) are examined? Does this analysis lend new insight for Trinitarian theologies?

[90]McFague, *Models of God*, 169–70.

[91]In Hebrew, *ruach* is female; in Greek, *pneuma* is neuter; in Latin, *spiritus* is masculine; and in German, *Geist* is masculine.

[92]McFague, *Models of God*, 169.

[93]Sallie McFague, *The Body of God: An Ecological Theology* (Minneapolis: Fortress Press, 1994), 141–50.

[94]McFague, *The Body of God*, 253.

principle that views the whole of evolutionary purpose for the ascendancy of human self-consciousness. For McFague, human life in the Spirit must first consider embodied life here on Earth, lived out in the praxis of inspired partnership with God and other creatures. Her own journey of experimentation with various models of God led McFague to turn to the Spirit for a model of life's diversity-in-unity in God.

While McFague maintains a cosmological horizon for a theology of Spirit, the following chapters focus on the relationship of Spirit language and the model of family or household (*oikos*). Exploration of the Spirit's functioning in the "household of God" (Eph. 2:19) provides a hermeneutic of mutual recognition necessary for the pneumatological interests of liberation, life, and diversity. By examining the Spirit's role in *patterns of governance* at the family and church level, a feminist analysis offers its own gifts to the turn to the Spirit in contemporary theology.

Beyond Household Monotheism

The second starting point for a feminist project comes from the pneumatological lead mentioned, but left undeveloped, in Moltmann's early book *The Trinity and the Kingdom*.[95] In this text, Moltmann argues for a social model of the Trinity based on moving beyond monotheistic models of God as Supreme Substance or Absolute Subject. These models, dominant in Western Christianity, privilege the divine sovereignty of the One and reflect the social orders of political and clerical sovereignty. The monarchical structure of the universe corresponds to the monarchical structures of the state and the church: one God–one Logos–one Cosmos–one Emperor–one Empire–one Christ–one Bishop–one Church. With echoes of McFague, Moltmann explains:

> As long as the unity of the triune God is understood monadically or subjectivistically, and not in Trinitarian terms, the whole cohesion of a religious legitimation of political sovereignty continues to exist. It is only when the doctrine of the Trinity vanquishes the monotheistic notion of the great universal monarch in heaven, and his divine patriarchs in the world, that earthly rulers, dictators and tyrants cease to find any justifying religious archetypes any more.[96]

Moltmann suggests that a return to Trinitarian thinking will help develop a theology of political freedom, reflected in "a community of men and women without supremacy and without subjection."[97]

But Moltmann neglects an additional form of social monotheism that extends his line of correlates: one Master–one Father–one Head of Household. He does recognize the possibility of what this feminist analysis terms *household monotheism* through a very brief reference to the social Trinity in family terms: "The image of the family is a favorite one for the unity of the

---

[95]Jürgen Moltmann, *The Trinity and the Kingdom* (San Francisco: Harper & Row, 1981).
[96]Ibid., 197.
[97]Ibid., 192.

Triunity: three Persons–one family."[98] By retrieving Gregory of Nazianzus' image of Adam, Eve, and Seth as an earthly image and parable of the Trinity, Moltmann stresses that the image of God is found in intersubjectivity, not in any individual subject.[99] Moltmann's connection between the Trinity, social models, and family provides a lead for a feminist exploration of family models and Spirit language. What Moltmann alludes to implicitly and uncritically, the following chapters make explicit–social models of the Trinity must include a critical family analysis as well.[100] Thus, what is the role of the Spirit in household monotheism? Because family and household also serve as models for the church, how does Spirit language function in ecclesiastical monotheism? What will nonpatriarchal understandings of family mean for theological construction? Is there a pneumatological way beyond household, church, and political monotheism?

A Feminist Gift

McFague's metaphorical theology and Moltmann's social Trinitarianism provide the starting points for a feminist turn to the Spirit beyond household monotheism. The project assumes that family life offers formative models for religious language. Historically, the family norm for Christian theology has been the male- or master-headed household, referred to in feminist theology as the patriarchal family or the "kyriocentric" household.[101] From a feminist perspective, Rita Nakashima Brock asserts, "Patriarchal family relationships are the bricks of the patriarch's theological house of worship."[102] Thus,

---

[98]Ibid., 199.

[99]Ibid.

[100]The lead from Moltmann echoes in the work of Miroslav Volf, who affirms the "conjunctive" relation between human communities and Triune relations. See his article "The Trinity is Our Social Program: The Doctrine of the Trinity and the Shape of Social Engagement," *Modern Theology* 14, no. 3 (July 1998): 403–23. Volf writes: "The conceptual construction of the correspondences cannot proceed on a one-way street starting from above–from the doctrine of the Trinity down to a vision of social realities. If the mode and the extent of the correspondences are not only determined by the character of the Trinity but also inscribed in the very fabric of social realities themselves, then the conceptual construction of the correspondences must go back and forth on a two-way street, both from above and from below. By describing God in whose image human beings are created and redeemed, the doctrine of the Trinity names the reality which human communities ought to image. By describing human beings as distinct from God, the doctrines of creation and of sin inform the way in which human communities can image the Triune God, now in history and then in eternity" (406–7). While Volf and Moltmann address societies, politics, and the Trinity, the analysis here extends the "two-way" conjunction to include families and Triune relations.

[101]The term *patriarchal* calls attention to the male-rule of the *paterfamilias,* the head of household. See Rosemary Radford Ruether, "Patriarchy," in *Dictionary of Feminist Theologies,* ed. Letty M. Russell and J. Shannon Clarkson (Louisville, Ky.: Westminster John Knox Press, 1996), 205–6. But the neologism–kyriocentric–calls attention to the ruling order of master or lord (*kyrios*) over slave. While contemporary discussion of family values tends to focus on gender relations, it is important not to lose sight of the historical oppression of servants and slaves within household orders, who in Western history have included persons of color or non-Western cultures. Moving beyond household monotheism needs to connect gender analysis with analyses of race, class, culture, and sexual orientation. On the concept of kyriarchy, see Elisabeth Schüssler Fiorenza, *Jesus: Miriam's Child, Sophia's Prophet* (New York: Continuum, 1994), 12–18.

[102]Rita Nakashima Brock, *Journeys By Heart: A Christology of Erotic Power* (New York: Crossroad, 1988), 4.

dismantling the bricks and re-firing them to reflect nonpatriarchal values makes available new opportunities for theological reconstruction. The hearth of feminist analysis presents the patriarchal family norm in its historical light and provides hope for contextual pneumatology from the standpoint of new family models.

Currently, the debate over family values in North American culture has set the "traditional" family model of male headship against the egalitarian model of partnership. Chapters 3 and 4 explore the debate between reformers and transformers of family values in North American society and churches, respectively. The debate rages between the norms of hierarchy and mutuality, raising the question, Can differences can be recognized without hierarchy, or must household unity involve uniformity under the proper head? The contemporary cultural debate shares deep connections with similar conflicts in early Christian churches between hierarchical and egalitarian models of household relations. The historical and theological analysis in chapter 6 shows that when each model is adopted for religious language, God the Spirit functions with a contrasting role. Within the patriarchal family model, Spirit language rightly orders household members under the ruling unity of the head of household. But in the egalitarian model, Spirit language functions to differentiate, yet unite, household members in relations of mutual recognition. Feminist analysis retrieves these pneumatological models for critical use in contemporary theological construction and societal transformation.

This chapter introduces the turn to the Spirit in contemporary theology and the starting points for a feminist analysis of Spirit models. While theological interest in God the Spirit is not new to this century, the World Council of Churches' 1991 Seventh Assembly in Canberra provided fiery sparks for an increased breadth of academic Spirit renewal. Following Canberra, theologians from diverse perspectives have begun offering rich resources for new paradigms of God the Spirit. The perspectives of McFague, Moltmann, and other theologians of the Spirit regarding liberation, life, and diversity will discover enrichment through the insight of a feminist pneumatology of mutual recognition. Examining the relationship of family and Spirit in theological discourse strengthens models of diversity-in-unity, whether in families, churches, or communities. The following chapters offer a gift from the diversity of the Spirit—a feminist pneumatology of mutual recognition based on the praxis of postmodern feminist families.

CHAPTER 3

Domestic Revolutions: Re-figuring Family Life

Many feminists are turning with renewed attention to the realm that has been seen for so long as paradigmatically not political. Ambivalent, as in the past, they value much of what families represent, but refuse to accept the continued reinforcement of women's subordination that for so long seemed almost synonymous with "family." They are responding to the multiple changes in family life that this *fin de siécle* has brought about—not so as to try to restore an overlauded and mythologized past, but so as to enable more egalitarian and more inclusive family forms and relations to develop in the future.[1]

Whose Family Values?

Common wisdom advises that unless one wants to spark a controversy, religion and politics are two topics of conversation to avoid around a dinner table. At the turn of the century, the subject of family values also warrants such a warning, not the least because family values so indelibly connect with both religion and politics. Mention family values and people definitely have opinions, and quite strong opinions at that! In fact, the reference to a "culture war" in North American society has become popular and commonplace.[2] While the image of war seems extreme and reductive, it does point toward two conflicting movements in North American family politics. On one side stand the social *reformers*, who view the second half of the twentieth century as a time of grave deterioration in moral character, social stability, and religious bearing. Reformers seek a return to the "traditional" family as the norm for family life. According to David Popenoe, the traditional family (or modern or nuclear family) may be formally defined as:

---

[1]Susan Moller Okin, "Families and Feminist Theology: Some Past and Present Issues," in *Feminism and Families,* ed. Hilde Lindemann Nelson (New York: Routledge, 1997), 24–25.

[2]James Davison Hunter, *Culture Wars: the Struggle to Define America* (New York: Basic Books, 1991).

a family situated apart from both the larger kin group and the work-place; focused on the procreation of children and consisting of a le-gal, lifelong, sexually exclusive, heterosexual monogamous marriage, based on affection and companionship, in which there is a sharp division of labor, with the female as full-time housewife and the male as primary provider and ultimate authority. Lasting for only a little more than a century, this family form emphasized the male as "good provider," the female as "good wife and mother," and the paramount importance of the family for child rearing.[3]

The term *traditional* implies that this particular family form constitutes the original or natural form of family, the foundation of our past and future societies. Similarly, references to the nuclear family also reinforce the image of an unchanging basic building block of social life. For many reformers, the traditional family provides the only faithful family structure for Christian re-ligious commitment. Reformers of the family adamantly agree with Connaught Marshner of the Heritage Foundation, "In regard to the family, one premise underlies all else: There is no alternative to the traditional family."[4]

On the other side of the debate stand social *transformers*, who recognize the historical adaptability of the family as a social institution and thus affirm a diversity of family forms, inclusive of, but not limited to, what they term the modern ("traditional") family.[5] Family transformer Judith Stacey advocates "brave, new families" and claims that "we are living…through a tumultuous and contested period of family history, a period after the modern family or-der, but before what we cannot foretell."[6] Transformers recognize the prob-lems and limitations of the modern family, yet remain committed to making changes for sustaining new family relations in the future. Reformers and trans-formers both lay claim to valuing family life, but their strategies and visions of family and society remain radically different. In talking about family values the question remains, Whose family values?

---

[3]David Popenoe, "Family Decline in America," in *Rebuilding the Nest: A New Commitment to the American Family,* ed. David Blankenhorn, Steven Bayme, and Jean Bethke Elshtain (Milwau-kee: Family Service America, 1990), 40. Popenoe is not a reformer in the sense used here of wanting to return uncritically to the traditional family norm, but his definition provides a good description of the reformist vision.

[4]Connaught Marshner, "Family Protection: The Imperative of the Future," in *Future 21: Directions for America in the 21st Century,* ed. Paul Weyrich and Connaught Marshner (Greenwich, Conn.: Devin-Adair, 1984), 148.

[5]Instead of referring to the traditional family, I prefer to use the term *modern family* in calling attention to the historical and contextual character of this family form. Maintaining the designation of traditional family continues reinforcing the normativity of this social structure and thus the deviance of alternative family structures. See Linda Nicholson, "The Myth of the Tradi-tional Family," in *Feminism and Families,* 27–42.

[6]Judith Stacey, *Brave New Families: Stories of Domestic Upheaval in Late Twentieth Century America* (New York: Basic Books, 1990). The second quote comes from Judith Stacey, "Backward Toward the Postmodern Family: Reflections on Gender, Kinship and Class in the Silicon Valley," in *Re-Thinking the Family: Some Feminist Questions,* ed. Barrie Thorne and Marilyn Yalom (Boston: North-eastern University Press, 1992), 93.

This chapter explores the controversy surrounding family values in North American society during the second half of the twentieth century. While family reformers return to a past hierarchical ideal, transformers seek new models of family democratization. The question is not which group, reformers or transformers, represents authentic family values, but what values form the core of each group's vision. Transformers remind us that the private boundaries, rigid gender roles, and inequities of power inherent in the modern family create an environment conducive to abuse and domination of family members. An uncritical return to this ideal of family values puts women and children at risk and places men in limited, but privileged, modes of participation. For a new century, a critical perspective on families needs to replace our nostalgic *familism.*

The exploration takes seriously the values and insights of postmodern feminist families in their struggles with re-figuring family life. The core values of equal regard, diversity, and shared authority re-figure family relations from the model of hierarchy to models of mutuality. In transforming models, the value of self-sacrifice shifts from the primary norm to transitional status, still necessary though, for the restoration of these democratic values. But the praxis of postmodern feminist families affirms another transitional value for developing mutuality in families—the value of self-assertion. By challenging the ideal of the modern family, postmodern feminist families create new spaces for reflection not only on family life, but on the values and social models underlying Christian faith and practice. Their struggles and joys create a new context for transforming theology beyond its reliance on models of household monotheism.[7]

Family or Families?

A defining moment in the debate between family reformers and transformers occurred in 1980 when former President Jimmy Carter changed the title of his proposed "The White House Conference on the American Family" to "The White House Conference on Families."[8] The shift from *family* to *families* acknowledged the complex, changing situation of the needs of families, but the wording generated controversy. For advocates of *families*, the change reflected "a politically charged battle with the potential for 'revisioning' and reconstituting our social relations and political life."[9] Conference reports acknowledged that "the roles and structure of families (and their) individual family members are growing, adapting, and evolving in new and different ways."[10] From the perspective of families, changes in family life need not be

---

[7]See chapter 2 for the discussion of theology's reliance on models of political and household monotheism.

[8]Irene Diamond, "Introduction," in *Families, Politics, and Public Policy: A Feminist Dialogue on Women and the State,* ed. Irene Diamond (New York: Longman, 1983), 1.

[9]Ibid.

[10]*White House Conference on Families–Families and Human Needs–Handbook* (Baltimore, 1980), 2, cited in Paula M. Cooey, *Family, Freedom and Faith: Building Community Today* (Louisville, Ky.: Westminster John Knox Press, 1996), 34.

interpreted as solely negative or destructive and women working outside the home should not shoulder the blame. In response, *family* reformers dissented by composing a Minority Report that insisted the title of future conferences return to the original plan, in order to recognize "that our nation was founded on a strong traditional family, meaning a married heterosexual couple with or without natural children."[11] Family or families? The difference represents more than playing with words. Family or families sets forth the boundaries between reformers and transformers in the cultural crisis of family values.

The controversy between family or families reaches all dimensions of society. In recent years, television has diversified its images of families with dramas and sitcoms across racial, class, and sexual spectrums. Yet on cable, The Family Channel provides an alternative with "family-friendly" programming (even though there are still plenty of Westerns and war films filled with violence and cultural stereotypes). News programming features segments designated specifically "For the Family." Magazine advertisers continue to use family images, depending on their intended audience, to sell anything from car tires to gourmet coffee. Political leaders square off with bestsellers promoting their own version of family values. In *The American Family*, former Vice President Dan Quayle and Diane Medved norm the modern family with its private responsibility for shaping moral character and the unique role of fatherhood.[12] In contrast, First Lady Hillary Rodham Clinton stresses public responsibility for nurturing the children of all families in her book *It Takes A Village*.[13] Democrats and Republicans alike present themselves as the political party of family values, yet differ dramatically in their approaches to issues such as abortion, welfare, tax reform, and domestic partnerships.

Religious leaders, too, have become involved in the battle over families. On one side the Christian Coalition's *Contract With the American Family* advances the male-headed modern family as the divinely ordained blueprint for a Christian society.[14] On the other side, Jim Wallis of the Sojourners community represents a politics of social justice for the poor and marginalized of all families in his response.[15] In the North American cultural war, the debate has become framed within the either/or: *family* or *families*.

Even Barney, the big purple dinosaur of PBS's children's programming, has been drawn into the struggle. Defining family as people who love one

---

[11]Diamond, 1.

[12]Dan Quayle and Diane Medved, *The American Family: Discovering the Values That Make Us Strong* (New York: HarperCollins, 1996).

[13]Hillary Rodham Clinton, *It Takes A Village and Other Lessons Children Teach Us* (New York: Simon and Schuster, 1996).

[14]Ralph Reed, *Mainstream Values Are No Longer Politically Incorrect: The Emerging Faith Factor in American Politics* (Dallas: Word Publishing, 1994), cited in Cooey, 30–42.

[15]Jim Wallis, *The Soul of Politics: A Practical and Prophetic Vision for Change* (Maryknoll, N.Y.: Orbis Books, 1994), cited in Cooey, 30–42. Cooey claims Wallis' inclusive, participatory position of the "People of God," based on the theological concept that all human beings are created in the image of God, is more helpful toward building democracy than Reed's exclusive and assimilationist position of "People of Faith."

another, Barney sings about families of all shapes and sizes. Each family is unique in an age of family diversity.

From the perspective of family reformers, Barney's song represents a dangerous relativistic ideology that whitewashes social deterioration and undermines faith, freedom, and even national security. As religious leader Jerry Falwell sounds the alarm for a family values apocalypse: "Need I say that it is time that moral Americans become informed and involved in helping to preserve family values in our nation?...We cannot wait. The twilight of our nation could well be at hand."[16] Calling forth a similar appeal for the traditional family as the cornerstone of Western civilization, Marshner claims "the American character, or more broadly, the character of Western civilization must be passed onto subsequent generations if our country as we know it is to survive."[17] Both family reformers and transformers of families agree that North American society stands at "the end of an epoch" for the cultural dominance of the modern family.[18] Whether this point is for better or for worse depends on the interpretive framework of each position.

Nuclear Fallout

Throughout the course of the family debate, statistics have been employed to contrast the closing decades of the twentieth century with the 1950s, viewed positively as a time of family stability and homogeneity. David Blankenhorn summarizes, "The Rubicon of the family debate centers on how one responds to the question, 'What are the dimensions and consequences of changes in the family during the past quarter century?'"[19] Most statistics convey a negative picture of family decline, including children placed increasingly at risk. In the 1950s and early 1960s, the majority (95 percent) of North American children were born to married couples, white and black.[20] Only 11 percent of children born in the 1950s would see their parents separate or divorce by the time they turned eighteen.[21] Between 1960 and 1982, the rate of divorce tripled, then leveled off at a point where today 50 percent of first marriages and 60 percent of second ones end in divorce.[22] In the same period, the proportion

---

[16]Jerry Falwell, *Listen America!* (Garden City, N.Y.: Doubleday, 1980), 142–43, cited in Susan Faludi, *Backlash: The Undeclared War Against American Women* (New York: Crown Publishers, 1991), 234.

[17]Marshner, 155.

[18]Popenoe, 40.

[19]David Blankenhorn, "American Family Dilemmas," in *Rebuilding the Nest*, 7–8. Blankenhorn contrasts the "optimistic" approach of Pat Schroeder's *Champion of the Great American Family* (New York: Random House, 1989) with the "pessimistic" approach of David Popenoe's *Disturbing the Nest: Family Change and Decline in Modern Societies* (New York: Aldine de Gruyter, 1988).

[20]Barbara Dafoe Whitehead, "Dan Quayle Was Right," *The Atlantic Monthly* (April 1993): 51.

[21]Ibid.

[22]Stephanie Coontz, *The Way We Never Were: American Families and the Nostalgia Trap* (New York: Basic Books, 1992), 3.

of children born to unmarried teenagers rose from 15 percent to 61 percent, while the total number of children growing up with only one parent doubled to a full quarter of all children under the age of eighteen.[23] After divorce, the average annual income of mothers and children is $13,500 for whites and $9,000 for nonwhites, compared to $25,000 for white nonresidential fathers and $13,600 for nonwhite nonresidential fathers.[24] Studies show children of single parents are more likely to have premarital births or marry as teenagers and then divorce.[25] In contrast to the intact, economically secure family of the 1950s, analysts link together the increasing rate of divorce, premarital births, and poverty in a cyclical trend with looming future implications.

Racist myths complicate the culture war over family values by giving the impression that family change primarily represents a crisis for families of color. Stereotypes of poor, young, female-headed families of color with large numbers of children draining national budgets and threatening stable white suburbs emerge in political rhetoric and media images. But Children's Defense Fund founder Marian Wright Edelman claims that while statistics of poverty and family change are higher, percentage-wise, in communities of color, *quantitatively* the family crisis is a white family crisis.[26] For example, in her 1987 assessment Edelman shows that while 4.3 million black children live in poverty (half of all black children), 8.1 million white children live in poverty (one-sixth of white children). Black teen birth rates remain higher than white rates, but white teens contribute 69 percent of all teen births. Five million black children live in single-parent families, but 9 million white children live in similar settings. From 1969 to 1984 the poverty rate for black children increased by one-sixth, while the poverty rate for white children increased by two-thirds. Edelman claims the crisis for black families has stabilized or grown more slowly than for white families, which she believes has been foreshadowed by trends among black families. By revealing a more accurate portrait of poverty and family change in the U.S., Edelman sounds the alarm for *all* "families in peril."[27]

Statistics further show that hunger, violence, homelessness, drug addition, and drug abuse increasingly afflict the most vulnerable members of society—children. While in earlier generations, older people were poorer, today children make up 40 percent of all poor Americans.[28] Family historian Stephanie Coontz presents the current bleak picture:

> More than 20% of American children live in poverty—one in eight children under age 12 actually goes hungry; almost 100,000 are homeless on any given night...Every day, 135,000 children take a gun to school; every fourteen hours, a child younger than age 5 is

---

[23]Ibid.
[24]Whitehead, 62.
[25]Ibid.
[26]Marian Wright Edelman, *Families in Peril: An Agenda for Social Change* (Cambridge, Mass.: Harvard University Press, 1987), ix, 24–27.
[27]Ibid.
[28]Lee Salk, Foreword, in *Rebuilding the Nest*, vi.

murdered…Homicide has now replaced motor vehicle accidents as the leading cause of death among children below the age of one. The violent-death rate of teenagers rose from 62.4 per 100,000 in 1984 to 69.7 in 1988, an increase of 12 percent. The teen suicide rate has quadrupled since 1950…In a recent national poll, one in seven Americans claimed to have been sexually abused as a child, while one in six reported being physically abused. One out of every ten newborns has been exposed to some kind of illicit drug.[29]

Edelman suggests that if these present trends continue, poverty will engulf one in every four children by the year 2000.[30] While acknowledging the complex causality of poverty, Popenoe attributes the increased vulnerability of children to not only changes in family structure, but to a change in "the social ecology of children."[31] Today, children are anxious about family stability. The source of routines and traditions has shifted from the family and other mediating structures to consumer culture. In contrast to the 1950s, children today spend increasing amounts of time on their own in multiple childcare options, in after-school programs, on the streets, or in front of computer screens and televisions, leading some analysts to speak of a "parenting deficit."[32] Even though Americans speak of family as the central element in their lives, analysis of family practices, governmental spending, health-care, and education provides evidence that Americans underinvest in their children.[33] Edelman concludes, "Young families of all races, on whom we count to raise healthy children for America's future, are in extraordinary trouble."[34]

Statistics in the family debate also focus on women and their changing involvement with work and home. Between 1960 and 1989, women's fertility declined by almost 50 percent, from an average of 3.7 children per woman to only 1.9.[35] Since the 1950s, more women with children have entered the work force beyond their homes.[36] In 1960, only 19 percent of married women

---

[29]Coontz, 2.

[30]Edelman, 82.

[31]Popenoe, 45.

[32]Don Browning, Bonnie J. Miller-McLemore, Pamela D. Couture, K. Brynolf Lyon, and Robert M. Franklin, *From Culture Wars to Common Ground: Religion and the American Family Debate* (Louisville, Ky.: Westminster John Knox Press, 1997), 55.

[33]Mark Mellman, Edward Lazarus, and Allan Rivlin, "Family Time, Family Values," in *Rebuilding the Nest*, 73; and Victor R. Fuchs, "Are Americans Underinvesting in Children?" in *Rebuilding the Nest*, 53–70.

[34]Marian Wright Edelman, *The Measure of Our Success: A Letter to My Children and Yours* (Boston: Beacon Press, 1992), 82.

[35]Popenoe, 40.

[36]Discrepancies exist as to the percentage of women today in modern families. In *Rethinking the Family*, Judith Stacey claims only 7 percent of families in 1986 could be considered "traditional" (93). She cites Andrew Cherlin, ed., *The Changing American Family and Public Policy* (Washington, D.C.: Urban Institute Press, 1988), 5; and Susan Householder Van Horn, *Women, Work and Fertility, 1900–1986* (New York: New York University Press, 1988), 152. But David Blankenhorn claims modern families comprise 33.3 percent of families, the largest single category in the 1987 Bureau of Labor Statistics report. Thus, in contrast to Stacey, Blankenhorn concludes that while trends indicate a decline, the modern family is still viable and credible for many people. See Blankenhorn, "American Family Dilemmas," in *Rebuilding the Nest*, 12–13.

with children younger than six entered the labor force (39 percent with children between six and seventeen); by 1986, this figure climbed to 54 percent (68 percent of those with older children).[37] But even as women take on more employment and men have begun to share parenting and domestic labor, in general, women continue to struggle with "the second shift" of domestic responsibilities.[38]

So how do we read the changes indicated by statistical analysis? Have the consequences of family change since the 1950s proved negative for the well-being of families? Do poverty and children at risk represent the nuclear fallout from the deterioration of nuclear families? Pessimists claim that the family, as an institution primarily concerned with the nurture and development of children, has declined, creating a situation of immense social cost.[39] Barbara Dafoe Whitehead argues that the longitudinal data now confirms the last twenty-five years as a failed "vast natural experiment" in family structural change, where the social metric has shifted from the well-being of children to adults.[40]   She concludes that children in disrupted families develop weak maternal and paternal bonds, live with greater risk for child abuse, achieve less in school, present behavioral problems, suffer from depression, have difficulty holding steady employment, and are more likely to become involved with violent and criminal activity. Whitehead concludes that the shifting value from the modern family to the diversity of families has not led to social progress, which is assumed by transformers of families, but has in fact undermined the American social fabric, with negative consequences extending into the next century.

Family reformers take the views of pessimists such as Whitehead and correlate them with the statistics on women working outside the home. As a result, advocates for the modern family blame the fragility of family life on working women. Paul Weyrich, founder of the Heritage Foundation claims, "At last the lie of feminism is being understood. Women are discovering they can't have it all. They are discovering that if they have careers, their children will suffer, their family life will be destroyed."[41] Family reformers believe women's primary social responsibilities consist of motherhood and the maintenance of family life as the "haven" in which children develop conscience and character.[42] They assume caring and nurture occur primarily within the private realm and thus interpret women's movement beyond the sphere of their "natural" competence as an abdication of family ties and love. The irony, though, of their argument comes forth in the punitive discourse of welfare

---

[37]Popenoe, 41.

[38]Arlie Hochschild, *The Second Shift: Working Parents and the Revolution at Home* (New York: Viking Penguin, 1989).

[39]Pessimism regarding the deterioration in family life need not imply a reformist response. Blakenhorn, while holding to a position of pessimism, incorporates equality for women in marriage and the workplace in his suggestions for strengthening family life and improving the family debate. See his "American Family Dilemmas," in *Rebuilding the Family*, 7–22.

[40]Whitehead, 52.

[41]Cited by Faludi, 230.

[42]Christopher Lasch, *Haven in a Heartless World: The Family Besieged* (New York: Basic Books, 1977), 138–40.

reform, where poor women become righteous (in the eyes of family reformers) when they become employed, relying on subsidized day care and state programs. This hypocrisy belies the racial and class assumptions underlying the "tradition" of the traditional family.

But family transformers interpret the sociological data less negatively. Decline in the percentage of modern families does not necessarily imply social regress and certainly cannot be viewed as the sole cause of children's vulnerability. Optimists respond that changes in families have led to greater freedom for women and men in regard to shared parenting and vocational satisfaction.[43] Acknowledging family diversity further sheds light on families previously discounted and invisible. Since the 1970s, gays and lesbians have begun to openly claim the rights of kinship within "families we choose."[44] While the majority of families involved married parents during the 1950s, not all of these families were traditional in form. Women of color and working-class women tell of their ongoing struggles with work outside and work within families.[45] Statistics on divorce and lower incomes also do not show what percentage of children and women live in safer, less abusive environments. The simplistic reduction of social problems to the character faults of poor parents and the employment of women outside the home mystifies the larger complex of economic, demographic, philosophical, and political changes, which must also be considered in evaluating the data on changes in family life. Thus, an adequate interpretation of the data considers the complex factors giving rise to the predominance of the 1950s family in the first place.

Domestic Revolutions

According to Coontz, the experience of modern families during the 1950s was a novel phenomenon resulting from post-war prosperity, cheap energy, a building boom, and expansive government benefits.[46] Thus, rather than view

---

[43]Diane Ehrensaft, *Parenting Together: Men and Women Sharing the Care of Their Children* (New York: The Free Press, 1987).

[44]Kath Weston, *Families We Choose: Lesbians, Gays, Kinship* (New York: Columbia University Press, 1991). See also idem, "The Politics of Gay Families," in *Rethinking the Family*, 119–39; *Gay and Lesbian Parents*, ed. Fredrick W. Bozett (New York: Praeger, 1987); Cheshire Calhoun, "Family Outlaws: Rethinking the Connections between Feminism, Lesbianism and the Family," in *Feminism and Families*, 131–50; Sidney Callahan, "Gays, Lesbians and the Use of Alternative Reproductive Technologies," in *Feminism and Families*, 188–204; Judith Stacey, *In the Name of the Family: Rethinking Family Values in the Postmodern Age* (Boston: Beacon Press, 1996), 105–44; and Joretta Marshall, *Counseling Lesbians* (Louisville, Ky.: Westminster John Knox Press, 1997).

[45]See Patricia Hill Collins, "Black Women and Motherhood," in *Re-Thinking the Family*, 215–45; Toinette M. Eugene, "'Lifting as We Climb': Womanist Theorizing about Religion and the Family"; and Jung Ha Kim, "A Voice from 'The Borderlands': Asian-American Women and their Families," in *Religion, Feminism & the Family*, ed. Anne Carr and Mary Stewart Van Leeuwen (Louisville Ky.: Westminster John Knox Press, 1996), 330–43, 344–57; and Mary Romero, "Who Takes Care of the Maid's Children? Exploring the Costs of Domestic Service," in *Families and Feminism*, 151–72.

[46]Coontz, 23–41, 68–92. Coontz writes, "By 1960, thirty-one million of the nation's forty-four million families owned their own home, 87 percent had a television, and 75 percent possessed a car. The number of people with discretionary income doubled during the 1950's...It was not family savings or individual enterprise, but federal housing loans and education payments (along with an unprecedented expansion of debt) that enabled so many 1950's American families to achieve the independence of homeownership" (25, 77).

the changes in family life as an unprecedented departure from a homogenous past epitomized by the 1950s, family history in North America can be detailed as a series of "domestic revolutions" over a period of several centuries.[47] The historical perspective does not dismiss the evidence for children's vulnerability, but sets the concern for families in a larger social context and leads to the possibility of new negotiations across the family divide. Historian Steven Mintz and anthropologist Susan Kellogg present a shared perspective:

> Although the family is seen as the social institution most resistant to change, it is, in fact, as deeply embedded in the historical process as any other institution. The claim that it is essentially a conservative institution–an island of stability in a sea of social, political, and economic change–is largely an illusion. If the family is a conservative institution in the sense that it transmits the moral and cultural values of one generation to the next, it is not conservative in the sense of being static. In structure, role, and conception, the American family has changed dramatically over time.[48]

Historical views of family life challenge static, timeless, and universal conceptions of family structures. In this light, the family pattern of the 1950s represents another contribution to the rule of variability, rather than the norm from which our current situation deviated. The perspective of family history provides a contextual approach to understanding the changes in family organization.

John Demos broadly sketches the changes in North American families. Three centuries ago, the European immigrant family–a "little commonwealth"–was considered the basic unit of society and church.[49] Personal identity meant nothing apart from family identity. Families provided self-sufficient agricultural units in which each member of the family, including women, children, youth, and the elderly, participated in sustaining the collective family economy. Family members worked literally in one another's presence and often at the same tasks. The functions of the family included workplace, school, hospital, and welfare agency under the headship of the father, whose control of property, discipline, craft skills, and marriage reinforced his paternal authority. This premodern or colonial family linked closely with the community, so much so that each was reflected in the other.

But during the late eighteenth and early nineteenth centuries, a domestic revolution occurred when the individual, understood as a propertied white male, became the basic unit of society. With the production of cash crops and factory goods, family economy shifted to the market economy of capitalism. Family life became dualistically structured between the masculine public sphere

---

[47]Steven Mintz and Susan Kellogg, *Domestic Revolutions: A Social History of American Family Life* (New York: The Free Press, 1988).

[48]Ibid., xiv.

[49]John Demos, *Past, Present, and Personal: The Family and the Life Course in American History* (New York: Oxford University Press, 1986), 3–40.

of rational self-interest, competitive self-sufficiency, and instrumental values, and the corollary feminine private sphere of domestic security, emotional warmth, and moral character. Thus, male productive labor separated from other family members, who were legally and politically represented in the public sphere by the male head of household. Women's productive and re-productive labor became domesticated within the private sphere imaged as a refuge within a cold, competitive world. While many poor and working class women and men continued laboring as domestics, factory workers, and share-croppers, middle-class women freed from household responsibilities by their new wealth, turned to nurturing children, shaping moral character, and creat-ing an environment of renewal and pleasure for their husbands. Women's fertility decreased and children's births were spaced closer together, which directed more financial resources toward the education of children, who ex-perienced greater freedom in marriage selection and vocational pursuits.

The first wave of feminism ignited out of the matrix of modern family values, social duty, and evangelical religion. The passion for nurture and care fueled a Victorian moral force that sought to change the public world itself into a larger home through women's reform movements.[50] But the modern ideal of private family life, with a mother devoted to children's emotional needs separate from the extended family, conflicted with the reality of fami-lies, particularly immigrant families, who survived through extended kin net-works dependent on the economic production of all family members.[51] Thus, the norm of domesticity arose within the upper and then middle classes of the eighteenth century, revealing the underlying racial, cultural, class, and gendered assumptions. The modern family ideal eventually emerged as a general social phenomenon in the mid-twentieth century after World War II, when more and more people gained access to the financial resources en-abling its mass instantiation.[52]

Demos claims that in our time, the struggles of postmodern family life indicate another domestic revolution. Now, nearly all the former functions of the family are professionally institutionalized beyond the purview of the home—medical facilities, nursing homes, social services, schools, banks, religious groups, and police. Today, families function primarily in terms of nurture, affection, happiness, and mutual interest. Child-rearing provides an important dimension, but more as an option toward parental fulfillment than obligatory social duty. Parents have fewer children and spend a shorter amount of their longer life spans rearing children. Work has become less the profession of the one male breadwinner than the economic necessity of adults and youth. The lines between work and home blur, creating new environments where people work out of their homes and businesses pursue family-friendly policies like

---

[50]Margaret Lamberts Bendroth, "Religion, Feminism, and the American Family: 1865–1920," in *Religion, Feminism & the Family*, 183–96.

[51]Linda Gordon, "Family Violence, Feminism and Social Control," in *Feminism and Fami-lies*, 262–86.

[52]Linda Nicholson, "The Myth of the Traditional Family," in *Feminism and Families*, 32–33.

flexible hours, parental leave, and on-site child care. Still, for many people, unattainable family wages, limited social resources, and increasing job demands place extraordinary burdens on already tenuous family relations. The stress leads Cornel West and Sylvia Ann Hewlett to assert that the economic, political, and social conditions of our day have in effect declared a "war" against parenting.[53] A new social alliance is needed between family, government, and economic systems.

The historical perspective discloses that families have undergone great changes in the last three hundred years. While economic factors figure prominently in changing the lives of families, the tension between communal and individual values makes a further impact. Market capitalism shifts the focus of family household activity from production and sustenance to consumption and individual pleasure. Thus, reformers and transformers both agree that individualistic consumer values undermine the nonmarket values of family life. Blankenhorn suggests that as a society, North Americans

> are increasingly unwilling, either through public behavior or private action, to value purposes larger than the self, and are especially unwilling to make those sacrifices necessary to foster good environments for children. I suspect that our "family deficit" is at least as dangerous to our long-term well-being as are our federal budget and trade deficits. Perhaps, also, the habits of heart and mind that produce the latter also create the former.[54]

Advocates for family transformation agree with Blankenhorn's concerns regarding the lack of vision and commitment in society, but they are more optimistic about our desire and will to envision social purposes larger than our individual selves. For Edelman, the answer lies in a renewed spiritual vision of compassionate commitment for people, businesses, and government.[55] For Coontz, businesses and government need to make as great an economic investment in child care, family-friendly work policies, and paid parental leave as they did to building canals and railroads in the early nineteenth century.[56] Public changes in a new domestic revolution for the next century include an enlarged vision of social generativity and attachment. For family transformers, this vision includes reexamining rigid dualistic gender roles and work spheres, heterosexual norms, the values of self-sufficiency and autonomy, and hierarchical relations between men and women and between parents and children. In the new domestic revolution, the "habits of the hearth" and home connect with a commitment to a transformed society as well.[57]

---

[53]Sylvia Ann Hewlett and Cornel West, *The War Against Parents: What We Can Do for America's Beleaguered Moms and Dads* (Boston: Houghton Mifflin, 1998).

[54]Blankenhorn, "American Family Dilemmas," in *Re-building the Nest,* 16–17.

[55]Edelman, *The Measure of Our Success,* 1–25.

[56]Stephanie Coontz, *The Way We Really Are: Coming to Terms with America's Changing Families* (New York: Basic Books, 1998), 74.

[57]The phrase "habits of the hearth" plays on the image from Robert N. Bellah and associates' work *Habits of the Heart: Individualism and Commitment in American Life* (Berkeley: University of California Press, 1985).

But reformers argue that the social problems beginning in the 1960s stem from women's inappropriate concern with self-fulfillment, autonomy, and economic advancement. Pitting children's well-being against women's well-being, reformers identify women's authentic source of fulfillment and expression within the domestic sphere. Nostalgia for the modern family involves paying up the family deficit by fathers' reclaiming their authoritative role as head of the family and mothers' making the sacrifice for other-concern. A return to modern family values can be heard in the admonishments of the Southern Baptist Convention's new "Faith and Message":

> The husband and wife are of equal worth before God, since both are created in God's image. The marriage relationship models the way God relates to his people. A husband is to love his wife as Christ loved the church. He has the God-given responsibility to provide for, to protect and to lead his family. A wife is to submit herself graciously to the servant leadership of her husband even as the church willingly submits to the headship of Christ. She, being in the image of God as is her husband and thus equal to him, has the God-given responsibility to respect her husband and to serve as his helper in managing the household and nurturing the next generation.[58]

Even though the statement uses the language of spiritual equality and calls all parents to renewed moral commitment, the language of male headship and female subordination nostalgically returns to the patriarchal model. Nostalgia can also be heard in the work of cultural critics such as Christopher Lasch, who proposes the unique disciplinarian authority of fathers as the solution to cultural narcissism and the intrusive control of social and governmental agencies.[59] Even in the situation of male absence from families,

---

[58]"Southern Baptist Employees Required to Heed Statement," *The Tennessean,* June 14, 1998, 4A.

[59]Family reformers often cite the work of Christopher Lasch, *Haven in a Heartless World: The Family Besieged* (New York: Basic Books, 1977); *The Culture of Narcissism: American Life in an Age of Diminishing Expectations* (New York: Warner Books, 1979); and *Women and the Common Life: Love, Marriage and Feminism* (New York: W. W. Norton & Company, 1997). Lasch places feminism's agenda against the best interests of the family, understood as the modern, bourgeois family. For Lasch, the physical and emotional absence of the father, due to changing modes of economic production, renders the father a weak and distant figure, thus no longer effective in his primary role as authoritative disciplinarian. Mother becomes the dominant figure of private life, yet because of her ambiguous role as object of fear and desire, she too proves an ineffective parent. Children are then left with unrestrained desire and without a model for self-restraint. Instead of internalizing the father's authority in terms of Oedipal repression and guilt, contemporary people pursue their own narcissistic gratification in accord with permissive parental standards. In his view, women have given up the haven to enter the heartless world, leaving future generations to their own pleasures. Thus, Lasch advocates a return to the paternal authority of the modern family. Without paternal authority as the primary mediating structure between social order and disorder, society will depend on larger forms of coercive control. Lasch's cultural pessimism gives him a reductionistic interpretation of feminism's agenda for family and social transformation as well as a stunted view of fatherhood. Criticisms of Lasch's work may be found in Guy B. Hammond, "Christopher Lasch and a Renewed Theory of the Family," *Perspectives in Religious Studies* 10 (Spring 1983): 15–32; and Don Browning, Carol Browning, and Ian Evison, "Family Values and the New Paternalism," *The Christian Century* 109 (June 3–10, 1992): 572–73.

nostalgic models of headship are recommended for men to assume their true leadership role and relieve women of their double burden in the private and public domains. Promise Keepers founder Bill McCartney advocates,

> You can talk around it, but the man has a responsibility before God. He must stand before God and give an account. Did you take spiritual leadership in your home? You know what a woman is told (in the Bible)? Respect your husband. O.K.? The way she would do that is that she would come alongside him and let him take the lead, and he in turn would lay down his life. He would serve her, affectionately and tenderly serve her.[60]

McCartney does not explicitly advocate domination, but as in the Southern Baptist's message, the servant model of leadership still requires dualistic structures of masculine-public-leadership and feminine-private-submission. Fellow Promise Keeper Tony Evans more strongly states the family problem that men have become "feminized" by not claiming their God-given role as "spiritually pure" family leaders.[61] He advises men tell their partners, "'Honey, I've made a terrible mistake. I've given you my role. I gave up leading this family, and I forced you to take my place. Now I must reclaim that role.' Don't misunderstand what I'm saying here. I'm not suggesting that you *ask* for your role back, I'm urging you to *take it back*."[62] Thus, while continuing to advocate a servant model of leadership, Promise Keepers, like other reformist movements, eschews family models based on mutuality. From the perspective of reformers, women who question the traditional model selfishly strike against the interests of children, spouses, society, and even God himself. For a new century, manhood and fatherhood can only be reformed nostalgically through the model of household monotheism.

Family reformers, like transformers, question social values of individualism and self-fulfillment, but their solutions to the family crisis neglect corporate and governmental responsibilities and place the burden of family (and social) well-being on the shoulders of women. Sociologists Barrie Thorne and Marilyn Yalom argue,

> Rather than challenge capitalist and patriarchal arrangements in the public sphere, however, defenders of the family retreat to an idealized family with the nurturant mother as its symbolic core. They demand that the family, and women, make up for everything the indifferent and hostile outer world refuses to do.[63]

While transformers envision another domestic revolution for the next century based on democratic values, reformers advocate a return to the

---

[60]Quoted in Ron Stodghill, "God of Our Fathers," *Time* (October 13, 1997): 59.

[61]Tony Evans, "Spiritual Purity," in *Seven Promises of a Promise Keeper* (Colorado Springs: Focus on the Family, 1994), 73–81.

[62]Ibid., 79.

[63]Thorne and Yalom, *Rethinking the Family*, 24.

patriarchal ideal of the modern family. From a reforming perspective of family history, the 1950s represent the great culmination of social progress and family stability. But a transforming perspective acknowledges the dynamic processes contributing to the formation of family life, including the serious limitations inherent in the modern family structure. Any re-visioning of family values must come to terms with the inequities of power in family life.

Remembering Family Violence

In the work of family reformers, the modern 1950s family provides the norm of security and stability in family life. Media images from the 1950s present typically happy and carefree families. The television programs *Father Knows Best* and *Leave it to Beaver* idealize family relations with a touch of humor, innocence, and Spic 'n' Span. In their advocacy for returning to the 1950s standard, reformers run the risk of discounting serious problems and limitations in the modern model. Without a critical view, they neglect the modern family's structural propensity to vulnerability, violence, and abuse. Placing family authority with the male head of household, a reformist position interprets any problem as the character fault of a particular family head or the fault of a family member who instigated the problem against the authority of the head. Reformists leave the structure of the modern family and the values that support it as unproblematic. But uncritically norming the modern family as the only appropriate model for family life continues placing family members at risk within a power structure that distorts relations.

In the years following the 1950s, accounts have come to light of domestic violence and sexual abuse hidden beneath the pleasantries of family life.[64] Only in the last two decades have changes in social consciousness, significantly prompted by the second wave of feminism and other advocacy groups, enabled a more open sharing of past abuse and the conditions contributing to the abuse. One survivor of childhood sexual abuse reflects,

> That day he touched me I wasn't doing anything wrong.
> I thought he loved me. I thought I was safe.
> It was just a day, like a normal day, just a day and then
> everything was changed.[65]

Tragically, while the home and hearth guarantee warmth, security, and nurture in the modern family ideal, for many survivors, families served instead as relations of isolation and anguish. Coontz summarizes, "Beneath the polished facades of many 'ideal' families, suburban as well as urban, was violence,

---

[64]For example, see Joy M. K. Bussert, *Battered Women: From a Theology of Suffering to an Ethic of Empowerment* (New York: Lutheran Church in America, 1986); Annie Imbens and Ineke Jonker, *Christianity and Incest*, trans. Patricia McVay (Kent, England: Burns & Oates, 1992); and Carol J. Adams and Marie M. Fortune, eds., *Violence Against Women and Children: A Christian Theological Sourcebook* (New York: Continuum, 1995).

[65]Catherine J. Foote, "That Day He Touched Me," in *Survivor Prayers: Talking With God About Childhood Sexual Abuse* (Louisville, Ky.: WestminsterJohn Knox Press, 1994), 18.

terror or simply grinding misery that only occasionally came to light."[66] According to the conventional values of the 1950s, domestic violence was not a crime, marital rape was a nonissue, and incest was diagnosed as "female sex delinquency."[67] Today the statistics of child abuse stagger the mind—one in four girls and one in six boys—thus, returning to a past family model without analyzing spousal and parental structures of power remains naïve and, in fact, dangerous.[68]

In confronting the limitations of the modern family ideal, transformers challenge the assumption of an altruistic father as head of the family. While the mother provides the nurturing core of the household, responsible for its inner life, ultimate decision-making power rests with the head. Economist Diana Strassmann explains that in the narrative of the "benevolent patriarch," the rational and disinterested head of household makes the best decisions for the conflicting needs of the household.[69] But a tension exists in the narrative. In the public economy, self-interest and market competition spark the man's motivation. In his other role, the male head of household functions idealistically out of concern for the interests of others around the private hearth. But the evidence of domestic violence and child sexual abuse challenges the ideal of benevolent headship, for family heads act out of self-interest, not only altruism. Thus, in inequitable power relations, the subordinated members receive inherent disadvantages. Strassman cites the research of Amartya Sen, who found unequal food distribution and undernourishment of female children in Indian patriarchal families.[70] Coontz confirms the self-interest of the family head in a North American context:

> Women and children bore the brunt of poverty within "traditional" two-parent families just as surely, if less visibly, as they do in modern female-headed households. Budget studies and medical records reveal that women and children in poor families of the past were far more likely to go without needed nutrients than were male heads of families.[71]

According to the evidence of abuse and violence in families, narratives of the benevolent patriarch actually serve the self-interest of the patriarch. Reformist strategies do not attend to the ways the modern family privileges the self-interest of the head.

The inequities of patriarchal decision-making power in the modern family model become compounded by the absence of accountability to family

---

[66]Coontz, *The Way We Never Were*, 35.

[67]Ibid.

[68]The statistics are cited in Christine E. Gudorf, "Sacrificial and Parental Spiritualities," in *Religion, Feminism & the Family*, 300–301.

[69]Diana Strassmann, "Not a Free Market: The Rhetoric of Disciplinary Authority in Economics," in *Beyond Economic Man: Feminist Theory and Economics*, ed. Marianne A. Ferber and Julie A. Nelson (Chicago: University of Chicago Press, 1993), 54–68.

[70]Amartya Sen, *Resources, Values and Development* (Cambridge, Mass.: Harvard University Press, 1984), cited in Strassman, 58–59.

[71]Coontz, *The Way We Never Were*, 4.

members for the head's decisions and behaviors. But this is also true for the relation of mother and child—hierarchical family order based on a unilateral dynamic of power gives the superior person total access to the inferior person without accountability. While the superior retains rights of order and authority, the inferior inherits obligations of obedience and deferral. Thus, subordinate family members have little recourse after violation. Modern family values of self-sufficiency and independence from kin or community relations foster an environment of isolation and the keeping of family secrets:

> I have been a keeper of secrets. I have been alone.
> I was told, "Tell no one." I was turned to stone.
> I was tortured in silence. I was quiet, afraid.
> He shouted "Shut up!" to my crying.
> He left me shattered, betrayed.[72]

Class assumptions supporting the modern family further reinforce the isolation.[73] In affluent cities and suburbs, class status correlates with moral achievement. Thus, for the sake of the family, the impact of abuse and violence is minimized and forced behind the appearance of family solidarity. How often we hear, "But they're such a nice family! He seems like such a good man! She would never do that!" Reformist advocacy esteems the modern family as the *good* family. The good head of household's superior moral management reflects in the orderly, appropriate appearances of dependent family members, who would never publicly or privately share the information that their interests are in fact not at the heart of family life.

As referred to earlier, the rigid social, political, religious, economic, and philosophical dualism between the public and private realms of family life compound the "brokenheartedness" of the modern family.[74] This dualism underwrites the narrative of the benevolent patriarch whose reasoning and action shifts according to the order of being—public market versus private hearth. In the public realm, where the head of household represents the interests of the family as a whole, modern justice involves the recognition of (his) individual rights and personal autonomy.[75] But in the realm of private life, the values of care, self-sacrifice, and other-concern structure family relations, implying a lack of justice values (rights and self-interest). Thus, where do children's rights or women's rights figure in the modern family model? The rigid boundary of privacy surrounding the modern family places the male head of household as the representative figure for the rights and interests of

---

[72]Foote, "The Keeper of Secrets," in *Survivor Prayers*, 47.

[73]Rayna Rapp, "Family and Class in Contemporary America," in *Rethinking the Family*, 49–67.

[74]Because power flows unilaterally in the patriarchal family, Rita Nakashima Brock characterizes this family order as a "broken-hearted family." See *Journeys by Heart: A Christology of Erotic Power* (New York: Crossroad, 1988), 25–49. See also chapters 5 and 8 of this book for a more in-depth presentation of Brock.

[75]Contrasts between the traditions of public justice and private care as related to gender are detailed in Susan Moller Okin, *Justice, Gender and the Family* (New York: Basic Books, 1989). See also Pamela D. Couture, "Rethinking Private and Public Patriarchy," in *Religion, Feminism & the Family*, 249–74.

the whole. Thus, he becomes the gatekeeper for concerns of family members and their relations to other family members and the community. Susan Moller Okin questions the safety of modern family boundaries: "The protection of the privacy of a domestic sphere in which inequality exists is the protection of the right of the strong to exploit and abuse the weak."[76]   Family analysts Kristine Baber and Katherine Allen concur: "The notion of traditional family boundaries is problematic because it allows myths to persist about how families are supposed to be and obscures what actually goes on in families. Privacy can be a mask for secrecy. A system that is shrouded in secrecy is not safe."[77]   Ironically, the wholesome discourse of the modern family ideal hides the fact of the home as the very place where personal violence and abuse are most tolerated and legitimated.

When family reformers advocate a return to models of past years, transformers of families question the uncritical appraisal of family values and structures. Survivors of family abuse and violence remind both reformers and transformers that there has not been a pristine family form beyond the ravages of domination. They tell reformers the return of male-headed models of authority will not necessarily provide the safety and security longed for in society. The modern family with its hierarchical power, benevolent patriarch, engendered realms, and private boundaries places family members at risk. Yet survivors challenge transformers to think beyond the concern of gender or government to the modes of power underlying family relations. Crucial voices in re-visioning the lives of families, abuse survivors remember family violence and stir the home fires toward another revolution in family life.

Giving Way to Common Ground

Recognizing violence and abuse stirs up the possibility of more complex understandings of family life from the nostalgic modern model. In a postmodern day, families need models that hold together the tensions between sociality and individuality, self-interest and self-sacrifice, choice and obligation, self-sufficiency and dependence, nurture and provision, and domestic work and paid work.[78]   In postmodern family life, the question of healthy family relations arises not as an either/or, either self-concern or other-concern, but *both* self and other. All family members must be recognized as having rights, interests, and subjectivities apart from those publicly recognized for the head of the family. Thus, families need new models that integrate the traditions of *justice* and *care* and apply them across the generations to

---

[76]Okin, *Justice, Gender and the Family,* 174.

[77]Kristine M. Baber and Katherine R. Allen, *Women and Families: Feminist Reconstructions* (New York: Guilford Press, 1992), 223.

[78]See the chapters by Pamela D. Couture, Bonnie J. Miller-McLemore, Christine E. Gudorf, Rob Palkovitz, Toinette M. Eugene, Jung Ha Kim, and Ivy George in *Religion, Feminism & the Family.* For an analysis of the ideology of self-sufficiency and the political-theological implications of shared responsibility between families and government policy, see Pamela D. Couture, *Blessed are the Poor? Women's Poverty, Family Policy, and Practical Theology* (Nashville: Abingdon Press, 1991).

children, youth, adults, and older adults. Past models of hierarchical leadership no longer address the needs of shared responsibility and accountability in families today. The time is ready for new models supporting the democratization of family life.

Pastoral theologian Don Browning and colleagues Bonnie Miller-McLemore, Pamela Couture, Brynolf Lyon, and Robert Franklin claim that during the 1990s the family debate changed from a battleground to a "common ground":

> Is the family declining or merely changing? This was a question asked repeatedly as the 1990s began. Before that, many social scientists and cultural liberals had believed that families were simply changing and that the new forms were just as good, and maybe better, than older ones. Religious, cultural, and political conservatives, however, believed that most family changes were harmful. But within a very few years, liberal political and cultural opinion makers had moved away from the idea that family changes were benign to a new concern over family disruption.[79]

Common ground advocates observe that beyond the polarized positions of conservatives (reformers) and liberals (transformers) a new awareness about families has emerged, which takes seriously the deteriorating sociological data on children, women, and men, yet places the data within larger economic, social, and political contexts. Families *are* in trouble, but neither a return to past models nor an easy acceptance of current trends will prove helpful for our current and future needs. Simplistic, nostalgic solutions need to give way to more complex and multidimensional strategies for increasing the "social capital" of families.[80]

Contributing to the formation of a common ground was the reclamation of family issues by the Democratic Party in the 1996 presidential campaign, which "changed the subject" away from conservative concerns of abortion and homosexuality toward the "ecology of institutions" strengthening family life.[81] New initiatives emerged from businesses, government, and religious institutions that called attention to the common concerns of children and their families. For example, one hopeful precedent may be seen in the episcopal initiative on "Children and Poverty" of The United Methodist Church seeking a renewed commitment from parents, citizens, churches, legislators, and economic leaders to addressing children's impoverishment.[82] Also during this time, analysts called fathers to responsibility and significantly redefined the

---

[79]Browning et al., *From Culture Wars to Common Ground*, 30. On intimations of an emerging centrist position in the family debate, see Don Browning and Ian Evison, "The Family Debate: A Middle Way," *The Christian Century* (July 14–21, 1993): 712.

[80]James S. Coleman, "Social Capital in the Creation of Human Capital," *American Journal of Sociology* 94 (1988): 95–210.

[81]Browning et al., *From Culture Wars to Common Ground*, 38–42.

[82]Council of Bishops of The United Methodist Church, *Children and Poverty: An Episcopal Initiative* (Nashville: The United Methodist Publishing House, 1996).

roles of fathers in families, which challenged the previous strategy of blaming mothers.[83] Thus, in contrast to pessimists and reformers who speak of family *decline*, the common ground advocates prefer to think in terms of family *crisis*, but one that is "simultaneously full of creativity and promise and full of danger and disruption."[84]

Meeting the challenges of the contemporary family crisis, common ground advocates propose a transvaluation in the "moral ecology" of family life.[85] In contrast to understandings of love as self-sacrifice or individual fulfillment, mutuality provides the new ethic for the postmodern democratization of families. But what will mutuality entail? Bonnie Miller-McClemore writes, "Something more than a revision of household roles and the construction of a family-friendly work environment is required for mutuality in contemporary families. Complex psychological, moral, and theological shifts are necessary."[86] The ethic of mutuality fosters new family values of equal regard and shared authority. Characterized by "mutual respect, affection, practical assistance, and justice between persons who value and aid one another with equal seriousness," equal regard involves children as well as adults, based on developmental needs and abilities *toward the goal of mutuality*.[87] New family values recognize children as persons of agency and initiative, rather than mere extensions or reflections of their parents' desires and wills. The value of shared authority refers to the distribution of power in a family, including decision making and determining the family's activities, goals, and commitments. Again, children can be incorporated into the shared authority of a family based on their developmental needs and competencies. Their preferences, desires, and insights make valuable contributions to the whole of family life. In contrast to the headship model of the reformist position, families of equal regard and shared authority seek more democratic, participatory models of organization.

But according to common ground advocates, the value of self-sacrifice still remains necessary to fulfill the ethic of mutuality.[88] The perspective of *critical* familism acknowledges that in the past, women and children shouldered the brunt of self-sacrificial modes of life. Thus, common ground advocates support the feminist criticism of analogies between Christian self-sacrifice and women's and children's subjectivities. They further acknowledge that Christian valuations of self-sacrificial ideals maintained the subordination of oppressed racial and ethnic groups in the past. But common ground advocates reject relational models that completely displace the value of self-sacrifice. A Christian

---

[83]Browning et al., *From Culture Wars to Common Ground*, 34–35. See also David Blankenhorn, *Fatherless America* (New York: Basic Books, 1995); and David Popenoe, *Life Without Father: Compelling New Evidence that Fatherhood and Marriage are Indispensable for the Good of Children and Society* (New York: Martin Kessler Books, 1996).

[84]Browning et al., *From Culture Wars to Common Ground*, 7.

[85]Ibid., 8.

[86]Bonnie J. Miller-McLemore, "Family and Work: Can Anyone 'Have it All'?" in *Religion, Feminism & the Family*, 282.

[87]Browning et al., *From Culture Wars to Common Ground*, 2.

[88]Ibid., 101–28.

theology of families must acknowledge the place of self-sacrifice in the lives of all family members. Privileging individual fulfillment jeopardizes the well-being of dependent, vulnerable family members and distorts the character of intimacy. In times of compromise or negotiation of difficult family concerns, an ethic of equal regard requires family members to displace self-interest in favor of the interests of the family or relationship as a whole. Thus, self-sacrifice provides a "transitional" value toward restoring mutual relations of equal regard and shared authority between people.[89]

But mutuality in families requires more than self-sacrifice to restore relations of equal regard. Common ground advocates understate the need for *self-assertion* as an additional transitional value for families committed to mutuality. As the advocates acknowledge, there are times in family life that call for self-sacrifice, but similarly, family life also involves times of asserting selfhood in restoring the fragile balance of power in relations. Self-assertion encompasses more than self-interest. Self-assertion means taking oneself seriously as a partner of value (and being recognized by others as a partner of value) in family relations when inequities need addressing or undervalued interests require attention. Thus, self-assertion brings together the traditions of justice and care, for a family in which members are not being cared for justly bears implications for the whole family, not just the individual members. Self-assertion becomes a transitional value toward caring justly for the whole. The modern family model values self-assertion for the head of household, but other family members' assertions, particularly in conflict with the head, are deemed problematic. The new postmodern model of family mutuality encourages and supports self-assertion for all family members. As explored in more detail in chapter 5, self-assertion, or willfulness, provides part of the common ground's "complex psychological, moral, and theological shifts" needed for mutual recognition in the lives of families.

The emergence of a common ground beyond the battlefields in the family crisis gives hope for *revaluing families.* While the common ground advocates primarily revalue a critical marriage culture, the values of mutuality, equal regard, and shared authority apply to the broader contexts of families. These new values, with the transitional values of self-assertion and self-sacrifice, comprise a horizon of commitment in the struggle toward democratizing family life. The intent of this chapter is not to set a standard or norm of one family model, but to aid all families in the identification of new family values for strengthening the lives of families. The commitment to families, rather than the family, introduces an additional new family value necessary for mutuality— the value of diversity.

Postmodern Feminist Families

Feminist analysis of family life challenges male headship as the defining essence of any family model. But what if family life is examined from the

---

[89]Ibid., 127.

experiences of women in families? Feminist researchers Baber and Allen place women as members of families in the center of their study on family life.[90] They acknowledge that families have been sources of exploitation and struggle for many women, but women continue finding fulfillment and sustenance in their families. Despite the family crisis, "relational commitment remains an organizing feature of women's lives. Indeed women are innovators in attempting to generate and sustain relationships that are rooted not in hierarchy but in relational qualities such as empathy, responsibility, and cooperation."[91] By shifting the focus to *women* in families, research uncovers the diversity of family contexts in the lives of women. The continued vitality of heterosexual marriage is seen, as well as the vitality of lesbians and their families, extended families, and women as leaders of households. The valuation of this diversity, including these families' joys and struggles, shifts the focus of family analysis from the ideal of the modern *family* to the ideal of postmodern feminist *families*.

According to Baber and Allen, the family crisis presents innovative opportunities and more open, honest understandings of the lives of families. While not minimizing the vulnerable impact of nuclear fallout, Baber and Allen affirm the praxis of women in families for whom mutuality sets the ideal. In their description of postmodern feminist families, the common ground values of equal regard and shared authority can be heard:

> Such families take the needs and interests of all family members seriously. Feminist families are those in which women's voices as well as men's are spoken, heard, and respected. Feminist families are safe, nurturing, and empowering to all family members; both women and men have equal access to opportunities and resources. These families protect the rights and ensure the well being of the vulnerable. They challenge the arbitrary awarding of power and privilege to certain members strictly because of gender, race, class, sexual orientation, and age.[92]

By valuing both individuality and relationality, postmodern feminist families take seriously the combined traditions of justice and care. Decision making is multilateral and thus authority is widely shared. But the praxis of postmodern feminist families endorses the new family value of diversity for reconstructing family relations and strengthening the corresponding values of equal regard and shared authority. For example, in families the ethic of equal regard does not merely extend to members based on a common identity; people do not have to be the same to regard one another equally. Equal regard presents a moral orientation shared by family members who may be very different, not only in age or sexual orientation, but in personality, goals, and interests. The new family value of diversity suggests that family members' differences can be a source of joy and not primarily a source of subversion or antagonism as in hierarchical models.

---

[90]Baber and Allen, viii.
[91]Ibid., 57–58.
[92]Ibid., 222.

By valuing diversity within families, postmodern feminist families contribute to a social environment in which diversity between families is affirmed. All families need not look like the modern family model in order to be valued and supported as families. Thus, strengthening connections between families enriches civic life. Families formerly marginalized or invisible can be recognized and included in the common ground of concern for families. Imaged less as a compilation of identical family units, social life constitutes a richly textured community where families gather for the flourishing of all. Baber and Allen advise:

> What is needed is not rejection of contemporary change but the development of creative strategies to encourage diverse groups to build bridges of understanding and common ground. Friendships, intimate partnerships and political coalitions across gender, race, class and sexual divisions are needed to challenge elitism and essentialism and to create a more democratic and just society for all.[93]

Postmodern feminist families contribute to the domestic revolution of the twentieth century continuing into the next decades. Part of the struggle for human democratization, postmodern feminist families connect with larger social and global movements. Reformist critics claim feminism upholds an antifamily agenda, but as Thorne and Yalom argue, "Feminists are seeking a realistic and complex understanding of families as part of a larger program of social change."[94] But the shift away from the hierarchical, private, class-bound, and rigidly engendered modern family has not been without cost and struggle. The crisis in family life creates situations of vulnerability and risk for women and men, and in particular, for children. Still, the crisis need not generate despair or pessimism. Amid the broader social ecology of institutional partnership with families, an emerging new ethos of mutuality creates opportunities for revaluing family life. New family values of equal regard, shared authority, and diversity help frame a commitment to the democratization of family life. On the forefront of this renewed commitment live postmodern feminist families.

This chapter traces the dynamics of the family crisis in North American society in the latter half of the twentieth century. As family history demonstrates, the changes of the current century have been part of a series of domestic revolutions in family life over several centuries. But in recent years, the polarized battleground between reformers and transformers of the 1960s, '70s, and '80s has given way to a common ground of concern for families. A paradigm shift is underway from the model of headship to models of mutuality. In these models, the value of self-sacrifice becomes reoriented to serve the interests of all family members, not only the privileged. But the transitional value of self-sacrifice works together with another transitional value—self-assertion. Together, they enable family members to live toward relations of equal regard, shared authority, and diversity. The praxis of postmodern feminist families

---

[93]Ibid., 223.

[94]Thorne and Yalom, *Rethinking Families*, 25.

provides evidence for the valuation of self and other, individuality and sociality, justice and care.

But the democratization of family life bears implications beyond itself. The full scope of the political, social, and economic implications extends beyond the focus of this study. The remaining chapters of this book examine the implications of refiguring families for congregational life and a theology of the Spirit. Since patriarchal models of family life metaphorically expressed theological understandings and ordered community life, a paradigm shift in family values impacts new ways of thinking about God and what it means to be the people of God. The next chapter traces the church revolution of the twentieth century from the model of male headship to models of mutuality. What are the ecclesiological and pneumatological implications for the *family of God* if families now value equal regard, shared authority, diversity, and self-assertion (and self-sacrifice)? How do new family values of postmodern feminist families help refigure congregational life?

CHAPTER 4

Church Revolutions:
Re-figuring Congregational Life

For this reason I bow my knees before the Father, from whom every family in heaven and on earth takes its name.[1]

Should the present form of the family disappear, the Christian church would necessarily undergo revolutionary changes.[2]

The Family of God

The family in the church, the church in the family. From the earliest of Christian communities until today, the language of family has helped form congregational identity and express theological meaning. In New Testament texts, Christians are addressed as brothers and sisters (Rom. 16:1–17), the church is compared with a household (1 Tim. 3:1–16), and the fatherhood of God is understood as establishing an ecumenical kinship for all families (Eph. 3:14–15). The conflictual development of the church-as-family model in the New Testament and early Christian history is explored in chapter 6. This chapter continues the exploration of re-figuring families by moving from the question of *family values* to the question of *church values*. Stanley Grenz and Roy Bell note the intimate relationship of church and family:

Christians readily speak about the church as a family. We heartily sing, "I'm so glad I'm a part of the family of God." Indeed, our shared allegiance to Christ as God's children means that we are a spiritual family. In addition to this foundational *theological* relationship, as an

---

[1]Ephesians 3:14–15. The text connects God as father (*pater*) with the fatherhood (*patria*) of all families in a kinship relation of patriarchal authority, origin, and order. While this text calls the *paterfamilias* (the head of the family) into relation with an authoritative higher power (and thus relativizes the absolute authority of household heads), the text grounds the male-headed social order in the order of creation and affirms the analogy between God the Father and family fathers. See E. Elizabeth Johnson, "Ephesians," in *The Women's Bible Commentary*, ed. Carol A. Newsom and Sharon H. Ringe (Louisville, Ky.: Westminster/John Knox Press, 1992), 338–42.

[2]W. Lloyd Warner, *The Family of God* (New Haven: Yale University Press, 1962), 266, cited by Janet Fishburne, *Confronting the Idolatry of Family: A New Vision for the Household of God* (Nashville: Abingdon Press, 1991), 34.

institution the church often functions *sociologically* and *psychologically* in a manner that resembles human families.[3]

With this close connection between family and church, congregations (and thus theology!) have much to learn from the transformations occurring in contemporary families.

This chapter explores how congregations, like families, are currently in the process of re-figuring themselves. In this century, the domestic revolution is paralleled by a corresponding church revolution. Women's ordination, the enfranchisement of the laity, and a new sense of church mission in relation to secular society have forced not only renovations, but new foundations for the household of God. The democratization of churches, mirroring the democratization of families, challenges male headship patterns and provides new models of Christian community. But mainline congregations have also struggled with bureaucratic inadequacies and financial pressures that have further caused congregations and denominational structures to examine their core values and purposes. Temptation lies in returning to a nostalgic identity with the past. But just as family transformers call attention to uncritical retrievals of past models, so should congregations develop a critical awareness. In the past, unilateral clerical authority, paternalistic structures, and the privatization of church life have led to abusive relations in the household of God, which the recent light on clergy sexual misconduct makes clear. Democratization of churches will require the transitional value of self-assertion to restore relations of equal regard, shared authority, and diversity in congregational life. The core value shift to mutuality in the lives of congregations, as well as families, will actually enable families and congregations to support one another toward more inclusive models of human community.

An Audible Icon

Across North America, the church and the family seem engaged in a campaign for mutual survival. From small rural parishes to urban mega-churches, building marquees colorfully advertise family-centered worship. Congregational planning committees envision family life centers equipped with gyms, day-care facilities, lounges, and classrooms. Religious bookstores market video resources that focus on the Christian family with biblically grounded advice for practical issues ranging from discipline to marital communication.[4] Struggles surrounding denominational sexuality reports, men's movements, abortion legislation, spousal authority, and homosexual ordination show that churches, too, have been engaged in a culture war. Christian coalitions, seeking to protect heterosexual social norms, boycott Walt Disney productions and lobby politicians in support of new covenant marriage options. The recent controversy in The United Methodist Church regarding the

---

[3]Stanley J. Grenz and Roy D. Bell, *Betrayal of Trust: Sexual Misconduct in the Pastorate* (Downer's Grove, Ill.: InterVarsity Press, 1995), 150. Emphasis added.

[4]Note the long-running popularity of Dr. James Dobson's *Focus on the Family* films, books, and videos (Colorado Springs, Colo.: Focus on the Family Publishing).

status of church discipline and the authority of pastors to officiate at same-sex covenant ceremonies represents not only the issue of ecclesiastical authority, but the challenge of family identity for congregations.[5] From the perspective of many people within congregations, the future of the family and the church remain intimately linked together. While some constituencies of mainline churches "draw the circle wide" in affirming the diverse realities of families, reformist family values promotion holds forth the traditional family, bread-winner father (the head) and homemaker mother with children, as the ideal and faithful kinship structure for the human community.[6]

Regulative beliefs concerning the close relation of church and family are borne out in the demographics of church populations. Research shows that Protestant churches in North America are, in general, composed of two rather complementary cohorts: people who are in traditional families and those who used to be.[7] Households underrepresented in contemporary Protestant churches, but experiencing growth in the general population, are young couples without children, families of gays and lesbians, single-headed households (mother or father), grandparent-headed families, and single persons. Women in nontraditional families with egalitarian attitudes toward gender roles tend toward lower rates of church attendance, church activity, belief in God, and prayer.[8] They may participate in noninstitutional women's religious groups or still consider themselves to be spiritual persons, but they perceive the insti-tutional church as less open and tolerant of their own values. One study of working couples shows that they believe churches exist more to pass on tradi-tional values of work and family than to help today's families "invent new patterns for their lives."[9] The hierarchical church structure, with its male-centered clerical authority, seems at odds with the values of these couples recasting religious symbolism and congregational life along more egalitarian

---

[5]"Methodist Pastor Acquitted," *The Christian Century* (April 1, 1998), 335–37. In light of Rev. Jimmy Creech's acquittal, the Judicial Council of The United Methodist Church ruled on August 11, 1998, that ministers conducting ceremonies celebrating homosexual unions are liable for church trial.

[6]Church resources acknowledging diverse family realities include: J. Ann Craig and Linda S. Elmiger, eds., *Family: Drawing the Circle Wide* (New York: Women's Division, General Board of Global Ministries, The United Methodist Church, 1994); Jorge Maldonado, *Even in the Best of Families: The Family of Jesus and Other Biblical Families like Ours* (Geneva: World Council of Churches, 1994); and Wallace Charles Smith, *The Church in the Life of the Black Family* (Valley Forge, Pa.: Judson Press, 1985). Conservative resources advocating male headship: Sherrill Burwell, "Im-proving and Strengthening Black Male-Female Relationships," in *The Black Family Past, Present, & Future: Perspectives of Sixteen Black Christian Leaders*, ed. Lee N. June (Grand Rapids, Mich.: Zondervan, 1991), 85–98; Al Janssen and Larry K. Weedon, eds., *Seven Promises of a Promise Keeper* (Colorado Springs, Colo.: Focus on the Family, 1994); John and Paula Sandford, *Restoring the Christian Family* (South Plainfield, N.J.: Bridge Publishing, 1979); William Sears, *Christian Parenting and Child Care* (Nashville: Thomas Nelson, 1991); and Charles K. Swindoll, *Growing Wise in Family Life* (Portland, Oreg.: Multnomah Press, 1988).

[7]Penny Long Marler, "Lost in the Fifties: The Changing Family and the Nostalgic Church," in *Work, Family, and Religion in Contemporary Society*, ed. Nancy Tatom Ammerman and Wade Clark Roof (New York: Routledge, 1995), 50.

[8]Lyn Gesch, "Responses to Changing Lifestyles: 'Feminists' and 'Traditionalists' in Main-stream Religion," in *Work, Family, and Religion,* 132.

[9]William Johnson Everett with Sylvia Johnson Everett, "Couples at Work: A Study of Pat-terns of Work, Family and Faith," in *Work, Family, and Religion,* 324.

lines. Research shows that congregations stand at a decisive point—either they maintain their identity along traditional lines and thus address only a select portion of the population, or they re-tradition their social and theological understandings about family, sexuality, marriage, and the church. As North American society struggles with changes in family life, congregations struggle with their own identities and missions.

The ties of church and family run deep. This may be seen in the statistics of Baby Boomers, for whom becoming a parent is often the point of entry back into church life.[10] In her study of four Episcopalian congregations, Joanna Bowen Gillespie discovered that family is the "audible icon" used to express congregational ideals and identity, even when young families are no longer the primary membership constituency.[11] She reflects:

> Home and church are the two most intimate institutions in human life, in that sense part of the "private" realm, their standards expressed in emotional values and language rather than in commercial or political terms. Family and religion operate powerfully but often unconsciously via invisible attitudes, values and mores.[12]

Because of the powerful embeddedness of family and church in emotional life, changes in the understanding of families will bring difficult challenges to congregations and theology. If the present ideal of the family changes, what transformations are in store for the Christian congregations?

The connection of church and family (or household) is evidenced in Christian religious language. Sallie McFague observes that family relations provide "imaginative pictures" for forging and sustaining our theological conceptions of God, the world, and God's relation to the world.[13] Christian traditions speak of God the Father, Jesus the Son, the church as the Bride, Christ the Bridegroom, the new birth of baptism, faith as filial obedience, and fellow Christians as brothers and sisters. The use of family language provides structure for relations of power in the church and determines patterns of leadership, authority, and ministry. Early church theologians are called church fathers; parishioners are addressed as children of God. Thus, social and ecclesiastical assumptions reflect one another through the metaphor of family. When challenges are made to these patterns, as in Chung Hyun Kyung's 1991 World Council of Churches address, differences within churches emerge between support for the traditional family model (reformers) and for more inclusive models of family (transformers).[14] For example, in response to the 1993

---

[10]Wade Clark Roof and Lyn Gesch, "Boomers and the Culture of Choice," in *Work, Family and Religion*, 70.

[11]Joanna Bowen Gillespie, *Women Speak: Of God, Congregations and Change* (Valley Forge, Pa.: Trinity Press International, 1995), 138.

[12]Ibid., 137.

[13]Sallie McFague, *Models of God: Theology for an Ecological, Nuclear Age* (Philadelphia: Fortress Press, 1987), 38.

[14]The controversy in the ecumenical household regarding Chung Hyun Kyung's address at the 1991 Seventh Assembly in Canberra is explored in chapter 1.

RE-Imagining Conference in Minneapolis, reformer Diane Knippers of the Institute on Religion and Democracy argued that rather than re-imagine family and sexuality, churches need to rebuild and renew *traditional* family life.[15] In contrast, transformer Melanie May, a "white, lesbian, feminist, Christian minister doing her work," admits she doesn't feel at home in most Christian churches, yet she still journeys toward a "homecoming" within the Christian faith because of the life-giving images, stories, and themes of a God who "yearns for human healing and wholeness."[16] Within the churches, reformers and transformers struggle for the future of congregational life.

But the relation between church and family goes beyond patterns of authority and order. Family language expresses deep and profound experiences of interconnection, intimacy, embodied life, and passion (all of which also involve aspects of power in relation). Gillespie suggests that family language, as religious language, connects to emotion because "deep spiritual longings or insights may be more comfortably couched in words that already contain emotional overtones: brotherhood, mother, sister, father God."[17] Central activities of congregational life relate to the domestic priorities of birthing (conversion and baptism), feeding (eucharist and potlucks), and nurture (pastoral care and small groups). Generational concerns include spiritual growth, Christian education, rites of passage, death, and memory. Within congregations, persons expect to be valued for their intrinsic worth. They anticipate that congregational life will express trust, hospitality, safety, and belonging. These characterizations of congregational life correlate to intimate concerns of family life and thus make family language a primary candidate for Christian communal self-understanding. As Edwin Friedman reflects, "The family is the true ecumenical experience of all humankind."[18]

While the analogy of family and church seems appropriate at first, there are limitations as well. The family, as a finite good, can become an idolatrous model, especially when the family becomes the end of religious loyalty. Janet Fishburne claims that North American churches still continue the Victorian "family pew" ethos in which a congregation is viewed as being composed of small, family units (each modern family on a pew), and the family is imaged as "a little church."[19] The Victorian cultural legacy connects home, hearth,

---

[15]Diane Knippers, "Re-Imagining Family, Liberty, and Ecumenism," *Good News* (March/April 1994): 38. In November 1993, "RE-Imagining: An Ecumenical Decade Event" was sponsored by the World Council of Churches in honor of the Ecumenical Decade of Churches in Solidarity with Women. The conference, which has now evolved into the Re-Imagining Community, examined themes such as God, Christ, community, ethics, sexuality, and family. Intense controversy was generated in reaction to the leadership, content of the presentations, and Sophia liturgies, which were labeled heresy and a threat to family values. See related articles in *The Christian Century* (April 6, 1994) and *Good News* (March/April 1994). For the journal *Re-Imagining*, contact reimagining@earthlink.net.

[16]Melanie May, *The Grace of Coming Home: Spirituality, Sexuality and the Struggle for Justice* (Cleveland: Pilgrim Press, 1995), xiv–xviii.

[17]Gillespie, 138.

[18]Edwin H. Friedman, *Generation to Generation: Family Process in Church and Synagogue* (New York: Guilford Press, 1985), 1.

[19]Fishburne, 19.

piety, and virtue with women's "natural" sphere of domesticity. Home is the locus of children's socialization in Christian piety and moral behaviors, with mothers considered the first and foremost teachers of piety. In the family pew ethos, a congregation is understood as being composed of pious families who attend church to receive reinforcement and direction concerning their spiritually (and culturally) formative work. But when the Victorian family is substituted for the kingdom of God, "religious familism" leads to the "domestic captivity" of congregational life and results in truncated visions of mission and ministry. [20] Instead, congregations should seek a *critical* religious familism, where all families receive pastoral care, faith formation, and the discernment of their gifts for ministry. Fishburne's vision is echoed by Justo Gonzales, who suggests that the household of God is more analogous to the extended, permeable, and inclusive constellation of relations comprising his Latino *familia*. He dreams, "How I wish the United Methodist church at large were able to see itself not as a conglomeration of families, each guarding its privacy and each trapped in the four walls of its own suburban home, but as the household of God, as the great *familia de Dios!* "[21]

In addition to idolatry, the analogy of family and church also bears pathological implications. If the church is like a family, then who are the parents, grandparents, and children? Who speaks, and who listens? How are decisions made and who takes responsibility? Peter Selby highlights the similarities between the relation of parents to children with the relations of pastors to parishioners.[22] Pathological danger exists in childlike idealization of congregations and the casting of church leaders, especially pastors (and their spouses), as parental caregivers. Like lone parents, pastors struggle with scant resources, few supports, limited energy, and an overabundance of people's needs. Laity seem willing to take on this division of roles, "for in many churches a willingness to be like a child in a family becomes almost an essential qualification for membership."[23] This dynamic, Selby notes, is complicated by the learned dependency in a family system where authorities preach, teach, and model paternalistic relations. Parishioners receive the message that they don't have to understand or worry about certain decisions and theological matters. But then, to further complicate things, the faith is supposedly simple and all a person needs to do is accept the faith and the rules! The analogy of church and family can lead to pathological distortions in the spiritual character of congregational life.

But the most serious problem with the family analogy is the prevention of congregational issues from being straightforwardly addressed:

> The feeling of impending disaster if children confront parents, and the sense, often imparted by their parents, that this will destroy the

---

[20]Ibid., 34–36.

[21]Justo L. Gonzalez, "The Great Family of God," *Circuit Rider* (November 1996): 12–13.

[22]Peter Selby, "Is the Church a Family?" in *The Family in Theological Perspective*, ed. Stephen C. Barton (Edinburgh: T & T Clark, 1996), 151–68.

[23]Ibid., 158–59.

unity and love within the family, means that for much of the time children are bound to adopt methods of attention-seeking, manipulation and repression to make their point. The regressive tendencies of many local congregations seem directly reminiscent of this experience: the dysfunctionality is often such that the result of membership of a local congregation will be to demean the person, making him or her less able, mature and capable than might otherwise have been the case.[24]

Selby warns against the dysfunctional limitations in the model of church as family. The analogy's power is in its ability to express belonging and care, but danger lies in the emotional vulnerability of dependent family members. As fearful children willing to repress their needs and avoid conflict with parents, laity can fall into the same pathological web with clergy and other authority figures in the congregation.

But the religious functioning of family models and metaphors need not reinforce existing personal family dynamics in the lives of church members. Images of the family of God, if used, should serve to transform the intimacies people naturally have into patterns of living that are intentionally inclusive. The new kinship in Christ extends human loyalties beyond the boundaries of family kinship. Selby explains his position:

> Therefore what ever hopes any of us may hold out for our children, the real issue for us is the hope God has in store for us and them alike in the divine family from which ours has to take its name and within which our families, like all our other loyalties, including of course, church loyalties, have to take their place.[25]

Selby joins Fishburne and Gonzales in advocating for a *transvaluation* of the relation between church and family. In God's great house, every kind of family structure is relativized to the inclusive vision of God's people. In order to work toward this vision, congregations need to establish realistic expectations between participants and explore alternative self-understandings for congregational life. Congregations can pursue an intentional mission to all families and develop theological sensitivities for the use of family images in scripture, theology, and hymnody. Without a transvalued understanding of family in Christian theology, Marjorie Thompson warns,

> we will succumb to our cultural habit of idolizing the family. When we sentimentalize or idealize any community, we make of it an idol...Unfortunately, as our social fabric tears and traditional structures crumble, increasingly wide segments of our religious culture resort to sentimentality and idealization with respect to the family.[26]

---

[24]Ibid., 157–58.

[25]Ibid., 167.

[26]Marjorie J. Thompson, *Family: The Forming Center: A Vision of the Role of Family in Spiritual Formation* (Nashville: Upper Room Books, 1989), 123.

Church Revolutions

With the close connection between family and church, it is no wonder that "as the family goes, so does the church."[27] The twentieth century has brought not only a major family revolution, but a church revolution as well. Women's challenges to male-headed family values are paralleled in the challenges of women, the "second sex," to church-family values.[28] Challenges of family headship may be seen in the struggle for women's ordination and partnership in leadership. Research shows that through the pioneering preaching of women like Sojourner Truth and Antoinette Brown, at least 3,400 women were ordained by the turn of the nineteenth century, but this represented only 3.3 percent of all employed European American clergy and 1.1 percent of African American clergy.[29] Backlash, discouragement, and lack of official recognition pressured the numbers to drop until after World War II, when U.S. denominations changed their practices. By 1958, forty-eight members of the World Council of Churches ordained women, and in 1963, Vatican II recognized the importance of women's participation in various fields of the apostolate.[30] The most recent statistics show that by 1995 the number had risen to 50,000 clergywomen, representing 9 percent of all U.S. clergy.[31] While criticism has been leveled at clerical "feminization" as one reason for decreasing membership in mainline churches, statistics refute this reason in that men still predominate in the profession.[32] In fact, as men have begun to share more equally in domestic responsibilities, men also have begun working toward mutuality in clerical leadership. Women's ordination offers one direction toward a more inclusive and whole household of faith.

But ordination is not the only dimension of family change. Women's lay ministries have also undergone transformation. Gillespie's generational study shows that older women (age 60+) gained their sense of congregational and spiritual identity in "philanthropic discipleship" such as making curtains for Sunday school rooms, cleaning the parish house kitchen, raising money for missions, and serving meals.[33] This traditional women's work has been under their own organizational responsibilities but lies behind the scenes in terms of the larger congregational picture. Domestic household management provides the analogy for older women's ministries in the household of faith. But women's philanthropic groups also have been responsible for educating the congregation about issues and causes. They have understood themselves as the organizational

---

[27]Marler, 38.

[28]Mary Daly, *The Church and the Second Sex* (Boston: Beacon Press, 1985).

[29]Paula D. Nesbitt, *Feminization of the Clergy in America: Occupational and Organizational Perspectives* (New York: Oxford University Press, 1997), 23.

[30]Ibid., 24.

[31]Ibid., 25.

[32]Ibid., 173–77.

[33]Gillespie, 195–212.

connection between the congregation and the community, society, and, in particular, foreign missionaries.

For women in the "bridge generation" (ages 41–60), church "volunteering" is one of other "jobs" in the community or in the paid work force.[34] Bridgers have less identity in church women's organizations, less involvement in national or denominational offices (though there are more opportunities for their leadership now), and more concern for individual spiritual fulfillment than the older generation. While they were involved with teaching during their own children's church years, they now serve in other leadership roles in the church, but these roles are not the only ones important to their identities.

The younger generation of women in Gillespie's study (ages 40 and under) have been defined by the currents of the 1960s and measure their congregational participation according to "choice" and "meeting personal needs."[35] The possibility of a full-time career and partnership in marriage creates many more opportunities for their identities and investments of time. Younger churchwomen carefully weigh their commitments and view giving as an individual matter separate from a sense of religious duty. This generation has even less denominational loyalty and commitment to organizational structures than older and bridging women. Worship for younger women needs to be contemporary in language and style and should reflect the practical concerns of daily life. They tend to receive their religious education on issues and causes from the sermon, yet have energy for short-term groups that more closely align with the needs of their families or themselves.

Gillespie's research could be interpreted as bad news for congregations based on maintaining a traditional correlation between church and family. Women are then faulted with the lack of availability for certain tasks, rather than questioning the tasks or re-structuring the whole sphere of congregational ministry. Women may have been busy with sacrificial "doing" in earlier years, but more recently, women are asking the "being" questions of spirituality, meaning, and commitment. Women today seek an inclusive recognition of gifts and equal distribution of responsibilities within a congregation. Changes in women's ministries prompt a deeper discernment of the character of the church—its "core" tasks and identity.[36]

In fact, changes for women—ordained and lay—in church household life are linked to the general transformation of the relation between clergy and laity. In this century, social democratization has influenced both family relations and ecclesiastical relations. Movements such as the "liberation of the laity," the "hour of the laity," or the "whole people of God" have challenged the dualistic, hierarchical relation of clergy and laity (as male over female and

[34]Ibid., 195–212.
[35]Ibid.
[36]Ezra Earl Jones, *Strategies for New Churches* (New York: Harper and Row, 1978).

parent over child) in the direction of partnership and accountability.[37] Loren Mead of the Alban Institute claims that the enfranchisement of the laity constitutes the "reinvention of the church," which is "the greatest change that the church has ever experienced in America; it may eventually make the transformation of the Reformation look like a ripple in a pond."[38]

One major factor in the transvaluation of the relation between clergy and laity is the rending of the "sacred canopy" between church and society.[39] Today, Christian congregations realize they no longer occupy the privileged, cultural center of Western society. Religious diversity, multiculturalism, justice movements, and secular influences have transformed the whole idea of a center and margins. But the situation is not necessarily bad news. Concerning the "disestablishment" of Christian culture, Douglas John Hall remarks that what "we are witnessing (and to some degree participating in) is nothing less than a radical re-formation/purification of Christianity, comparable in magnitude only to the alteration which occurred at the other end of this same process, when the church moved into Caesar's court."[40] Given the changes in society, churches in North America discover themselves in a situation more comparable to the early churches than the churches of the last century.[41] In the former apostolic paradigm, Christian communities encountered an indifferent or antagonistic world and had to call forth the gifts of all church members to meet the mission contexts right beyond the community boundaries. Then the reign of Constantine (313 C.E.) signified a church revolution to the Christendom paradigm, in which Christianity and culture were united and the mission contexts comprised the outermost margins of the empire. Christians were expected to be good, obedient citizens and pay their taxes for the empire, which was maintained by official authorities. In the latter years of the Christendom paradigm (this century!), laity have still been expected to support the hierarchy, leave theological matters to their superiors, give money to support foreign missions, and be loyal to their denomination. The Christendom paradigm continues to operate on the assumption of an institutional church culturally united with powerful political and economic institutions. But

---

[37]For resources see Anne Rowthorn, *The Liberation of the Laity* (Harrisburg, Pa.: Morehouse, 1986); Peter Coughlin, *The Hour of the Laity: Their Expanding Role* (Newtown, N.S.W., Australia: E. J. Dwyer, 1989); William K. McElvaney, *The People of God in Ministry* (Nashville: Abingdon Press, 1981); Hans-Ruedi Weber, *Living in the Image of Christ: The Laity in Ministry* (Geneva: World Council of Churches 1986); John Cobb, *Lay Theology* (St. Louis: Chalice Press, 1994); and James C. Fenhagen and Celia Allison Hahn, *Ministry for a New Time* (New York: Alban Institute, 1995). The classic early work is by Hendrick Kraemer, *A Theology of the Laity* (London: Lutterworth Press, 1958).

[38]Loren B. Mead, *The Once and Future Church: Reinventing the Congregation for a New Mission Frontier* (New York: Alban Institute, 1991), 68.

[39]Peter Berger, *The Sacred Canopy: Elements of a Sociological Theory of Religion* (New York: Anchor, 1990).

[40]Douglas John Hall, *Thinking the Faith* (Minneapolis: Augsburg Press, 1989), 201–4. Hall uses the categories of diaspora and establishment in correspondence to what Mead terms apostolic and Christendom. Hall writes of "the end of the Constantinian era" in which religious ideology and empire were one (200–207).

[41]Mead, *The Once and Future Church,* 9–22.

these days, cultural establishment for congregations has given way to disestablishment.

Mead argues that the paradigm of Christendom was built on "clerical-ism," a great achievement for a worldwide church, but one that has taken "power and authority unto itself, away from the church it is intended to serve."[42] He acknowledges that many clergy don't want this authoritarian, self-serving power, but the institutional structures still support a system in which clergy "overfunction" and laity "underfunction" toward a dysfunctional end.[43] Like Selby, Mead compares the Christendom relation of clergy and laity to the relation of parents and children. In this family dysfunctionality, higher levels of church administration communicate to lower levels using "parent tapes" that order, direct, and command.[44] "Good" congregations and lay people are rewarded for their compliance and held up as model leaders. But "childish" others resort to behaviors such as resentment, criticism, fighting, fleeing, and ignorance.

Today, congregations struggle with change from the Christendom to the post-Christendom paradigm, which if not negotiated with vision and hon-esty, leads to ongoing decline. Some congregations covenant together through small-group ministries meeting weekly for serious examination of spiritual formation. Many congregations have committed themselves to in-depth Bible study as a way of re-gaining theological clarity and evangelical integrity. Oth-ers risk even radical change like selling their buildings and moving into a mall coffeehouse for Generation X connections. But many congregations continue blindly and fearfully, clinging to assumptions from the family pew ethos of the past. Mead believes a new dialogue between clergy and laity as "apostolic people" can reorient ministry for a third mission revolution.[45] In the new paradigm, clergy function as "catalysts of religious authority" that enfranchise laity to fulfill their apostolic ministries in communities, businesses, families, and other places of connection with the world.[46] Of primary importance is the theological formation of the laity, for in the post-Christendom era, laity become the "deeply grounded specialists" on the missionary frontier.[47]

But the ideals of enfranchisement of the laity and democratization of con-gregational life lead to deeper challenges for the transvaluation of clergy/laity relations. In light of the contemporary re-figuration of families, criticism of clericalism can go beyond what Mead envisions. If the relation between clergy and laity is no longer imaged as that of parents and children, then is the relation more like the one of spouses who have rejected dualistic, rigid roles in favor of shared work? In the democratization of families, roles and authority

---

[42]Loren B. Mead, *Transforming Congregations for the Future* (New York: Alban Institute, 1994), 96.

[43]Loren B. Mead, *Five Challenges for the Once and Future Church* (New York: Alban Institute, 1996), 1–15.

[44]Mead, *Transforming Congregations*, 99.

[45]Mead, *Five Challenges*, 14–15.

[46]Ibid., 14–15, 69.

[47]Mead, *The Once and Future Church*, 56–58.

lines are re-figured in participatory, shared directions. Mutuality implies the permeable, flexible sharing of responsibilities and opportunities–nurture, economic provision, domestic labor, creativity–not the complementariness of roles, even if the roles are regarded equally. Challenges to the modern family norm lead to the recognition of families as multiple, diverse constellations. If the criticism of role essentialism is directed from the family to the church, then the question of a given, essential structure or form of congregational life must be examined. In the new church revolution, must congregations maintain the categories of clergy and laity to still be church?

Feminists such as Rosemary Radford Ruether, Elisabeth Schüssler Fiorenza, and Val Webb claim that the ecclesiological distinction between clergy and laity rests on deep, dualistic assumptions concerning authority and dependence, as in the patriarchal parent/child relation.[48] The language of lay "empowerment" continues to draw upon this dualism to the extent that there are those with power, right knowledge, and authority to give these gifts to others. The issue is not that power, knowledge, and authority are inappropriate dimensions of congregational life. The question is, From whom does power, knowledge, and authority arise? How is it sustained, negotiated, and claimed? Ruether writes:

> What we see in all forms of paternalism and clericalism is the relationship of a dependent adult to a dominant adult being assimilated into that of a child to a male parent. Because the power exercised by the father is presumed to be benevolent and wise, it is psychologically and culturally difficult to criticize it. Deep resonances of childhood guilt are evoked to keep such a relationship in place. The dependent person is made to feel both ungrateful and ostracized for rejecting paternal authority. Thus it is difficult to articulate the inappropriateness of such father-child relationships between adults and to name their function as *disempowerment*.[49]

Ruether's criticism of clericalism can be extended to include the relation of children to a female parent. Women entering the ministry or priesthood have challenged the male headship model of church-family life, but the democratization of families presses ahead with the challenge to clerical headship as a whole. While ordained women may hold to less rigid or unilateral ways of relating, the parental implications still remain, and the household office still supports some model of hierarchical headship. These days, children grow up and often become caretakers of parents as they grow older. But the distinction between clergy and laity continues with separate functions. Why,

---

[48]See Elisabeth Schüssler Fiorenza, *The Discipleship of Equals: A Critical Feminist Ekklesia-logy of Liberation* (New York: Crossroad, 1993); Rosemary Radford Ruether, *Women-Church: Theology and Practice* (San Francisco: Harper & Row, 1985); and Val Webb, *Ministry and Ordination in the Uniting Church in Australia: An Historical, Contextual and Constructive Theological Study* (Ann Arbor, Mich.: UMI Dissertation Services, 1996). I am grateful to Val for her critical comments and support in reading this chapter.
[49]Ruether, 76. Emphasis added.

as Webb wonders, is the question of ordination the one we hesitate to ask?[50] What new models of ministry in God's household will help meet the challenges of a new millennium?

Changing to new paradigms is never easy. Struggling with questions and new possibilities is difficult; it puts the whole household under stress. Like family reformers, nostalgia for a comfortable, secure past is heard within the church household as well. Mead remarks, "For many people the problem would be solved if we could return to that strong, hierarchical model when Herr Pastor was Herr Pastor and the rector was truly the 'ruler.'"[51] Church revolutions, like family revolutions, create a crisis in re-negotiating identity, values, and relations. With such great stress on families, the church's identity with family increases, as people seek in congregational life what has been lacking or denied in their own experiences of family. In recent years, congregations have responded to strong desires for belonging by fostering intimate, caring relationships among congregational members. But the inherent danger in the new church revolution is that nostalgia for the ideal family will compound with nostalgia for the ideal family-church, reinforcing the family pew ethos and resisting opportunities for congregational and theological transformation.

Betrayal of Trust in the Household of God

Nostalgia is a powerful emotion. When faced with ecclesiastical longings for the past glories of the church, Mead (echoing Stephanie Coontz) remembers that "they were not better times, they preserved many kinds of injustices and inequities."[52] We don't have to look far to realize that the church as a family has its own share of domestic abuse. Marie Fortune warns congregations, "Unfortunately just as there is potential for abuse in families, there is potential for abuse in the church that views itself as family."[53] In recent years, clergy sexual misconduct has come to light as a major problem for churches of every denomination. Newspaper and magazine headlines continue to report new cases. Victims, survivors, and complainants include women, children, youth, and men as well.[54] Congregations, the secondary victims, struggle for years to come to terms with the abuse and initiate steps toward healing. Denominational authorities pay out enormous sums in settlement, yet the scars run deeper than money indicates. Although preliminary, statistics regarding the extent of clergy sexual abuse remain indicting:

---

[50]Val Webb, "Is it Permissible to Ask Why We Ordain at All?" *Uniting Church Studies* 3, no. 1 (March 1997): 13–46.

[51]Mead, *The Once and Future Church,* 33.

[52]Mead, *Five Challenges,* vii.

[53]Marie M. Fortune, *Is Nothing Sacred? When Sex Invades the Pastoral Relationship* (New York: Harper & Row, 1989), xiv. See also Peter Rutter, *Sex in the Forbidden Zone: When Men in Power— Therapists, Doctors, Clergy, Teachers and Others–Betray Women's Trust* (London: Mandala, 1990).

[54]Men may have been children or youth when involved in an abusive relation with clergy, but cases involving clergywomen and adult male parishioners are also coming to light. The sexual abuse of male parishioners by male clergy needs to be recognized as well. See Nils C. Friberg and Mark R. Laaser, *Before the Fall: Preventing Pastoral Sexual Abuse* (Collegeville, Minn.: The Liturgical Press, 1998), 44–58.

Clergy sexual abuse...is much more prevalent than is commonly supposed. Some estimates even exceed the 5 to 13-percent figure ascribed to male psychotherapists. Preliminary statistics indicate that somewhere from one out of eight to one out of three clergy have crossed sexual boundaries with their parishioners. Of all extramarital contact self-reported by clergy in one study, over two-thirds was with a counselee, staff member, lay leader/teacher, or other congregant. Thirty-one percent of clergy in the same study reported that they experienced *no* consequences for extramarital contact, and only 4 percent said their churches ever found out about what they had done. Over 76 percent of clergy in another study reported knowing of a minister who had sexual intercourse with a parishioner.[55]

Preliminary statistics indicate that sexually abusive relations between clergy and congregational members are not an aberration, but a pervasive problem requiring serious examination.

Clergy sexual misconduct represents a devastating betrayal of trust occurring between institutionally recognized religious leaders and members of religious communities who look to the leaders for particular ministerial responsibilities, usually during times of crisis or vulnerability.[56] Associated with sacred, holy power to represent the church and God, priests and clergy bear the fiduciary responsibility to exercise their power and authority of office in ways that address others' needs and do not exploit congregational members. One woman shares her story of betrayal:

I had gone to him for spiritual and emotional counseling during an extremely vulnerable time in my life, after the death of my husband. It never occurred to me that I should ask the question, "Can I trust this man?" After all, he was a beloved pastor and prominent person in the community. And in my frame of mind, I was completely trusting.[57]

The survivor points to the tragedy of the betrayal—the pastoral relation began because of the healing needs of the person in crisis, but then the expectations of the relation become reversed so the clergy's own needs become

---

[55]Pamela Cooper-White, *The Cry of Tamar: Violence Against Women and the Church's Response* (Minneapolis: Fortress Press, 1995), 128.

[56]Important resources include Pamela Cooper-White, "Soul Stealing: Power Relations in Pastoral Sexual Abuse," *The Christian Century* (February 20, 1991): 196–99; Richard M. Gula, *Ethics in Pastoral Ministry* (New York: Paulist Press, 1996), 74–75; Nancy Meyer Hopkins, *The Congregational Response to Clergy Betrayal of Trust* (Collegeville, Minn.: The Liturgical Press, 1998), 11–16; Nancy Meyer Hopkins and Mark Laaser, eds., *Restoring the Soul of a Church: Healing Congregations Wounded by Clergy Sexual Misconduct* (New York: Alban Institute, 1995), 55–115; Peter Horsfield, "Forgiveness and Reconciliation in Situations of Sexual Assault," *Occasional Paper Seven*: Uniting Church in Australia, Commission on Women and Men (April 1994); Nancy Nason-Clark, "The Impact of Abuses of Clergy Trust on Female Congregants' Faith and Practice," in *Wolves within the Fold: Religious Leadership and Abuses of Power*, ed. Anson Shupe (New Brunswick, N.J.: Rutgers University Press, 1998), 85–100; and Neil and Thea Ormerod, *When Ministers Sin: Sexual Abuse in the Churches* (Alexandra, N.S.W., Australia: Millennium Books, 1995).

[57]Quote used with permission.

paramount. But clergy sexual misconduct is not just a problem of having an affair or of questionable morals. The sexual betrayal (in terms of child abuse, sexual harassment, or adult exploitation) becomes "an abuse of power," motivated by fear and insecurity and resulting in the domination and control of others for personal gratification and false security.[58] In the end, the betrayal of trust entails not only physical and emotional damage, but spiritual devastation as well. Survivors claim their experiences of terror, isolation, and abandonment can be compared with losing one's soul. A survivor explains her spiritual confusion and loss after the abuse:

> I trusted God not at all. Sometimes I doubted that a God even existed. I had heard of God's love and truth and honesty through sermons delivered by this man, and later he had expressed his love for me. I had believed the whole package. Now I knew that much of it was a lie. Which parts could I believe and which parts were not the truth? I couldn't separate them out![59]

For congregants, what starts as a betrayal of trust in the pastoral relationship becomes compounded by the additional perception of betrayal by God.

As the women's movement brought family violence out of bedrooms and basements, now survivors bring church violence out of sacristies, choir lofts, and offices. While cases involving clergy and church staff remain prominent, lay church leaders have also been indicted with abuse cases. With the intimate connection between family and church, parallels have been made between male clergy sexual abuse and spousal abuse. But an additional analogy rises from the research and sharing of stories—church sexual abuse can be compared with incest in families.[60] The abuse by clergy or other congregational leaders involves a unilateral relationship between a powerful, trusted authority figure and a dependent person of little power. Comparable characteristics between family abuse and church abuse include age difference, intrinsic trust, unequal power, authoritative qualities, intellectual and educational differences, natural tendencies to obey and please, psychological vulnerability on the dependent's part, and the parent's or clergy's own wounds and sense of vulnerability often exacerbated by stress.[61]

Comparisons between family incest and clergy sexual misconduct can also be found in the responses of others to knowledge of the abuse. Survivors speak of being enmeshed in complicated behaviors such as denial, secrecy, blaming the victim, misnaming the problem, shooting the messenger, and idealizing the violator.[62] In pastoral abuse, often complainants and survivors

---

[58]James Newton Poling, *The Abuse of Power: A Theological Problem* (Nashville: Abingdon Press, 1991), 27.

[59]Quote used with permission.

[60]Marie M. Fortune and James N. Poling, *Sexual Abuse by Clergy: A Crisis for the Church,* JPCP Monograph no. 6 (Decatur, Ga.: Journal of Pastoral Care Publications, 1994), 38–41.

[61]Richard Irons and Katherine Roberts, "The Unhealed Wounders," in *Restoring the Soul of a Church,* 40. Irons and Roberts claim that in clergy sexual misconduct, the clergyperson is generally ten or more years older than the congregant.

[62]Fortune, *Is Nothing Sacred?* 46–98, 108–29. See also Ann-Janine Morey, "Blaming Women for the Sexually Abusive Male Pastor," *The Christian Century* (October 5, 1988): 866–69.

are pressured to remain silent and forgive the violator quickly, without public acknowledgment, so the "problem" can be resolved and the institution relieved of taking disciplinary action. The truth of the violation is never told, and the conditions for repeat offenses are then in place. No wonder great nostalgia exists in congregations for the good old days when congregations didn't have to talk about such things—but then, of course, they didn't happen either!

The analogy of church as family highlights the power inequity between clergy offenders and survivors (some survivors of clergy sexual misconduct are clergy as well). But the family analogy also highlights other cultural factors that contribute to abusive congregational environments. Drawing on Fishburne's earlier analysis, the Victorian legacy of the family constituting the private sphere of society finds parallels in the way congregational life is valued. The warm, domestic hearth has been associated with the warm hearth of churches. Thus, congregations are valued more for the personal, intimate character of fellowship than for their public, denominational designations. But while the values of hearth and home foster belonging and intimate warmth, the alliance of privacy with congregational life paradoxically helps create a "culture of secrecy and abuse."[63] Challenges to the church household system thus become judged as damaging and disloyal from persons within and as beyond the jurisdiction of persons outside. Cara Beed describes the problem of privatization:

> The culture of secrecy effectively locks the victims of abuse into consciously hiding the abuse, isolating the victim from peer and other support. The culture of secrecy depends on the strength of the auspicing organisation to maintain control over the dissemination of information about the pastoral activities of its workers. Maintaining secrecy depends also on the extent to which the organisation is able to limit the sharing of experiences by victims/clients/participants…Commitment to the group…is impressed on victims, as a means of ensuring their silence (rather than damage the organisation).[64]

The modern family analogy for congregational life promotes a model of great access to the emotional, spiritual, and physical lives of congregants by leaders. When boundaries are violated, the domestic ideology contributes to the toleration of sexual misconduct and the enforcement of secrecy, control, and disinformation.

But the greatest problem with the analogy of domestic and ecclesiastical abuse is found in a theological environment that supports abusive, unilateral relations. James Poling and Marie Fortune claim that in the family incest drama, a child submits to the father's will, takes on the responsibility or guilt, and

---

[63]Cara Beed, *Cultures of Secrecy and Abuse: A Paradox for Churches* (Hawthorn, Victoria: RossCo Print, 1998).
[64]Ibid., 11.

sacrifices her- or himself for the sake of the relation.[65] In the church, substitutionary understandings of atonement reinforce a sacrificial selfhood in relation to God and others in authority. From sermons, liturgies, and stained-glass windows, God the Father is presented as all-knowing, wise, and beyond question in terms of his motives and desires. Humans must respond with obedience, submission, and unquestioning loyalty to his will as mediated and explained by clergy and other authorities. God's unilateral power over the world is presented as benevolent, but wrathful when the human partner fails or raises problems. In the church sexual misconduct drama, congregants are expected to sacrifice themselves, like Jesus, the obedient one, for the sake of the violator, congregational unity, and God's will. To assert otherwise jeopardizes the relation and risks exposing, punishing, and shaming people. But like an obediently suffering Jesus, a suffering God remains problematic, for victims are still encouraged to suffer like God without seeking justice for the abuse. In theologies of unilateral power, the absolutely asymmetric relation between God and the world is mirrored in the relation of church leaders and congregational members.

Fortune and Poling suggest that in this distorted family drama, "the Holy Spirit is like the non-offending parent who has been silenced or is colluding, a third figure for identification."[66] While they do not pursue the implications of this insight, Fortune and Poling allude to the Spirit's enmeshment with the unilateral power of the Father, the sacrificial selfhood of the obedient Son, and the unassailable unity of the church family. Chapter 6 pursues the connection of Spirit language and family models in New Testament texts and the work of early church theologians. This research will show that in communities structured according to the male headship family model, the Spirit plays the role of maintaining order, consolidating unity, and conforming the human will to the will of the divine Head (and "His" representative). Within congregational cultures of secrecy and abuse, the Spirit's connection with justice, truth, and self-assertion becomes neglected or repressed. Poling and Fortune rightly claim, "The religious drama is acted out as a family drama."[67] But the reverse is also true; the family drama is acted out as a religious drama. The two, family and church, are intimately connected and need more thorough theological exploration.

Spirited Survivors

Like the survivors of family sexual abuse who challenge contemporary nostalgia for the traditional family, spirited survivors of the family of God (and their supporters and advocates) challenge nostalgic models of congregational life. On the one hand, survivors and support groups bring forth complaints for review and action. Trials within the church and in the criminal or civil justice system press for review, accountability, and restitution. On the other hand, survivors contribute proactively toward educating congregations

---

[65]Fortune and Poling, *Sexual Abuse by Clergy*, 29–43.
[66]Ibid., 38.
[67]Ibid.

about boundaries, developing better processes of investigation and review, writing codes of ethics, initiating new structures and procedures in congregational ministries, and shaping new theologies. But while great strides have been made, congregations remain at risk until the entire vocation or identity of the people of God has been re-visioned. It would be naïve and simplistic to think lay leadership is the only solution, or that lay authorities are not also susceptible to the abuse of sexual power. But the enfranchisement of the laity provides one essential part of a holistic transformation. Reflecting on her own bittersweet experience of working with congregational and denominational processes as a complainant and then educator, a survivor asserts, "There is no question but that I am a much stronger person now, but it's a lesson I would not wish on anyone."[68] The prophetic gifts of spirited survivors provide an immensely valuable teaching moment for congregational life.

In new models of mutual ministry, clergy have their responsibilities as well. Clergy—male and female—must acquire the skills and competencies necessary for maintaining pastoral boundaries and exercising trustworthy leadership. Clergy are professionally responsible for the boundaries of sacred trust, yet this is not to say the pastoral relation is inherently hierarchical or based on unilateral power.[69] In fact, respecting boundaries enables clergy (and leaders in congregations with role or institutional power) to develop an awareness about misusing vulnerable relations, and it calls forth new models of authority and power between all congregational members who care for one another. In addition, attending to the spiritual needs of congregants through acknowledging boundaries does not require clergy to sacrifice their own needs. The issue for clergy and ministry leaders is becoming aware of one's own needs and then clarifying the appropriate relationships in which to care for these needs. Karen Lebacqz and Ronald Barton argue for a model of "relational power" where the focus of boundaries serves the empowerment of others.[70] Addressing the therapeutic relation, but applicable to pastoral relations as well, they write:

> Keeping boundaries is not simply a reflection of patriarchal hierarchy, but a recognition of the vulnerability and pain of clients. Keeping boundaries serves the purpose of therapy, which focuses on healing

---

[68]Used with permission.

[69]Marie M. Fortune, "Is Nothing Sacred? The Betrayal of the Ministerial or Teaching Relationship," *Journal of Feminist Studies in Religion* 10, no. 1 (Spring 1994): 17–26. Fortune's position differs from Carter Heyward, who associates the need for clerical boundaries with a traditional, patriarchal ethic that undermines mutuality. See Heyward's book *When Boundaries Betray Us* (San Francisco: HarperSanFrancisco, 1994). Heyward writes in an exchange with Fortune, "Can a professional healing relationship be mutually intimate and ethical at the same time? Fortune says no. I say yes." Fortune replies, "I believe that a professional relationship cannot at the same time be pastoral, therapeutic and healing—and mutually intimate. When pastor and congregant move from the professional, pastoral relationship to a mutually intimate relationship, they give up the pastoral relationship." See "Boundaries or Barriers? An Exchange," *The Christian Century* (June 1, 1994): 579.

[70]Karen Lebacqz and Ronald G. Barton, "Boundaries, Mutuality and Professional Ethics," in *Boundary Wars: Intimacy and Distance in Healing Relationships,* ed. Katherine Hancock Ragsdale (Cleveland, Ohio: Pilgrim Press, 1996), 96–110.

that pain, enhancing the value of the client, and restoring power to the client. The maintenance of boundaries does not mean that professional and client are in a hierarchical, abusive relationship. It means that hospitality is being honored.[71]

Lebacqz and Barton claim that congregational understandings of mutuality need to broaden in ways that do not simply equate professional relations with friendship, erotic love, or sister- and brotherhood.[72] Ministries of sacred trust such as spiritual direction, congregational care, healing, prayer, and liturgical leadership may be embodied in ways characterized by relational power in contrast to unilateral power. Clergy have their share of work to do in broadening understandings of mutuality.

Yet renovation in the household of God requires the participation of all congregational members. On the one hand, clergy can examine their use and misuse of authority. On the other hand, laity can recognize, cultivate, and exercise their own power-in-relation. Certainly a church revolution based on the household transformation of both clergy and laity bears much struggle, pain, and difficulty. But without transforming the self-conscious identity and vocation of all Christians in congregations, parent-child models will continue operating with dysfunctional consequences. While children and dependent others in congregations need leaders to decide, direct, and act for them (to certain degrees), the democratization of church life can incorporate developmental and special needs within the *more encompassing horizon* of equal regard, shared authority, and diversity. In the previous chapter we saw that self-assertion provides a necessary value in families toward restoring and maintaining mutuality in relations. With the eruption of clergy sexual misconduct into the public consciousness of congregational life, laity are realizing opportunities for self-assertion toward a transvaluation of the whole people of God. According to spirited survivors, the time is right for a church "come of age."[73]

A New Hearth for the People of God

The family of God is in the midst of a church revolution. Will nostalgia be the overriding church value of the future or will a new reformation emerge as envisioned by Mead, Hall, Fortune, and others? In this century changes in family formation have significantly influenced and challenged congregations of the family pew ethos. Parallels between the re-figuring of congregational and family life can be seen in the changes involving clerical leadership, women's discipleship, and the relation between clergy and laity. As families struggle with new models of mutuality, congregations also struggle with democratizing church life. Congregational transvaluation requires a new

---

[71]Lebacqz and Barton, 108.

[72]Ibid., 108–9. See also Karen Lebacqz and Ronald G. Barton, *Sex in the Parish* (Louisville, Ky.: Westminster/John Knox Press, 1991); and Karen Lebacqz, *Professional Ethics: Power and Paradox* (Nashville: Abingdon Press, 1985).

[73]The allusion is to Bonhoeffer's understanding of living responsibly and ethically in a "world come of age." See Dietrich Bonhoeffer, *Letters & Papers From Prison*, ed. Eberhard Bethge (New York: Macmillan, 1979), 341.

configuration of power among household members along with the creation of new patterns and structures. The changes toward mutuality in congregational life can be viewed as a both/and development. Those with greater institutional power will need to examine the transitional value of sacrifice, while those with less institutional power can assert themselves and become more completely and meaningfully involved with ministry.

Rebecca Chopp suggests that congregations need a new "poetics of community," where poetics means "not a mere continuation of older images, ways of speaking, or metaphors for community, but new forms, pictures, images and sounds of community."[74] Today, the church revolution provides opportunities for re-figuring congregational life in ways other than the conventional piety of the Victorian hearth. If, as Rita Nakashima Brock claims, "patriarchal family relationships are the bricks of the patriarch's theological house of worship," then the post-Christendom paradigm requires new poetic bricks for a new hearth in God's household.[75]

A poetics of community for the whole people of God entails a critical appraisal of the male headship model enshrined in Ephesians 3:14–15 (cited earlier), where God the cosmic Father (*pater*) substantiates the fatherhood of male heads of household (*patria*) in the created order of human families and congregations. Gonzales directs the image of family away from the nuclear family toward the extended kinship model of Hispanic and Hispanic American families. Likewise, Wallace Charles Smith advocates the church-as-family analogy in the extended family model of African and African American families.[76] These images of church retain, yet extend, the bonds of belonging and kinship so powerful in the family analogy.

But a new poetics of community must also take into consideration the potential limitations of family as a viable model for congregational life. Family images continue to beg the question about parental leaders and childlike followers. Thus, the image of church as family can be supplemented by diverse images of community life. The language of community affirms the public dimension of congregational life and thus promotes clarity around boundaries. Diverse community images also help with de-centering and relativizing all family relations in relation to God's horizon of faithful discipleship. Problems exist when family is the sole or primary model for congregational life. Even the move to *families* (as opposed to the family) or *familia* retains the potential for continuing some form of the family pew ethos (where the church serves only the needs of families or *familia*, rather than families or *familia* ministering in the world). The family or household of God, even interpreted through the poetics of a *critical familism*, needs the additional richness of multiple images, symbols, tastes, and sounds of community life.

---

[74]Rebecca S. Chopp, *The Power to Speak: Feminism, Language, God* (New York: Crossroad, 1991), 85.

[75]Rita Nakashima Brock, *Journeys By Heart: A Christology of Erotic Power* (New York: Crossroad, 1988), 4.

[76]Smith, *The Church in the Life of the Black Family*, 58–59.

New bricks build community space for spiritual vitality and transformation. A new hearth for the household of God provides energy for ministry in the world in contrast to the idealistic, Victorian hearth standing as the warm center of people withdrawn from the world. In a day of congregational disestablishment, a new hearth symbolizes the relational power for engagement with the diversity of cultures in North American (and global) society. Church values for new hearths include justice, care, mutuality, self-assertion, proper trust, openness, equal regard, and shared authority. These bricks replace the family values of unilateral power, paternalism, secrecy, repression, and subordination. In a new hearth, structures of leadership are re-shaped and re-fired so they serve and are accountable to household members who depend on them for community wholeness and functioning.

But new bricks require new theological mortar. The transvaluation from clerical paternalism to apostolic enfranchisement challenges theology to contextualize its work within the new revolution of congregational and family life. In the lives of families, the concept of the paternal head representing the whole family or household in the public realm has changed. Likewise, theology needs to change its own view of congregational life represented publicly by the clergy (and other staff). The re-figuring of congregational life means a change in focus from the word only as the pastor's speaking, acting, and presence, to the Word proclaimed in the speaking, acting, and presence of the whole congregation in worship and ministry. Energy for this abundant life is the gift of the Spirit, who inspires openness, challenge, risk, and transformation.

Additional theological mortar cementing the new bricks of congregational life can be found in organic, holistic understandings of power and holiness, which challenge Christendom models of headship. In the latter, the church is imaged as the body related dualistically and subordinately to Christ, the head, represented by clerical authorities. Echoing the benevolent patriarch's domestic economy, the Christendom model relies on the Head's superior reasoning abilities for ordering the easily misdirected, willful, and passionate members of the body below. Power flows from Christ through the leaders to the laity, who are then empowered to live according to the will of the Head (and the head of the church). But if the Head is considered part of the whole body, and if the body's powers of reason, affection, imagination, and desire are perceived as a "consortium of powers," then the whole body in all its diversity and interdependence is necessary for living out the life of Christian community.[77] Different members bring forth gifts or powers that are not available independently or singularly. James Whitehead and Evelyn Whitehead express the meaning of mutuality in the consortium model: "We count on each other for the release of our full power."[78] Thus, the consortium model avoids the association of clergy with the head and laity with the body, even if

---

[77]James D. Whitehead and Evelyn Eaton Whitehead, *The Emerging Laity: Returning Leadership to the Community of Faith* (New York: Doubleday, 1986), 66–96.
[78]Ibid., 87.

the two are viewed as working in interdependent partnership. No one person represents the Holy, only the whole community engaged with all its baptismal gifts. With new theological mortar, the whole people of God become the sign of the Holy.

For re-figuring congregations in a post-Christendom age, the image of the Triune community can replace the privilege of headship in the heart or hearth of congregational life. Rather than a unilateral order of Father over Son, and Father and Son over Spirit, the Holy Community of Creator, Christ, and Spirit enfranchises congregational life as a consortium of power and holiness. Here, Trinitarian values of equal regard, shared authority, proper trust, and diversity-in-unity (like the new values of families) inspire re-figured congregations who embody these values in ministries, families, neighborhoods, and beyond. The theological mortar of Triune mutuality challenges the household monotheism of congregations based on the "traditional" father-headed family and Father-headed Triune family. New bricks for the new hearth can be strengthened together through a Triune mortar, which points toward a community of people "without supremacy and without subjection."[79]

The purpose of this chapter has been to critically draw forth the contemporary relation between family life and congregational life. In recent years, congregations have turned to images of kinship and family for re-figuring their identities and missions in North American society. But will these new identities and missions maintain the Victorian ethos of the family pew, or will the re-figuring of relations in families enable congregations to actually recover vital dimensions of ministry and theology?[80] In the family revolution of this century, the ethic of mutuality with its corresponding family values of equal regard, shared authority, proper trust, self-assertion, and diversity-in-unity have come forth as the common ground for the renewal of commitment to families. In a similar pattern, the church revolution of this century has also embraced the ethic of mutuality for a common ground of commitment to congregational life. But like families, the danger of nostalgia lures congregations back to paternalistic configurations of power and holiness, which may appear to solve cultural struggle and chaos. Congregations, though, should heed the testimony of spirited sexual abuse survivors. Enfranchised by God's spirit, the whole people of God can fire new bricks for a new hearth in which the abundant life of God may blaze forth in all its fullness.

---

[79]Jürgen Moltmann, *The Trinity and the Kingdom: The Doctrine of God* (San Francisco: Harper and Row, 1981), 192.

[80]Delwin Brown claims that change in Christian traditions, while often provoked from circumstances and events outside the tradition, is accomplished primarily by the recovery and re-formation of elements internal to the tradition. See his *Boundaries of Our Habitations: Tradition and Theological Construction* (Albany, N.Y.: SUNY Press, 1994), 26–27. While the family and church revolutions have been generated in part due to historical factors beyond Christian traditions, opportunities for recovering and reforming neglected theological dimensions, such as Spirit, mutual recognition, and dignity, will enable creative change within Christian traditions.

CHAPTER 5

A Maternal Interlude

Maternal voices have been drowned by professional theory,
ideologies of motherhood, sexist arrogance, and childhood
fantasy. Voices that have been distorted and censored can only
be developing voices. Alternately silenced and edging toward
speech, mothers' voices are not voices of mothers as they are,
but as they are becoming. As mothers struggle toward
responsible thinking they will transform the thought they are
beginning to articulate and the knowledge they are determined
to share.[1]

"What are we here to teach you, Mum?"[2]

An Issue Whose Time Has Come

The last two chapters explored the dynamics of changing family models
in contemporary North American society and churches. The case was made
that the inclusive postmodern norm of *valuing families,* in contrast to the exclusive norm of *family values* (as in the modern, private family of male headship)
creates an opportunity for renewed reflection on how family models and household metaphors have functioned within Christian theology. But before moving too quickly into the specific inquiry between family models and Spirit
models, further exploration of the patriarchal family will enhance the theological analysis.

This chapter gathers critical resources for pneumatological exploration
based on a feminist maternal standpoint. The conscious connection of the
two adjectives—feminist and maternal—is vital. In a mutually critical correlation, feminist theorizing addresses women in relation to their families while
maternal theorizing addresses the historical legacies of gender construction.
But the maternal connection makes an additional contribution to feminist
analysis. In a patriarchal social order, mothers mediate relations of power
between fathers and children. Their vulnerability on what Rita Nakashima

---

[1]Sara Ruddick, *Maternal Thinking: Towards a Politics of Peace* (New York: Ballantine Books, 1989), 40.

[2]Quick Lamb asks his mother Oriel this question in Tim Winton's novel *Cloudstreet* (Ringwood, Victoria: Penguin Books, 1998), 269.

89

Brock terms "the fulcrum of power and powerlessness" creates the possibility of a unique, bifocal awareness.[3] While feminist analysis gives voice to the abuse of male power over women, a feminist *maternal* analysis further recognizes, self-critically, the potential abuse of power by mothers over children. Thus, a feminist maternal standpoint seeks out holistic transformations of family systems.

The first sections of this chapter explore hermeneutical issues in claiming a feminist maternal standpoint. In recent years, specifically identified maternal voices have challenged the construction of mother as *other* in discourses of literature, religion, ethics, and more.[4] But maternal voices are developing voices, "alternately silenced and edging toward speech."[5] What obstacles and complications do maternal voices face? The first sections make the case for maternal voices as timely partners in theological exploration. The latter sections explore the work of theorists Sarah Ruddick, Jessica Benjamin, and Alice Miller, who analyze the patriarchal family as a distorted system of family life. The deconstructive resource of poisonous pedagogy (Miller) joins the constructive resources of proper trust (Ruddick) and mutual recognition (Benjamin) in providing critical concepts for evaluating patriarchal Spirit models. These resources further aid in constructing a feminist maternal pneumatology of mutual recognition.

The interlude takes seriously "maternal thinking" in the work of contemporary theological reflection.[6] Maternal thought arises critically from the

---

[3]Rita Nakashima Brock, "Poisonous Pedagogy, Ethical Terror, and Maternal Thinking," paper presented at the American Academy of Religion, San Francisco (November 24, 1992): 20. Quote used by permission of the author.

[4]On mother as *other*, see Nancy Chodorow, *The Reproduction of Mothering: Psychoanalysis and the Sociology of Gender* (Berkeley: University of California Press, 1978); Patricia Hill Collins, *Black Feminist Thought: Knowledge, Consciousness, and the Politics of Empowerment* (London: Routledge, 1991), 43–90; Brenda O. Daly and Maureen T. Reddy, eds., *Narrating Mothers: Theorizing Maternal Subjectivities* (Knoxville: University of Tennessee Press, 1991); Cathy N. Davidson and E. M. Broner, eds., *The Lost Tradition: Mothers and Daughters in Literature* (New York: Frederick Ungar Publishing, 1980); J. Cheryl Exum, *Fragmented Women: Feminist (Sub)Versions of Biblical Narratives* (Valley Forge, Pa.: Trinity Press International, 1993); Nancy Hartsock, *Money, Sex and Power: Toward a Feminist Historical Materialism* (Boston: Northeastern University Press, 1985), 155–251; Kathryn Allen Rabuzzi, *Motherself: A Mythic Analysis of Motherhood* (Bloomington: Indiana University Press, 1988); and Joyce Treblicot, ed., *Mothering: Essays in Feminist Theory* (Savage, Md.: Rowman & Littlefield, 1983).

[5]Ruddick, 40.

[6]Ibid., 13–27. Theologians taking maternal experience seriously for theological construction include Rita Nakashima Brock, *Journeys by Heart: A Christology of Erotic Power* (New York: Crossroad, 1988); Anne Carr and Elisabeth Schüssler Fiorenza, eds., *Concilium: Motherhood: Experience, Institution, Theology* (Edinburgh: T & T Clark, 1989); Christine E. Gudorf, "Parenting, Mutual Love, and Sacrifice," in *Women's Consciousness, Women's Conscience: A Reader in Feminist Ethics*, ed. Barbara Hilkert Andolsen, Christine E. Gudorf, and Mary D. Pellauer (Minneapolis: Winston Press, 1985), 175–91; Catherine Keller, *From a Broken Web: Separation, Sexism and Self* (Boston: Beacon Press, 1986); Sallie McFague, *Models of God: Theology for an Ecological, Nuclear Age* (Philadelphia: Fortress Press, 1987); Bonnie J. Miller-McLemore, *Also a Mother: Work and Family as Theological Dilemma* (Nashville: Abingdon Press, 1994), 229–47; Sally B. Purvis, "Mothers, Neighbors and Strangers: Another Look at Agape," *Journal of Feminist Studies in Religion* 7 (Spring 1991): 19–34; Letty M. Russell et al., *Inheriting Our Mothers' Gardens: Feminist Theology in Third World Perspective* (Philadelphia: Westminster Press, 1988); and Delores S. Williams, *Sisters in the Wilderness: The Challenge of Womanist God-Talk* (Maryknoll, N.Y.: Orbis Books, 1993).

everyday practices of nurturing and caring for children. While maternal thinking is not exclusively the domain of mothers or women, in the past women did most of the mothering labor, and today many women continue to affirm mothering as one of the most significant dimensions of their lives. This is not to say that mothers do or should think alike or that they share the same experiences. Maternal thinkers speak from diverse, complex contexts and in ways that confront as well as extend one another. But because maternal identities and the practices of caring for children have been devalued, mystified, and marginalized in theological discourse, claiming space for particular reflection is now warranted. As Bonnie Miller-McLemore remarks: "The foremost religious thinkers have seldom taken seriously the knowledge that a mother and child might have about divine and human love, justice, power, and grace, or *the complexities that accompany their attempts* to realize these values."[7]

The exploration of Spirit models within the metaphorical framework of family and household pauses for a maternal interlude in identifying problematic practices of family life. Maternal voices now join with other critical perspectives in constructing a new hearth for the household of God. While past theological reflection incorporated mothering more in terms of an absent presence, for our day, "children and mothering are an issue whose time had to come, and it has come."[8]

Maternal Voices

While new to academic theology, maternal voices are not new to Christian traditions. When Sojourner Truth made her challenge, "I have borne thirteen chilern and seen em mos' all sold off into slavery, and when I cried out with a mother's grief, none but Jesus heard—and ar'nt I a woman?" she raised a womanist maternal voice with christological implications.[9] When Elizabeth Oakes Smith and other first-wave feminists sought to "restore the divine order to the world," they spoke not only as feminist voices, but also as feminist maternal voices with theological significance.[10] Throughout church history, women's maternal voices contributed to the daily vitality of Christian traditions.

But in recent years, questions have been raised for feminist theology concerning the place of families in its vision. Miller-McLemore writes:

> Most feminist theologians have agreed with the general feminist view that the patriarchal family no longer has a place...Much of this

---

[7]Miller-McLemore, 38. Emphasis added.

[8]Ibid., 83.

[9]Deborah Gray White, *Aren't I a Woman? Female Slaves in the Plantation South* (New York: W. W. Norton, 1985), 14. For the christological dimensions of Sojourner Truth's theology, see Jacquelyn Grant, *White Women's Christ and Black Women's Jesus: Feminist Christology and Womanist Response* (Atlanta: Scholars Press, 1989).

[10]Catherine A. Brekus, "Restoring the Divine Order to the World," in *Religion, Feminism, & the Family*, ed. Anne Carr and Mary Stewart Van Leeuwen (Louisville, Ky.: Westminster John Knox Press, 1996), 166–82.

reflection, however, has not received the kind of attention or codification it needs. Few feminist theologians have actually identified alternative family models.[11]

Extending feminist theology's family reflections in the direction of constructive theology presents a corresponding challenge. These challenges exist in part due to feminism's questionable relation to motherhood. Critics often portray feminists as antinatal and antifamily (see chapter 3). Complaints have been made that feminism has not wanted to deal with the issue of motherhood, resulting in mothers' marginalization in the eyes of the women's movement.[12] Women of color claim that feminists evidence an antagonistic relation to family life, in contrast to their own experiences of families as spaces of alternative identity, freedom, and cultural formation. Patricia Hill Collins suggests, "The relationship between mothers and children can serve as a private sphere in which cultures of resistance and everyday forms of resistance are learned."[13]

But interpreting contemporary feminism and motherhood as mutually exclusive interests misrepresents both feminism and motherhood. In the mid-1960s and early '70s, feminism advanced a *protest* movement and was not the only group raising critical questions about families in society.[14] Generally speaking, feminist voices for equality and opportunity were not rejecting the maternal commitments of women's lives; they were deconstructing the male privilege inherent in institutions of mothering, family, and partnership. Feminists made the important distinction between motherhood as a patriarchal institution and motherhood as a relationship to children.[15] Miller-McLemore explains the difficult position of feminists with critical perspectives on family life:

> Feminists have had good reason to feel reluctant about speaking for the values of rearing children and motherhood...Women have paid, and continue to pay dearly for nurturing children, costs that men have not known. The constraints of nurturing children are real. Reproductive difference, a potential source of power, is at the same time the source of women's greatest vulnerability.[16]

Opening up creative alternatives in contrast to the conventional family model meant an urgent priority for feminism on advocating the equal status of women and men. But even as a protest movement, feminism's agendas reflected family concerns of health care, birth control, breastfeeding, economic

---

[11]Miller-McLemore, 85.

[12]Sylvia Ann Hewlett, *A Lesser Life: The Myth of Women's Liberation in America* (New York: William Morrow, 1986), 184–85.

[13]Collins, 51.

[14]Lauri Umansky, *Motherhood Reconceived: Feminism and the Legacies of the Sixties* (New York: New York University Press, 1996), 18–19.

[15]Adrienne Rich, *Of Woman Born: Motherhood as Experience and Institution* (New York: W. W. Norton, 1986), 13.

[16]Miller-McLemore, 83.

opportunities, and child care, which, while different from conventional norms, still included visions of community inclusive of children and mothers.[17] Regarding the perceived antagonism between feminism and families, Miller-McLemore concludes:

> If motherhood and children received criticism and little theoretical attention hitherto, it was more a matter of emphasis, priority, and self-protection than hostility and rejection. The questioning of the inherent biological and psychological differences of motherhood, and of the essential place of children in women's lives, was a means, not a foregone conclusion.[18]

Thus, the turn in feminist theology to a more self-consciously maternal standpoint represents a *trajectory of critical awareness* inherent in feminism's history. Far from adding an alien or contradictory identity, recognizing feminist maternal voices today brings forth with clarity issues that have been and remain vital not only to women's flourishing, but to human flourishing as well. People may be skeptical and critical of the "dreaded f-word," but when viewed as part of a larger revolution in social change, feminism and motherhood need each other.[19] Today feminist theologians return with new eyes to Valerie Saiving's classic 1960s feminist declaration, "I am a student of theology; I am also a woman," and claim Saiving's maternal voice heard between the lines, "I am also a mother."[20] The time for feminist *maternal* voices has come.

An Unknown Place

In her "Poem for My Sons," Minnie Bruce Pratt writes about the costly journey of mothering two sons.[21] During the children's early years, their father continued his literary work, but Pratt struggled with debilitating deliveries, nursing complications, and sleepless nights in which she lost her vocational call as a poet. In order to return to poetry, and her sons, Pratt found her voice anew, but this meant a transformation in identity from the warm, dutiful mother of childhood lullabies to a willful woman of lesbian vision. Yet now she stands at "an unknown place," where she and her sons face each other in the possibility of mutual recognition.[22] She risked stepping out on the journey and the invitation to join her has been offered to her sons. Will they recognize their mother as the wise poet and passionate traveler? Or will they retain the image

---

[17]Umansky, 52–76.

[18]Miller-McLemore, 83.

[19]Val Webb, *Why We're Equal: An Introduction to Feminist Theology* (St. Louis: Chalice Press, 1999), 1.

[20]Miller-McLemore, 84–92. For Valerie Saiving's essay, see "The Human Situation: A Feminine View," *Journal of Religion* 40 (April, 1960): 100–112.

[21]Minnie Bruce Pratt, *No More Masks! An Anthology of 20th Century American Women Poets,* ed. Florence Howe (New York: Harper Perennial, 1993), 379–80.

[22]Ibid., 380.

of the young woman of lullabies? Will they now be able to meet together in the poetic "re-crossing" of mother and sons?[23]

Maternal voices are identities in process. They speak of many different experiences and address many different struggles from a broad range of social contexts. For example, following the choice of Orpah (Ruth 1:8), who returned to her mother's house, Miller-McLemore tells of the powerful experience of lactation and the "empathic, connected knowing" it entails:

> I know physically through a muscular ache. Apart from the ache, I can scarcely know. In this knowing, few abstractions come between myself and the other, mouth to nipple–no bottle, no instrument to measure birth size or fetal movement. As with pregnancy, lactation subverts artificial boundaries between self and other, inside and outside.[24]

In contrast, Jane Lazarre speaks of the tightly-woven "mother knot" she experienced with the birth of her bi-racial son, Benjamin, and the struggles of organizing parental child care collectives to enable a gradual return to her writing career:

> For two days every week I would be in New York attending classes. For two days and one night every week I would be away from Benjamin...I turned and waved goodbye to James holding Benjamin in his arms. A bottle would have to suffice since I would be too far away to return, a baby-sitter would feed him and change him and perhaps kiss him. And wanting nothing more than to run back and hold him to me, I boarded the train.[25]

Poet Audre Lorde speaks of creating new ways of living in the world as family: "As parents, Frances and I have given Jonathan our love, our openness, and our dreams to help form his visions. Most importantly, as the son of lesbians, he has had an invaluable model–not only of a relationship–but of relating."[26] Susan Maushart shares the abundant joys of nurturing children but also talks honestly of the "Masks of Motherhood" used in an unacknowledged maternal conspiracy of fear, shame, and silence:

> What human beings need to know about mothering is perhaps the greatest story never written. The journey to motherhood is an odyssey of epic proportions, and every woman who undertakes it a hero. Celebrating our role at the very core of humanity means learning to sing every line of that epic freely, the lamentations along with the hymns. When the Masks of Motherhood do crack through, they will have been eroded by tears that have been shed and shared, by the

---

[23]Ibid.

[24]Miller-McLemore, 147.

[25]Jane Lazarre, *The Mother Knot* (Boston: Beacon Press, 1976), 62–63.

[26]Audre Lorde, *Sister Outsider: Essays and Speeches* (Freedom, Calif.: Crossing Press, 1984), 79.

tremor of secrets unclasped, by the booming laughter of relief. What lies beneath the brave and brittle face of motherhood is a countenance of infinite expressiveness, a body of deepest knowing.[27]

Yet from her womanist experience, Delores Williams tells of black women's "surrogacy roles" when economic survival depends on nurturing children and adults other than their own families:

> Two kinds of social-role surrogacy have negatively affected the lives of African-American women and mothers: coerced surrogacy and voluntary surrogacy. Coerced surrogacy, belonging to the antebellum period, was a condition in which people and systems more powerful than black people forced black women to function in roles that ordinarily would have been filled by someone else...After emancipation, the coercion associated with antebellum surrogacy was replaced by social pressures that influenced many black women to continue to fill some surrogacy roles...For poor black women voluntary surrogacy could mean that, as domestics employed by white families, these women could still perform nurturing tasks for white children.[28]

When mothers share their voices, the great diversity of mothering experiences is heard—biological mothering, mothering by partners, "othermothering," coerced mothering, "diverted" mothering, and more.[29] While still in process, maternal voices learn from one another and recognize their diverse contributions to holistic social transformation.

In light of such diversity, creating space for maternal voices risks at least two dangers. First, a maternal standpoint faces the challenge of any specific identity politics. For example, what does feminist theology mean when it speaks of *women's* experience? Does feminist theology conflate the condition of some women with the complex conditions of other women through unacknowledged assumptions about universality?[30] Or what does it mean for black theology to speak of *black* experience? Does black theology draw on the lives

---

[27]Susan Maushart, *The Mask of Motherhood: How Mothering Changes Everything and Why We Pretend it Doesn't* (Sydney: Vintage Australia, 1997), 318–19.

[28]Williams, 61.

[29]Collins, in *Black Feminist Thought,* explains the expression "othermother": "Within African American communities, fluid and changing boundaries often distinguish biological mothers from other women who care for children. Biological mothers, or bloodmothers, are expected to care for their children. But African and African-American communities have also recognized that vesting one person with full responsibility for mothering a child may not be wise or possible. As a result, othermothers—women who assist bloodmothers by sharing mothering responsibilities—traditionally have been central to the institution of Black motherhood" (119). Sau-ling C. Wong uses the concept of "diverted mothering" to describe the experience of women (and men) of color caring for persons in situations of employment that usually involve the illusion of equality and mask a power differential. See her chapter "Diverted Mothering: Representations of Caregivers of Color in the Age of Multiculturalism," in *Mothering: Ideology, Experience, and Agency,* ed. Evelyn Nakano Glenn, Grace Chang, and Linda Rennie Forcey (New York: Routledge, 1994), 67–91.

[30]Elizabeth V. Spelmann, *Inessential Woman: Problems of Exclusion in Feminist Thought* (Boston: Beacon Press, 1988), 3–4.

and experiences of African Americans as an "ontological totality" without differences?[31] A *maternal* standpoint risks making universal claims about an assumed common identity, *mother,* or the experience named *mothering.* Essentialist claims end up conflating the complexity of maternal voices and marginalizing or effacing those who tell different stories. Critical theory, with its positional subject and infinite deferral of meaning, confronts a feminist maternal standpoint with the danger of creating another "regime of truth," maternal truth.[32]

But critical theory faces its own challenges from feminist critics. Does the infinite deferral of meaning risk de-politicizing feminist concerns and maintaining oppressive relations and institutions?[33] Not identifying maternal voices as such perpetuates their distorted subjectivities as the *(m)others* that sexism, racism, classism, heterosexism, and other systemic oppressions depend on. Concerning the pragmatic strategy of self-definition, Jana Sawicki makes the following observation:

> What is certain is that our differences are ambiguous; they may be used either to divide us or to enrich our politics. If we are not the ones to give voice to them, then history suggests that they will continue to be either misnamed and distorted, or simply reduced to silence.[34]

A feminist maternal standpoint, as a critical strategy of subjectification, refuses to let maternal identity remain as other. But the key to this strategy is in maintaining the tension between subjectification and openness to others in ongoing transformation. bell hooks holds critical theory and identity politics in tension in her "yearning" for "new and varied forms of bonding" across the boundaries of race, class, and gender.[35] From within this tension she asks, "How do we create an oppositional worldview, a consciousness, an identity, a standpoint that exists not only as that struggle which also opposes dehumanization but as that movement which enables creative, expansive self-actualization?"[36] Maternal thinking aims to create an oppositional worldview

---

[31]See Victor Anderson, *Beyond Ontological Blackness: An Essay on African American Religious and Cultural Criticism* (New York: Continuum, 1995).

[32]Concerning "regime of truth," see Michel Foucault, *Power/Knowledge: Selected Interviews & Other Writings 1972–1977* (New York: Pantheon Books, 1980), 112. Concerning critical theory and the social construction of difference see Michele Barrett, "The Concept of 'Difference,'" *Feminist Review* 26 (1987): 29–41; Judith Butler, *Gender Trouble: Feminism and the Subversion of Identity* (New York: Routledge, 1990); Gayle Greene and Coppelia Kahn, eds., *Making a Difference: Feminist Literary Criticism* (London: Routledge, 1985), 57–112; Colette Guillaumin, "The Question of Difference," *Feminist Issues* 2 (1982): 33–52; Luce Irigaray, *This Sex Which Is Not One* (Ithaca, N.Y.: Cornell University Press, 1985), 23–33, 68–85; Toril Moi, *Sexual/Textual Politics: Feminist Literary Theory* (London: Routledge, 1985); and Chris Weedon, *Feminist Practice & Poststructuralist Theory* (New York: Basil Blackwell, 1987).

[33]Elizabeth Meese, *Crossing the Double Cross: The Practice of Feminist Criticism* (Chapel Hill: University of North Carolina Press, 1986), 83–84.

[34]Jana Sawicki, *Disciplining Foucault: Feminism, Power and the Body* (London: Routledge, 1991), 32.

[35]bell hooks, *Yearning: Race, Gender and Cultural Politics* (Boston: South End Press, 1990), 31.

[36]Ibid., 13.

from which emerging practices and identities of mothering can be explored. Just because an authentic maternal identity cannot be established, the struggle for maternal thinking need not be abandoned.

While "feminism(s)" more accurately represents the complexity of feminism, feminist maternal thinking likewise embraces its character as irreducible *maternalism(s)* to avoid the danger of monistic universality.[37] The emerging diversity need not threaten knowledge but leads to richer dialogical, multifaceted theological reflections and movements for social change. In light of the danger of conflating knowledge, a feminist maternal standpoint, as a critical hermeneutic of subjectification, contributes to a stronger objectivity of knowledge. While some feminists like hooks and Meese turn to critical theory for a de-centering strategy, Sandra Harding claims standpoint theory entails its own self-critical assumptions.[38] In contrast to modern epistemologies and their placement of an objective knower outside the frame of knowledge, standpoint theory places knowers *within* the same historical frame of reference as the objects of knowledge. Thus, a feminist maternal standpoint recognizes the different social locations of other women's maternal standpoints. Each of these contexts (and more) provides standpoints from which to criticize dominance, including the dominance of other maternal standpoints. The goal of standpoint epistemology, evident in a feminist maternal perspective, is not value-neutral knowledge of reality as it is, but "less partial and distorted accounts of nature and social life."[39] Harding explains:

> Feminist standpoint theory is not in itself either essentialist or nonessentialist, racist or antiracist, ethnocentric or not. It contains tendencies in each direction; it contains contradictions. And its logic has surprising consequences: the subject/agent of feminist knowledge is multiple and contradictory, not unitary and "coherent"; the subject/agent of feminist knowledge must also be the subject/agent of every other liberatory knowledge project.[40]

In facing the first danger of reifying another regime of truth, a feminist maternal standpoint affirms an open, self-critical engagement in process with other voices struggling for identity and recognition.

The second danger a feminist maternal standpoint encounters is reinscribing the very same norms it seeks to overcome. Elizabeth Meese names this problem the "double cross," in which feminist identity betrays its own

---

[37]Elizabeth Meese, *(Ex)Tensions: Refiguring Feminist Criticism* (Urbana, Ill.: University of Illinois Press, 1990). Meese writes, "I want feminism(s) to be a space from which difference can speak and be spoken with respect, a space where we can write and or speak with one another rather than for or against each other. From this unfeasible but critical figuration issues a call for many voices and perspectives, choreographed into (con)figurations at some future moment; otherwise we risk double-crossing one another, believing that 'we' (me and those most like me) are writing the discourse of liberation" (28).

[38]Sandra Harding, *Whose Science? Whose Knowledge? Thinking from Women's Lives* (Ithaca, N.Y.: Cornell University Press, 1991), 138–87.

[39]Sandra Harding, "Rethinking Standpoint Epistemology: What is 'Strong Objectivity?'" in *Feminist Epistemologies*, ed. Linda Alcoff and Elizabeth Potter (New York: Routledge, 1993), 72.

[40]Harding, *Whose Science?* 180.

best intentions.[41] In a day of contesting family values, identifying particular maternal perspectives risks linkage with the private, apolitical, sexist, racist, classist, and heterosexist assumptions of the nostalgic 1950s family norm. The dualisms a feminist maternal standpoint originally seeks to de-center—male/female, white/color, public/private, heterosexual/homosexual, active/passive, mind/body, work/love—may return as newly re-centered. But once again, as Sawicki pointed out, not speaking from explicitly maternal voices risks mis-naming, distorting, and silencing maternal identities within contemporary society. So are feminist maternal voices damned if they do and damned if they don't? Either way, risks and dangers are involved. Miller-McLemore provides insight: "The critical task will be to distinguish [maternal] interpretations that play into the hands of societal backlash against women, in the name of 'family values,' from those that support women by fostering alternative values."[42] Ongoing critical work and vigilance must meet the dangers of re-inscribing patriarchal family values.

Feminist maternal voices create emerging spaces for an oppositional worldview that *values families.* In articulating a feminist maternal standpoint, conflating diverse voices and re-inforcing dualistic values remain threatening dangers. The challenge, though, may be met as did Pratt, in stepping out of bounds into this unknown place to create a future not only for oneself, but also for children, partners, friends, and families. Together, feminism and motherhood receive critical enhancement from one another in the hope of creating an existence we can all pray to. Certainly, a feminist maternal standpoint does not create this existence alone. In openness and self-critical awareness, feminist maternal voices join a larger choreography of struggling journeyers who also share this fragile, vulnerable, and beautiful world. But a feminist maternal standpoint, in its open and self-critical identity, brings forth the crucial issue of maternal abuse of power.

The Fulcrum of Power and Powerlessness

While recognizing the diversity of feminist and maternal voices, the feminist maternal perspective I speak from in this pneumatological project takes maternal power in relation to children as its central focus. My voice represents a middle-class, European American, married, heterosexual feminist currently living and teaching in Perth, Western Australia.[43] I have two children, Aaron and Will, ages 8 and 3, respectively. Pregnancy for me was neither a horrifying loss of individuation and agency nor a playful fluid dissolution of

---

[41]Meese, *Crossing the Double Cross,* 69–87.

[42]Miller-McLemore, 95.

[43]Australians also struggle with the tension between family values and valuing families. See Hugh Mackay, *Reinventing Australia: The Mind and Mood of Australia in the '90's* (Pymble, N.S.W., Australia: Angus & Robertson, 1993). While I think that my pneumatological analysis will interest Australian theologians, I am too new to make cultural comparisons and contrasts. The research in this book reflects the U.S. social context, and for now, I continue to identify myself with its formative orientation.

my identity.[44] I was just aware of the profound connection between self and other—my child—yet strangely enough, "the other is both my self and not my self...I am one, but two."[45] In pregnancy, my identity became irrevocably interfaced with the lives of my children.

But nothing prepared me for the post-natal impact of children. With each of their births, I became terrified of the profound power I held in relation to these two vulnerable and tenacious children. On the one hand, I celebrated the creative influence I would make on their lives and passions. But on the other hand, I feared I would also be one from whom they might learn emotional and physical pain, deprivation, violence, and cruelty. Motherhood made me acutely aware of the immense formative power—physical, psychological, social—that parents hold over the lives of their children. How could such precious persons be the ones most vulnerable to my power for creation and destruction? Certainly parents are not the only ones; peers and other adults have influence as well.[46] But maternal identity must recognize its inherent, ambiguous connection with power. Now, whatever I theorize or theologize about the oppression of women within families and society must be done in the full awareness and accountability of my own possibilities for abusive, oppressive relations with Aaron and Will. They are the ones who have taught me the intricate dynamics of mutual recognition.

A feminist maternal hermeneutic acknowledges that while privileged men have power over women within patriarchal society, mothers and othermothers also exist in positions of power over their children. This complex, multiple-subject positionality for women may lead to mothers' and othermothers' passive complicity in domination of their children or direct responsibility for family distortion and violence. As keeper of the hearth in the patriarchal family drama, the mother plays a pivotal role between father and children. Deferentially, she subordinates herself to the will of the father and socializes children in the dutiful values of patriarchy. Mothers potentially extend oppressive relations involving distorted self-domestication as well. Dorothy Allison shares the story of her mother's shameful regret toward the end of her life regarding the abusive relations of their family. Physically ailing, her mother remained economically dependent on Allison's stepfather (whom she loved) even though she worked throughout her life.

> "Baby," she said in a voice even softer than her whisper. Moisture appeared in the fine lines at the corners of her eyes. Her pupils looked strange, the irises cloudy, her expression confused. "I never meant for you to be hurt," she said. "I thought I was doing the right thing..."

---

[44]Linda M. G. Zerilli, "A Process without a Subject: Simone de Beauvoir and Julia Kristeva on Maternity," *Signs* 18 (Autumn 1992): 111–35.

[45]Miller-McLemore, 143.

[46]Patricia A. Adler, *Peer Power: Preadolescent Culture and Identity* (New Brunswick, N.J.: Rutgers University Press, 1998).

"I know." I said it softly looking into her eyes. I said, "I know, Mama. I know. Don't do this. There's no use to it. You did what you had to do."

"All those years," she said. "At first I just wanted to protect you, then I wanted a way to make it up to you. I wanted you to know you were never any of the things he called you." Her face was wet, no discrete tears coursing along her cheeks, just a tide of grief slowly slipping down to her chin.[47]

For years, Allison struggled with the damage of incest, physical violence, and emotional abuse at the hands of her stepfather. Who was to blame? Allison thought she was the one. But how could she heal without further confronting the complex, tragic legacies of her mother and aunts with their partners? Allison's story conveys the costly dangers of maternal complicity in abusive family relations.

Thus, a feminist maternal hermeneutic provides opportunities for women (and men) to reflect on parental power from the pivotal position of motherhood. Rita Nakashima Brock shares her insight:

> Maternal thinking opens doors for examining the multiple voices that allow us both to identify with those who are vulnerable and to accept responsibility for our power because mothers sit on *the fulcrum of power and powerlessness,* of hope and despair, and of abuse and empowerment.[48]

From the fulcrum of power and powerlessness, mothers and othermothers can become advocates and protectors of themselves and their children against oppression's ravages and distortions. Instead of extending abusive authority, critical maternal praxis creates marginal, alternative spaces for identities beyond the ones initially fostered by parental distortion and effacement. Surviving, resisting, and transforming the consciousness of all family members will comprise new values for families. As one of the mothers in Gloria Naylor's *The Women of Brewster Place* tells her daughter, "The one lesson I wanted you to learn is not to be afraid to face anyone, not even a crafty old lady like me who can out talk you."[49] A feminist maternal hermeneutic takes as its standpoint the daily, ordinary struggles of mothers, othermothers, and children. This standpoint acknowledges the potential for both maternal complicity and resistance in patriarchal families and other oppressive social systems.

Recognizing the fulcrum of power and powerlessness means mothers and othermothers can reflect on their diverse family experiences beyond the simple dichotomy of victim and oppressor. Brock's wise words are again helpful at this point:

---

[47]Dorothy Allison, *Skin: Talking About Sex, Class and Literature* (Ithaca, N.Y.: Firebrand Books, 1994), 245–46.

[48]Brock, "Poisonous Pedagogy," 20. Emphasis added.

[49]Gloria Naylor, *The Women of Brewster Place* (New York: Penguin Books, 1983), 87.

We are asked to identify as one or the other, but what if we are both? Most of us are both and we are more than both. We live in complex relationships of power in which the abuse of other human beings and our environment are part of our potential, even as we are vulnerable to the abuse of others.[50]

From a feminist maternal standpoint, mothers and othermothers must identify themselves not simply as innocent victims, but as participants in larger institutions of domination. The complexity must not be underestimated. In some dimensions of their lives, mothers and othermothers act with power, yet in other respects they experience themselves caught in systems of power-lessness. Thus, feminist mothers and othermothers "lose their innocence" and accept responsibility for minimizing evil with the hopeful "knowledge that we have some power, even if only minimal, to contribute to life-giving forces."[51] In maternal thinking, mothers and othermothers must face their own responsibility for constructive and destructive power in relation to their children. A feminist maternal standpoint does not reduce all distinctions between family members to a single, universal participation in sin or evil, but acknowledges the complexity and multifaceted character of participation toward accountability and active compassion.

But the commitments of postmodern feminist families do not guarantee that women will not abuse their positional power with children. The inherent asymmetry of the parent-child relationship presents an ongoing struggle for mothers, othermothers, and all persons who care for children by embodying life-giving power. Feminist maternal thinking promotes a thorough analysis of patriarchal family values and seeks practical transformation of the ways families *continue to practice and extend* these values under the guise of alternative models. Challenging the normativity of the patriarchal family is not enough. Equality and mutuality in parental relations is not enough. A feminist maternal standpoint addresses the family values giving structure to the whole household.

Theoretical Sources for a Feminist Maternal Standpoint

The next three sections present the theoretical resources for the analysis of Spirit language and family models in chapter 6. These concepts critically evaluate the patriarchal family model and guide feminist maternal practice toward alternative family ideals. The focus on child-rearing may seem like a strange detour beyond the bounds of appropriate theological method. Certainly, religious language draws on images of fathering, mothering, and childhood, but how critically have these relations been examined for their theological importance? Brock claims, "Child-rearing, as the responsibility

---

[50]Rita Nakashima Brock, "Losing Your Innocence but Not Your Hope," in *Reconstructing the Christ Symbol: Essays in Feminist Christology,* ed. Maryanne Stevens (New York: Paulist Press, 1993), 43.
[51]Ibid., 46–47.

largely of women, has not been regarded as a serious theological issue."[52]
The following sections gather together theoretical resources for a feminist
maternal evaluation of patriarchal family values. The resources will then enable a critical analysis of pneumatologies based on the imagery of a patriarchal household order.

The three theorists for a feminist maternal standpoint share the view that
the patriarchal family, with its values of male headship, unilateral power, and
subordination, distorts relations between family members. For Sara Ruddick,
Jessica Benjamin, and Alice Miller, children should not be treated as extensions of the family head, but as others in their own right, who grow and mature in interdependent relations with family members.   From this shared
intersubjective perspective, the theorists support forms of maternal praxis that
value and even encourage self-assertion, willfulness, and agentiality in children. First, Ruddick contrasts the patriarchal value of blind trust with her
maternal concept of *proper trust* and advances the training of children as a
work of conscience. Second, Benjamin characterizes the patriarchal family as
a system of distorted recognition and offers instead the goal of *mutual recognition*. Miller, the third theorist, details the patriarchal values constituting *poisonous pedagogy* and warns against maternal complicity. The positive concepts
of proper trust and mutual recognition and the negative concept of poisonous
pedagogy advance critical theological reflection for a feminist maternal
standpoint.

Proper Trust

In her book *Maternal Thinking: Towards a Peace Politics*, Sara Ruddick presents her hope for "a revisionist history of human flesh under the aspect of
natality."[53] In contrast to viewing human reason as dispassionate and non-
interested, Ruddick claims that through maternal thinking, reason can actually be strengthened by passion and loyalty. Caring for children has hardly
been esteemed in philosophical history as a resource of human reason. But
Ruddick envisions an alternative logic to the militaristic reasoning of patriarchal orders. In maternal thinking, critical reflection on the life activities of
child care presents ideals that structure maternal practice and determine what
is reasonable within the practice. According to Ruddick's pragmatic understanding of truth, the maternal ideals of preservation, growth, and social acceptability lead to the corresponding work of preservative love, nurture, and
training.[54]

For the purposes of this maternal interlude, the focus will be on Ruddick's
practices of nurture and training. Both practices entail "a metaphysical attitude welcoming change" and an understanding of human nature as "hospitable

---

[52]Rita Nakashima Brock, "And a Little Child Will Lead Us: Christology and Child Abuse,"
in *Christianity, Patriarchy and Abuse: A Feminist Critique*, ed. Joanne Carlson Brown and Carole R.
Bohn (Cleveland: Pilgrim Press, 1989), 42.
[53]Ruddick, 205–17.
[54]Ibid., 17–23, 65–126.

to goodness."[55] Thus, for parents, fostering growth "is to nurture a child's developing spirit—whatever in a child is lively, purposive, and responsive."[56] Ruddick's philosophical use of the term *spirit* at this point is significant because of its sensual root meaning in embodied life, similar to theological understandings of spirit as breath, life, energy, and wind (*ruach*). Ruddick explains:

> The term "spirit" may be misleading. To speak paradoxically, from a maternal perspective, *the spirit is material.* A child's body, from its birth is enspirited. A primary experience of preservative love is an admiring wonder at what a new body does. An enspirited body is in turn, a source and focus of mental life.[57]

Neither clay nor puppets, in maternal thinking, children dance with the breath of life. Children whirl in the constant development of thoughts, feelings, bodies, and abilities. From Ruddick's perspective, a child's spirit demands nurture, not distortion.

But most parents encounter difficulties in the everyday attempts of fostering growth. Minimizing the trouble and intensity of nurture, parents and caregivers may respond to changing spirits with rigid, authoritarian control. Instead of nurturing growth, parents end up stunting or squelching their children's spirits. Ruddick identifies this distortion with patriarchy, where the child's growth in spirit takes a subordinate position to the father's authority and control within the family. Yet from a beneficent view of children, the present developmental challenges work toward health and integration through a relational orientation between parent and child. Eliminating temporary challenges by fiat may maintain the order in a parent's life, but this exempts children from accomplishing developmental tasks necessary for continual maturation. The crucial issue is whether spirit is *chaos* in need of restraint and order or *life* in need of direction and affirmation. Ruddick suggests the latter, and thus, as a child develops, change and all its challenges may be welcomed. The maternal practice of nurture stands in sharp contrast to family values of control, rigidity, and domination.

Because fostering growth raises the question of ends, Ruddick presents her third ideal, social acceptability and its practice of training. While members of families, children are also parts of neighborhoods, communities, institutions, and nations. Thus, maternal practice educates children for productive, creative participation in these networks. Ruddick's peace politics distinguishes between training as domination (leading to passivity and conformity) and training as a work of conscience. For the former, nature is the enemy, resulting in models of control and subordination. Training as domination assumes an extension from parent to child, which eliminates the child's

---

[55]Ibid., 89, 103.
[56]Ibid., 82.
[57]Ibid., 83. Emphasis added.

need for self-authority. In contrast, training as a work of conscience affirms an internalized authority in children. Ruddick advises:

> As a mother attempts to convert, tame, or dominate a child's rebellious will, it becomes almost impossible for "difference" to find a voice. When, in contrast, training is a work of conscience and a child's conscientiousness is a criterion of a training's success, mothers aim to *maintain in themselves and develop in their children* responsibility for reflective judgment.[58]

The irony of maternal practice is that a mother must use her own authority to teach children that they cannot count ultimately on her own or anyone else's authority. Self and other must remain in tension. Thus, children need assistance and respect in developing their capacities for critical thinking, action, and judgment. For Ruddick, training as an act of conscience requires nurturing willfulness in children. Only if children are esteemed as others in their own right (and not extensions of their parents) can they develop as agents, initiators, or dissenters.

The key to forming willful conscience is proper trust. Ruddick defines her concept:

> Proper trust is one of the most difficult maternal virtues. It requires of a mother clear judgment that does not give way to obedience or denial. It depends on her being reliably good willed and independent yet able to express and to accept from her children righteous indignation at trust betrayed.[59]

The maternal virtue of proper trust challenges the values of blind trust and unquestioning obedience in models of unilateral power. These patriarchal values undergird coercive training models in which the battle of wills must be won by those in authority at all cost. Proper trust establishes increasing mutuality in family relations, where children and parents can express anger, disagreement, and frustration without the fear of severing relations or retaliatory violence. In particular, proper trust recognizes maternal betrayal or failure and makes forgiveness and reconciliation possible. Ruddick sets forth her hope for children and their caregivers:

> If, when their mothers fail them, as they inevitably do, children deny their hurt and rage so that they can continue "trusting," they are in effect giving up on their mothers. By contrast, when they recognize and protest betrayal, they reaffirm their expectation that their mother has been and can again become worthy of trust.[60]

In maternal thinking, the concept of proper trust supports a social vision in which conflict resolves peacefully without the distortion of selfhood and with dignity for both parent and child.

---

[58]Ibid., 117. Emphasis added.
[59]Ibid., 119.
[60]Ibid.

Sara Ruddick contributes to a feminist maternal standpoint by taking seriously the daily work of nurture and conscience formation that parents and caregivers engage in with their children. These practical modes of thinking extend beyond child-rearing to other social contexts as well. Through a focus on embodiment, Ruddick re-claims the character of spirited life according to the values of willfulness and agentiality. Since family relations inevitably involve conflict and failure, the concept of proper trust supports honest communication without domination. Ruddick's theory has been criticized as essentialistic in correlating mothering and mothers with peaceful and non-militaristic orientations.[61] While Ruddick acknowledges the difficulties of defining maternal thought, she further tends toward a nonambiguous politics and vision of family life by reducing the ambivalent dimensions of maternal identity and practice.[62] Yet despite these criticisms, Ruddick's concept of proper trust offers a critical tool for analyzing the values of the patriarchal family model and resourcing a feminist maternal standpoint. Proper trust forges the possibility of mutual recognition between family members.

Mutual Recognition

In *The Bonds of Love: Psychoanalysis, Feminism, and the Problem of Domination,* Jessica Benjamin deconstructs the patriarchal family as a social system of distorted recognition.[63] For a feminist maternal standpoint, Benjamin provides *mutual* recognition in families as a constructive theoretical resource. According to Benjamin, humans live within a paradoxical tension—people depend on others to recognize their own assertions of individuality and vice versa. Thus, the problem of domination in relations expands beyond the mere intrapsychic problem for psychoanalysis, which views the individual as a discrete, closed unit with a complex internal structure. An intersubjective paradigm re-casts domination as a problem between selves and others; thus under patriarchy, the paradoxical tension for family members breaks apart into dualistic relations—only one asserts and the other only recognizes. Benjamin explores how the bonds of love in families twist and tighten into forms of relational bondage.

She begins by questioning the psychological images of need-driven infants in relation to their mothers. In these developmental theories, the mother-child relation emerges from unbounded oneness and exclusively focuses the narrative of self-differentiation on heroic separation of the child from the mother. Benjamin thinks monistic paradigms make the erroneous assumption that "we grow out of relationships rather than becoming more active and sovereign within them."[64] In contrast, Benjamin presents the infant as

---

[61]Linda Rennie Forcey, "Feminist Perspectives on Mothering and Peace," in *Mothering: Ideology, Experience and Agency*, 370.

[62]Ibid., 364.

[63]Jessica Benjamin, *The Bonds of Love: Psychoanalysis, Feminism, and the Problem of Domination* (New York: Pantheon Books, 1988).

[64]Ibid., 18.

actively seeking relational attunement with others.[65] Rather than failed self-differentiation, intersubjective attunement represents the successful outcome of actively organizing experiences of self-being-with-another. Benjamin explains the difference an intersubjective perspective makes for developmental theory:

> Once we accept the idea that infants do not begin life as part of an undifferentiated unity, the issue is not only how we separate from oneness, but also how we connect to and recognize others; the issue is not how we become free of the other, but how we actively engage and make ourselves known in relation to the other.[66]

By re-conceptualizing the mother-child relation within an intersubjective framework, Benjamin places mutual recognition at the heart of the bonds of family love.

But seeing anew the infant requires a corresponding development in understanding the mother as a subject in relation. Not merely an object for growth or gratification of the child's ego, the mother's own selfhood plays a vital role in the processes of recognition: "The mother cannot (and should not) be a mirror; she must not merely reflect back what the child asserts; she must embody something of the not-me; she must be an independent other who responds in her different way."[67]

Maturing differentiation for mother (or othermother) and child in relation requires maintaining the vulnerable balance between self-assertion and other-recognition. Benjamin explains:

> Recognition is the essential response, the constant companion of assertion. The subject declares, "I am, I do," and then waits for the response, "You are, you have done." Recognition is thus reflexive; it includes not only the other's confirming response, but also how we find ourselves in that response. We recognize ourselves in the other.[68]

In the concept of mutual recognition, differentiation follows the narrative of discovery rather than disengagement. The other in reflexive relation is a real subject, rather than an instrumental object for identity formation. Benjamin's maternal epistemology entails different subjects constructing a shared reality through mutual recognition. Because we recognize ourselves in and through the other, Benjamin concludes, "The other plays an active part in the struggle of the individual to creatively discover and accept reality."[69]

Reciprocity between self and other leads to the paradox of recognition: One's own independent existence depends on the recognition of others. In mutual recognition, assertion and recognition stand in paradoxical tension.

---

[65]Benjamin constructs her theory of mutual recognition on the infant research of Daniel Stern in his book *The Interpersonal World of the Infant* (New York: Basic Books, 1985).

[66]Benjamin, 18.

[67]Ibid., 24.

[68]Ibid., 21.

[69]Ibid., 45.

Loss of the paradox through denying dependency or objectifying the other results in alienated forms of differentiation, which Benjamin names "the dialectic of control":

> If I completely control the other then the other ceases to exist, and if the other completely controls me, then I cease to exist. True independence means sustaining the essential tension of these contradictory impulses; that is, both asserting the self and recognizing the other. Domination is the consequence of refusing this condition.[70]

Within the patriarchal family, the tension of mutual recognition breaks down and splits into polarities. The male family head asserts himself without responsive openness to family members. Children and mother respond with recognition, but without their own differentiated assertions. Domination results from the father's denial of his dependency and masterful control of mother and children.

But Benjamin quickly points out that the power of patriarchal domination is more than the prohibition of others' assertions. Domination *twists* desire, so that submission to powerful male figures also includes an identification with them as personifications of the fantasy of omnipotence.

> In ideal love, as in other forms of masochism, acts of self-abnegation are in fact meant to secure access to the glory and power of the other. Often, when we look for the roots of this ideal love, we find the idealized father and a replaying of the thwarted early relationship of identification and recognition. Often, too, we find that the parental constellation reveals a split between the missing father of excitement and the present, but devalued, mother.[71]

As the desires of family members twist, the bonds of family love become confining, rigid forms of order. The playful space of multiple desires between self and other collapses into a mirroring of the powerful subject (who asserts) in the dualistically defined other (who recognizes). Reduced to a self-referential system of the authoritative head's desire, the patriarchal system replicates itself when male children learn to identify with male authority figures (repudiating connection with female nurturers) and female children learn to identify with maternal subordination. Both sexes end up seeking distorted recognition through conformity with the idealized family head.

Benjamin's concept of mutual recognition makes an important theoretical contribution to a feminist maternal hermeneutic. Instead of the heroic developmental myth of separation and mastery, mutual recognition provides a narrative for maturing, multiple relations of being-with-self-and-other. While Benjamin's analysis of social domination reduces the dynamics of oppression to an interpersonal system, her affirmation of differentiation in relationships

---

[70]Ibid.

[71]Ibid., 117.

through interdependency revitalizes the paradoxical tension of family life.[72] We develop as persons within relations, rather than grow out of relations. But restoring mutual recognition to family relations of twisted desire and self-subordination requires initially the self-assertion of family others. For Benjamin, the *(m)other* must make a difference. Thus, working toward mutual recognition inevitably incorporates confrontation and conflict between family members. Benjamin advises with hope, "Mutual recognition cannot be achieved through obedience, through identification with the other's power, or through repression. It requires finally, contact with the other."[73] Vital to a feminist maternal standpoint, conflict and confrontation become means for the greater end of mutual recognition in family relations.

Benjamin's analysis helps resist and re-direct nostalgia for the family model of male headship. Mutual recognition in families requires modeling both assertion and recognition between parental partners. But Benjamin's ideal of mutual recognition between parent and child may not always be accessible. While not wanting to place all the responsibility on mothers, Miller-McLemore observes the reality of children's demands:

> Mutual love is the ideal. But particularly with children, mutual love does not begin mutually, and their care involves a certain measure of parental self-loss and self-renunciation. In the interlude, in the larger network of care, many hands must rock the cradle and share the burdens of self-giving and dependence…When the less adept and dependent child cannot give back, the necessity to give, in response to the needs of a child, depends upon a broader context of give-and-take.[74]

Benjamin would agree, but because she fears the patriarchal assumption that *maternal* identity must shoulder the burden of recognizing others' needs and assertions, she privileges maternal identity formation. Unfortunately, by privileging maternal assertion, Benjamin overlooks maternal complicity in the breakdown of mutual recognition within families. Maternal assertion without a corresponding acknowledgment of maternal recognition (recognizing the assertions of children) contributes to the domination of children. The patriarchal dualism involving the assertion of the head and the recognition of others can become replicated as a matriarchal dualism—the mother asserts, and children only recognize. Proper trust reminds us that children also need to assert themselves and receive recognition by parents and caregivers for authentic mutual recognition. In order to attain a better understanding of

---

[72]Evelyn Nakano Glenn writes, "Mothering takes place in social contexts that include unequal power relations between men and women, between dominant and subordinate racial groups, between colonized and colonizer. Thus mothering cannot escape being an arena of political struggle." See her chapter "Social Construction of Mothering," in *Mothering: Ideology, Experience and Agency*, 17.

[73]Benjamin, 40.

[74]Miller-McLemore, 166.

maternal complicity in domination, we need to turn to the child's perspective through the theory of Alice Miller.

Poisonous Pedagogy

Psychoanalyst Alice Miller conceived the concept of poisonous pedagogy not through years of research or independent insight, but through "countless conversations" with her son, who helped Miller become aware of the deep-seated assumptions regarding child-rearing that she internalized during her own childhood.[75] Miller's book, *For Your Own Good*, analyzes European child-rearing texts from the sixteenth through the nineteenth centuries. Even though these texts are old, Miller asserts that the family values of poisonous pedagogy still permeate major areas of our lives. The "very omnipresence [of poisonous values] makes it difficult for us to recognize them. They are like a pernicious virus we have learned to live with since we were little."[76]

Poisonous pedagogy constitutes explicit and implicit family practices that teach children to repress their own needs and desires, resulting in personal conformity to the will of family authorities. In the child-rearing texts Miller studied, fathers carry the responsibility for discipline because mothers—basically weak—cannot be trusted with teaching obedience. Miller quotes L. Kellner, who in 1852 gave the following observation:

> In the family it is usually weak mothers who follow the philanthropic principle, whereas the father demands unconditional obedience without wasting words. In return it is the mother who is most often tyrannized by her offspring and the father who enjoys their respect; for this reason, he is the head of the whole household and determines its atmosphere.[77]

The texts contrast sharply with the Victorian valorization of women's expertise in virtue formation. Yet in poisonous pedagogy, as in Victorian domesticity, mothers still support and follow the patriarchal head of household in his general oversight. Thus, in the logic of poisonous pedagogy, mothers and other caregivers must conform as well as children.

Fundamentally a philosophy (and theology) of coercive power, poisonous pedagogy reinforces the blind trust and unquestioning obedience of children. Like weeds from a garden, spontaneity, self-concern, obstinacy, willfulness, or strong feelings must be rooted out from children when they first appear. The manuals admonish family authorities to take confidence in the divine ordination of their pedagogical mission. Since obedience and self-sacrifice are the qualities most desired by God in his children, earthly fathers are justified

---

[75]Alice Miller, *For Your Own Good: Hidden Cruelty in Childrearing and the Roots of Violence* (New York: Noonday Press, 1983), xviii. Miller also gives credit to her second analyst, Gertrud Boller-Schwing.
[76]Ibid., 271.
[77]Ibid., 40.

in applying any form of treatment toward early signs of sin and wickedness. Without swift punishment, the very souls of children remain in jeopardy. Thus, breaking the child's will functions as the fundamental metaphor in poisonous pedagogy. Miller quotes from a 1748 German text, "An Essay on the Education and Instruction of Children":

> It is quite natural for the child's soul to have a will of its own, and things that are not done correctly in the first two years will be difficult to rectify thereafter. One of the advantages of these early years is that then force and compulsion can be used. Over the years children forget everything that happened to them in early childhood. If their wills can be broken at this time, *they will never remember afterwards that they had a will*, and for this very reason the severity that is required will not have any serious consequences.[78]

The child-rearing manuals advise strategies of humiliation, corporal punishment, physical deprivation, cruelty, and the withdrawal of love for breaking the child's will and creating a docile, malleable, and receptive person, for his or her own good. In families constituted by poisonous power, children equate love with obedience and goodness with conformity. Suffering or outrage become the fault of children, who learn the inconsequentiality of their own needs. Miller shows that the coercive assumptions of poisonous pedagogy, learned by children as truths, are in effect lies.

But the outcomes of poisonous pedagogy mislead those with power. Because strong feelings and honest responses challenge authority, poisonous pedagogy teaches children to repress feelings of rage, pain, and betrayal. According to Miller, the central mechanism of this defense is the creation of "false selves" through the process of "splitting."[79] Oriented toward authorities, the false self cloaks the hurt that continues within the child. Dorothy Allison tells of pulling deeply within herself during her "punishment" and disconnecting herself from her thoughts and feelings. Her story expresses the self-contempt and inner rage kept at bay by the false self she created to endure her stepfather's poison:

> I tried not to make him angry. I ran his errands. I listened to him talk, standing still on one leg and then the other, keeping my face empty, impartial...Got to stand still for him, his hands, his big hands on his little body. I would imagine those hands cut off by marauders sweeping down on great black horses, swords like lightning bolts in the hands of armored women who wouldn't even know my name but would kill him anyway. Imagine boils and blisters, and wasting diseases; sudden overturned cars and spreading gasoline. Imagine vengeance. Imagine justice. What is the difference anyway when both

---

[78]Ibid., 13.
[79]Ibid., 79.

are only stories in your head? In the very day of reality you stand still. I stood still. Bent over. Laid down.[80]

False selves display the subordination and conformation desired by authorities, but as Allison's story shows, false selves mask the brokenhearted subject of distorted recognition. Miller's concept of the false self with its repressed anger applies not only to interpersonal or family relations. In his autobiography, Nelson Mandela shares a reflection that exemplifies Miller's concept on a societal level. In response to South Africa's indoctrination education of black children, Mandela writes,

> The consequences of Bantu Education came back to haunt the government in unforeseen ways. For it was Bantu Education that produced in the 1970s the angriest, most rebellious generation of black youth the country had ever seen. When these children of Bantu Education entered their late teens and early twenties, they rose up with a vehemence.[81]

From the perception of authority, children and subordinated others evidence the aims of obedience and conformity, but what remains at heart goes without recognition.

Miller observes that while necessary for survival and psychological space, the creation of false selves leads to con-fusion in relations of domination. In fused relations, the authoritarian selfhood of the parent has difficulty distinguishing itself from the false selfhood of the child. Parental power thus becomes dependent on the child's powerlessness. Rita Nakashima Brock, who looks to Miller's work for her own theological reconstruction, describes fusion as the antithesis of connection:

> Fused relationships operate by the deception that two selves are one, that one self can cause the feelings and reactions of others. Such fusion pulls selves off center. Each believes the other must be a certain way for it to feel secure. Hence much anger is focused on changing the other, rather than on taking care of the self. The lack of separate selves results in a loss of connection. The distinctive, unique self of the other is not experienced clearly.[82]

Fused relations revolve around the needs of the parent, yet fusion continues cyclically throughout generations, so that adults tragically require of their children what was demanded of them—meeting parental needs and serving as objects of projected self-contempt.[83] In fused relations of parents and children,

---

[80]Dorothy Allison, *Trash* (Ithaca, N.Y.: Firebrand Books, 1988), 37–38. Allison continues her story in *Skin*, 13–36. See also her semiautobiographical novel *Bastard Out of Carolina* (New York: Dutton, 1992).
    [81]Nelson Mandela, *Long Walk to Freedom* (Boston: Little, Brown, 1994), 148.
    [82]Brock, *Journeys by Heart*, 29–30.
    [83]Miller, 98–99.

distortion, fear, and falsehood bind the generations, perpetuating family secrets and extending modes of control.

Miller's concept of poisonous pedagogy serves as an additional theoretical resource for analyzing the dynamics of the patriarchal family from a feminist maternal standpoint. Like Ruddick, she reductively assumes the genesis of social violence and domination in family dynamics, rather than theorizing family poison as one aspect of complex, multilayered social disorders.[84] But poisonous pedagogy and its correlative notions of coercive power, breaking the will, and false selves provide insight into the ways mothers and othermothers can perpetuate violence in families. Through the cyclical pattern of fusion, subordinated children discount and repress their own needs; yet when they become parents themselves, they demand from their children what was abusively demanded of them. Thus, unilateral power, blind trust, and con-fused conformity represent the fundamental family values of poisonous pedagogy. A feminist maternal standpoint recognizes potential maternal complicity in embodying these values, even in postmodern feminist families. But in the model of male headship, the risk of complicity is even greater, since mothers maintain a subordinate relation in regard to their spouses, the final authority. The potential for maternal abuse increases when mothers and othermothers live within the family fulcrum of power and powerlessness.

To stop the cycle of violence, Miller invites parents to turn from their own pedagogies of poison and learn from their children. Miller is not condoning further self-sacrifice on the part of mothers or othermothers through this suggestion. But instead of unilaterally controlling relations, parents can seek empathetic relations with their children by acknowledging needs, encouraging initiative, and respecting feelings and thoughts. Since poisonous pedagogy undermines the possibility for mutual recognition, restoration entails untwisting fused wills and recognizing the child-other as a center of desire and individuality within her or himself. Miller was confronted by her own son, who then struggled with her toward a new relationship. We can empathize with her hope for the future of families:

> I can imagine that someday we will regard our children not as creatures to manipulate or to change but rather as messengers from a world we once deeply knew, but which we have long since forgotten, who can reveal to us more about the true secrets of life, and also our own lives, than our parents were ever able to. We do not need to be told whether to be strict or permissive with our children. *What we do need is to have respect for their needs, their feelings, and their individuality, as well as for our own.*[85]

---

[84]In a book review in *Social Work* (July-August 1984), Mary Pharis reflects on Miller's work, "Less satisfying is Miller's complete reliance on a psychodynamic explanation for every instance of abuse...A more ecological model might better serve to explain why not all parents in Germany evolved into child abusers" (412).

[85]Miller, xiv. Emphasis added.

What Are We Here to Teach You, Mum?

In Tim Winton's novel *Cloudstreet*, Quick Lamb and his mum, Oriel, were out prawning one night.[86] It had been years since she and her oldest son spent time together, alone, by the sea. The talk turned to family matters—hurts and losses. Quick didn't like dredging up all this personal talk, but Oriel told him that family was all they had. She really wanted to know whether she had been a good mother. So Quick took the risk and told her what he thought. Oriel needed to hear she was "flamin' bossy":

> She laughed. I'm glad you see things my way.

> Quick pulled with her to the beach, and helped empty the net of its cargo of jellyfish and gobbleguts and other useless small fish. He had a boyish impulse to kick her in the shins and run, just to have her after him, awful and reliable with it.

> The strong are here to look after the weak, son, and the weak are here to teach the strong.

> What are we here to teach you, Mum?

> Too early to say.[87]

Families shape us, for better and for worse. In families we learn about love and laughter, abuse and power, trust and betrayal. A feminist maternal standpoint starts from the joys and pains, delights and dangers of mothers, othermothers, and children struggling day to day toward relations of mutual recognition. While deeply personal, these relations of sweat and bone also reflect the great complications of social, political, and economic factors. Definitely, like Oriel, it is "too early to say" that mothers and othermothers have learned all they need to know or voiced all they need to say. In the story, Oriel eventually discovers her own weakness, while her children find their strengths. In fact, through the strength of her children and extended family, Oriel embraces reconciliation with her own painful past. In a tentative process, maternal voices risk stepping out to an unknown place, with the hope that in valuing families, they contribute with others to the larger project of life's flourishing.

And maternal voices are making diverse contributions across a wide range of fields. Confronting the dangerous nostalgia for traditional family values, a maternal interlude gathers resources for analyzing poisonous dynamics of the patriarchal family. A feminist maternal standpoint asserts that motherhood and feminism sustain mutual concerns necessary for confronting the societal backlash against women. In light of escalating youth violence, family values advocates press for male headship in families and paternal authority in discipline with greater urgency. But calls for evaluating and renewing men's

---

[86]Winton, 267–69. *Prawn* is the Australian word for what North Americans term *shrimp*.
[87]Ibid., 269.

participation in family life must not happen at the expense of re-subordinating women and children. Certainly, the struggle against domination toward inclusive human societies demands analyses of social institutions larger than families. Economic, political, and environmental analyses must continue. But ultimately the struggle in all these areas must move through our understandings of families, for families provide one of the formative structures of human community.

The theoretical resources of Ruddick, Benjamin, and Miller provide insight into the distortions inherent in families structured by unilateral power. Together, they detail the household dynamics of an "economy of the Same," in which subordinate family members merely reflect the desire and will of the household head.[88] The concept of poisonous pedagogy helps us understand how relations become falsely fused through coercive headship and repression of subordinate family members. For Alice Miller, the patriarchal family constitutes a deadly system in which threat, fear, emotional abuse, and even physical retribution affect obedient conformity. Domestic violence, incest, and ecclesiastical sexual misconduct connect with the dynamics of poisonous pedagogy—lack of empathy, neglect of the needs of vulnerable others, coercive loyalty, false selves, unquestioned obedience, and self-sacrifice for the supposedly altruistic authority. Jessica Benjamin characterizes this relational dysfunction as the breakdown of recognition that can only be restored through others' being recognized as different. In her contribution to a feminist maternal standpoint, the paradoxical tension of assertion and recognition must be maintained mutually for both self and other. Thus, the concept of mutual recognition challenges poisonous trust and obedient conformity. For Sara Ruddick, proper trust and conscience formation necessitate nurturing empathy, willfulness, conflict resolution, and honest expression in families. The theoretical resources of proper trust and mutual recognition stand positively in contrast to the negative concept of poisonous pedagogy. Together they serve as tools for analyzing the dynamics of the patriarchal family model.

In this chapter, maternal voices present contexts from which to reflect critically on the patriarchal family with its dynamics of domination and subordination. Since the damage and healing of women is so closely linked with the damage and healing of children, a feminist maternal standpoint asserts the identity of being "also a mother." But what happens when the damage of children results from poisonous maternal power? How can feminism and maternal thinkers begin to theorize together about women's participation in the abuse of power? Here I have claimed that a feminist maternal standpoint

---

[88]Luce Irigaray, *This Sex Which Is Not One*, trans. Catherine Porter (Ithaca, N.Y.: Cornell University Press, 1985). I am re-directing Irigaray's presentation of patriarchal specularization to include relations in the entire household: "Now this domination of the philosophic logos stems in large part from its power to reduce all others to the economy of the Same. The teleologically constructive project it takes on is always also a project of diversion, deflection, reduction of the other in the Same. And, in its greatest generality perhaps, from its power to eradicate the difference between the sexes in systems that are self-representative of a 'masculine subject'" (74).

offers a self-critical contribution to the debate about families. Positioned on the fulcrum of power and powerlessness, feminist maternal reflection acknowledges the danger of maternal complicity with oppressive family values and holds women accountable, no longer innocent, for their own use of power in relation to children.

Valuing families is an issue whose time has come. Moving into the future with commitment and imagination makes critical analysis of the patriarchal norm a vigilant task. But critical analysis also furthers theology's constructive work because, as we will see in the following chapter, the patriarchal family model historically funds the religious imagination of Christian traditions. Family metaphors of the almighty Father, obedient Son, errant children, orderly household, and unifying Spirit resonate within a patriarchal family model. If it is true that "at the center of patriarchal Christianity is a 'broken-hearted' patriarchal family structure," then for our time, theological reconstruction requires new models of social relations, particularly family relations.[89] A feminist maternal standpoint, drawing on the resources of proper trust, mutual recognition, and poisonous pedagogy, stokes the fire for this re-constructive work.

---

[89]Brock, *Journeys By Heart*, xii. Brock plays with the metaphor of brokenheartedness in order to present a soteriological shift from human sin (and the need for atonement) to human damage (and the need for healing). The term *heart* offers "a metaphor for the human self and our capacity for intimacy" and "involves the union of body, spirit, reason, and passion through heart knowledge, the deepest and fullest knowing" (xiv).

CHAPTER 6

Spirit's Domestication
in the Household of God

If God's inner relationships are the prototype for our human
relationships, and if "the personal is the political" (to use the
familiar feminist slogan), then no doctrine of the Trinity,
however construed, can be wholly devoid of political, spiritual
and sexual implications. The perfect relations found at these
other levels will create the texture of relationship as it cuts
through any theological system. The task of a Christian feminist,
then, will be to ferret out those connections and implications,
and if necessary, criticize and redirect them.[1]

Poisonous Pneumatology

From a feminist maternal standpoint, the breakdown of mutual recognition in patriarchal families creates relations in which family authorities assert
themselves and everyone else can only recognize. Characterized as poisonous pedagogy, this unilateral flow of power fosters conformity among family
members, blind trust of family authorities, and repression of efforts for personal differentiation. The particular wills and interests of family members
twist in reference to the will and interest of the family head for whom family
members only serve as an extension of identity.

This chapter shifts the focus from *poisonous pedagogy* in the patriarchal
family to *poisonous pneumatology* in the patriarchal household of God. The analysis builds on Rita Nakashima Brock's insight that "patriarchal family relations
are the bricks of the patriarch's theological house of worship."[2] Brock's insight corresponds with Sallie McFague's observation that in spite of Christian
adherence to the Mosaic First Commandment, the paternal metaphor for God
has become an idolatrous and intransigent patriarchal model with implications for patterns of governance at the national, ecclesiastical, business, and
family levels.[3] In recent years, feminist theologians have devoted energy to

---

[1]Sarah Coakley, "'Batter My Heart...'?" *Harvard Divinity Bulletin* 23 (Fall–Winter 1994): 12–17.
[2]Rita Nakashima Brock, *Journeys by Heart: A Christology of Erotic Power* (New York: Crossroad,
1988), 4.
[3]Sallie McFague, *Metaphorical Theology: Models of God in Religious Language* (Philadelphia:
Fortress Press, 1987), 9.

re-imagining God the Father and Jesus the Son, but with the renewed interest in pneumatology, new opportunities arise for feminists to re-imagine the Spirit as well. The following analysis addresses patriarchal patterns of governance in early Christian churches and ancient Mediterranean families, but from the relatively unexplored angle of Spirit talk.

Drawing on Elisabeth Schüssler Fiorenza's "feminist critical hermeneutics," I claim the early Jesus movement included house-churches where free women and slaves participated as full disciples and served in leadership roles.[4] In this case, the language of Spirit functioned to empower alternative social networks of mutuality, inclusivity, and diverse gifts. While "tension, ambiguity and anomaly" mark women's inclusion in scriptural texts, a feminist critical reading shows that Christian faith was not essentially patriarchal from the beginning.[5] Originally, family metaphors adopted by the churches challenged the Greco-Roman model of household structured according to the rule of the *paterfamilias.* But as churches integrated the socio-political theory of Aristotelian household management into their corporate lives, family metaphors helped return the "household of freedom" to an "economy of domination."[6] In this move, Spirit language twists to serve an ordering, conforming, and disciplining function within the constitution of God's "large house" (2 Tim. 2:20–21).

This chapter first investigates family values in the ancient Mediterranean world. Aristotle's theory provides the hierarchical logic of household and civic order, supplemented by the moral logic of kinship honor and shame. Religious practices of the domestic cult bind together the public and private spheres into one comprehensive vision of social harmony. The investigation then moves to the formation of early Christian communities according to two themes—family relativization and family re-entrenchment. As the Aristotelian tri-part hierarchy of masters over slaves, husbands over wives, and fathers over children becomes normative (however benevolently), household churches relinquish egalitarian energies for conventional patriarchal patterns of governance. In this process, the charismatic gifts of church household members are sacrificed for exclusive institutional offices.

---

[4]Elizabeth Schüssler Fiorenza describes her method in *In Memory of Her* (New York: Crossroad, 1986): "Androcentric texts and documents do not mirror historical reality, report historical facts, or tell us how it actually was. As androcentric texts, our early Christian sources are theological interpretations, argumentation, projections and selections rooted in a patriarchal culture. Such texts must be evaluated historically in terms of their own time and culture and assessed theologically in terms of a feminist scale of values. A careful analysis of their androcentric tendencies and patriarchal functions, nevertheless, can provide clues for the historical discipleship of equals in the beginning of Christianity. These clues can help us to construct a historical model of interpretation that does justice to the egalitarian as well as the patriarchalizing tendencies and developments in the early church" (60).

[5]Elaine Mary Wainwright, *Towards a Feminist Critical Reading of the Gospel According to Matthew* (Berlin: Walter de Gruyter, 1991), 353.

[6]Letty Russell, *Household of Freedom: Authority in Feminist Theology* (Philadelphia: Westminster Press, 1987). For formative work on this pneumatological transformation, see Nancy M. Victorin-Vangerud, *From Economies of Domination to Economies of Recognition: A Feminist Pneumatology* (Ann Arbor, Mich.: UMI, 1996).

The third section of the chapter turns to the Spirit. The shift in ecclesiastical models from the egalitarian community to a patriarchal and "kyriocentric" (master-centered) household incorporates a corresponding shift in the way Spirit language functions.[7] By domesticating gifts and subordinating household members under one head, the Spirit is cast in the role of underwriting and bringing about the order of the church within the order of the Father and the Son. Four short studies involving Paul, Clement of Rome, Tertullian, and John of Chrysostom reveal an increasingly poisonous association of Spirit language and household order. Domesticated and subordinated within the patriarchal household of God, the "docile and useful" Spirit creates a docile and useful church.[8]

Ancient Mediterranean Family Values

The analysis of family metaphors and pneumatology begins with an examination of the social context of ancient Mediterranean family life.[9] In contrast to our modern notion of family as "nuclear" family, both Greek and Roman languages use concepts of family more closely related to an extended household. The family domain provides a center of production for men and women, rather than a haven or withdrawal from economic and political life. In Greek, the word *oikos* refers to a domestic association inclusive of material possessions, physical space, and all members (wives, children, relatives, slaves, and servants) under the authority of the head. In Latin, *familia* includes persons and possessions under the authority of the oldest male in direct line, the *paterfamilias*, with relatives (*agnati*) including all males connected by a common ancestor. The Latin term *domus* includes descendents through women as well, but a wife, while subordinate to her husband, is still considered under the authority of her *paterfamilias*. Freed slaves, workers, renters, friends, and lodgers may be included too. The *paterfamilias* exercises legal power, *patria*

---

[7]Elisabeth Schüssler Fiorenza, *Jesus: Miriam's Child, Sophia's Prophet* (New York: Continuum, 1994), 14.

[8]In using the phrase "docile and useful" persons, I am following Michel Foucault's understanding of discipline in *Discipline and Punishment: The Birth of the Prison,* trans. Alan Sheridan (New York: Vintage Books, 1979). He writes, "Discipline may be identified neither with an institution nor with an apparatus; it is a type of power, a modality for its exercise, comprising a whole set of instruments, techniques, procedures, levels of application, targets; it is a 'physics' or an 'anatomy of power,' a technology…Generally speaking, it might be that the disciplines are techniques for assuring the ordering of human multiplicities. It is true that there is nothing exceptional or even characteristic in this; every system of power is presented with the same problem. But the peculiarity of the disciplines is that they try to define in relation to the multiplicities a tactics of power…in short to increase both the *docility and the utility* of all the elements of the system" (215–18). Emphasis added.

[9]See Halvor Moxnes, "What Is Family: Problems in Constructing Early Christian Families," and Eva Marie Lassen, "The Roman Family: Ideal and Metaphor," in *Constructing Early Christian Families: Family as Social Reality and Metaphor,* ed. Halvor Moxnes (London: Routledge, 1997), 14–36, 103–20. See also Carolyn Osiek, "The Family in Early Christianity," *The Catholic Biblical Quarterly* 58 (1996): 1–24; and Carolyn Osiek and David L. Balch, *Families in the New Testament World: Households and House Churches,* Family, Religion, and Culture Series (Louisville, Ky.: Westminster John Knox Press, 1997).

potestas, over all members of the *familia* until his death. Of course, these terms refer to households of wealth that are architecturally designed to segregate by gender (Greek homes) and status (Roman homes).[10] Archeological evidence from Ostia, Pompeii, Herculaneum, and Ephesus shows that depending on wealth, household structure assumes a variety of styles–the large mansion (*domus*), courtyard house, single-roomed dwellings, or apartments, and homeless conditions.[11] Yet the ideal on which the institutional and moral logic rests is the *oikos, familia* and *domus*.

Aristotle's Household Management

In ancient Greco-Roman society, Aristotle's *Politics* provides the theory behind household management (*oikonomia*).[12] According to Aristotelian theory, domestic households form the fundamental building blocks of the city-state. Each household constitutes a primary association for the basic, everyday life purposes of household members. Three relations of rule comprise a household: master over slave, husband over wife, and father over child. According to nature, the male head of household rules by virtue of his superior reason and knowledgeable skills of mastery, marriage, and procreation. Every other member of the household has a particular role or function, and the head knows how to most effectively implement each part for maximum activity.

But the three relations of rule differ. The rule of master over slave is absolute, since the slave is without reason, just as the soul rules over the body. Wives and children are free, yet possess limited deliberative faculties; thus, husbands rule over wives with the rule of a statesman and over children with a kingly rule. In all three relations, the head is by nature fit for rule and the inferior others fit for subordination. Thus, the subjects of rule require the *paterfamilias'* ruling in order to gain satisfactory participation in the whole. The *paterfamilias* also requires the proper functioning of household members for his own livelihood. From Aristotle's perspective, the relations of rule are beneficent, based on the natural abilities of different human beings. While all household members participate in virtue (*arete*), they do so according to specific qualities of their roles. Ruling men may be just and courageous, but women manifest virtue in silence. Aristotle's model requires only one ruler or head of an association; for a household member to step outside the order and take on a different role sabotages the natural order and instigates internal corruption. As Arius Didymus, court philosopher for Augustus Caesar and popularizer of Aristotle, warns, "Seditions...occur...whenever those with equal

---

[10]Osiek and Balch, 24–31, 221. The atrium and front parts of the house were open to the public during the main part of the day for business and hospitality. Women's rooms and women's dining areas were located further back for security. While slaves served in all parts of the house, they were associated with the areas of storage, washing, or cooking and slept in dark cells also used for storage.

[11]Santiago Guijarro, "The Family in First-Century Palestine," in *Constructing Early Christian Families,* 42–65. See also Osiek and Balch, 5–35.

[12]Aristotle, *Politics: Books I and II,* trans. Trevor J. Saunders (Oxford: Clarendon Press, 1995), 1–21.

rights are compelled to be unequal, or when those who are unequal have equality."[13]

Aristotle's theory builds on the household unit in society. Several households make up a village, and since every household has a ruler, a ruler of the village is needed as well. Then villages make up the state, and again the notion of rulership presents itself. But rulership on the state level exists among equals, the elite male citizens, and thus is potentially reciprocal, since political rule serves only a beneficial service for securing what extends beyond basic, bodily, everyday-life purposes—the good life of leisure and philosophy.[14] But even though political rulership is theoretically between equals, the hierarchy of the domestic household mirrors the hierarchy of the state. As a head of household rules his domestic association (*oikos*), so should a political leader rule the state association (*polis*). Caesar complements his use of kingly and divine metaphors for self-designation with the paternal metaphor *Pater Patriae* conferred on him in 45 or 44 B.C.E. Similarly, Augustus Caesar is declared *Pater Patriae* in 2 B.C.E. The analogy is clear: The father of the ideal Roman family is also the ideal father of the empire.[15] In ancient Mediterranean society, the household with its patriarchal/kyriocentric structure provides the fundamental structure for the macrocosmos, ruled over ultimately by the emperor.[16]

Family Honor and Shame

Aristotle's theory formulates the institutional or hierarchical logic of ancient Mediterranean family values, but to more fully understand the social context, the moral logic of family honor and shame must be explored. In ancient Mediterranean society an individual relates to society, not as an individual, but through a kinship network that determines one's status, honor, and responsibilities. Halvor Moxnes explains the way kinship systems influence social structure:

> In a kinship system everybody has his or her place. This system replicates other systems like the contrast between inside and outside, pure and impure, etc. Thus the question of origin becomes a question of social control. The individual is considered first and foremost as part of a family, not only of the small, "nuclear" group, but also of a lineage. Family is the main source of honor, and consequently, it becomes important to uphold family honor, to behave according to the family honor. Within this system it is a fault to diminish one's family, but also to overextend oneself, to go beyond that which is acceptable.[17]

---

[13]David Balch, "Household Codes," in *Greco-Roman Literature and the New Testament*, ed. David Aune (Atlanta: Scholars Press, 1988), 43.

[14]See Bertrand Russell's discussion of Aristotle's citizens as "cultured gentlemen" in *History of Western Philosophy* (London: George Allen & Unwin, 1961), 196–205.

[15]Lassen, 111–12.

[16]Moxnes, 36.

[17]Ibid., 8.

The centrality of kinship in society fosters the creation of a "dyadic personality" in which a family member's worth requires the social acknowledgment of that worth.[18] Thus, the relation of honor to the individual and the family is a two-way street. One acquires honor (or shame) through the family by one's birth and by the achievements of other family members. But one also brings honor (or shame) upon the whole family according to one's own success, failure, or indiscretion.

Personal honor is derived from maintaining family honor at all cost. Loyalty extends primarily to intrafamilial relations, in particular to the *paterfamilias*. People outside the kinship system compete for the limited social goods available.[19] In this agonal society, every invitation, debate, challenge, business transaction, gift, or marriage presents opportunities to enhance the family's honor. Thus, conflict within the *familia* becomes a major source of grief. Philip Esler explains, "This sense of collective honor within a family means that it is particularly shameful if the members themselves fall out and fail to present a united front to a harshly judgmental public."[20] Family dissension and conflict reflect negatively on the *paterfamilias'* ruling ability, which makes sibling cohesion, unity, and obedience valuable for social control.

Because the cultural dualism of public/domestic is associated with sexual difference, ancient Mediterranean women and men acquire honor through different means.[21] For elite men, successful oratorical challenge in the public arena–the *polis*–is rewarded with honor. Women gain honor through chastity, subordination, and seclusion within the private household (*oikos*).[22] But the two are interrelated. The hymen symbolizes female honor; thus, women must maintain the sanctity of their biological and social spaces. Symbolized by the testicles, male honor requires protecting female space and crossing the boundaries of other men through challenge, gain, or female sexual violation. Thus, female honor depends ultimately upon male honor.[23] If insiders or outsiders transgress the public/domestic boundaries of the family, shame ensues.

---

[18]Bruce J. Malina, *The New Testament World: Insights from Cultural Anthropology* (Louisville, Ky.: Westminster John Knox Press, 1993), 28–89.

[19]Ibid., 90–116.

[20]Philip F. Esler, "Imagery and Identity in Gal. 5:13 to 6:10," in *Constructing Early Christian Families*, 124.

[21]There are difficulties in making this generalization about women's social reality in ancient Mediterranean culture. Oseik and Balch, in *Families in the New Testament World*, show that in reality women did function in the areas of political influence, business ownership, patronage, and other public roles, even as gladiators. They write, "[Women] were not invisible, but on the contrary very visible, even as the language of public male discourse and political structures tried not to acknowledge that visibility, but rather to render women socially invisible" (58). The seclusion of women was an elite ideal. Most women struggled to survive in the peasant class (comprising 93 percent of the empire), where they were engaged in both public and domestic production (37).

[22]Karen Jo Torjesen, *When Women Were Priests: Women's Leadership in the Early Church and the Scandal of Their Subordination in the Rise of Christianity* (San Francisco: HarperSanFrancisco, 1993), 155–75.

[23]Malina, 49–50.

'Round the Family Hearth

The hierarchical structure of ancient Mediterranean kinship and the values of family honor consolidate through religious practices of the domestic cult.[24] Greeks venerate Hestia, the goddess of the hearth. Romans worship Vesta as the goddess of the hearth, along with the Lares (deified spirits of dead ancestors) and the Penates (storehouse deities who guarantee the food supply). Household shrines are located in the dining room, kitchen, atrium, or gardens, and all household members—children and slaves, but especially the *paterfamilias* and *materfamilias*—engage in daily, monthly, and other regular sacrifices together. Family life and family structure mediate religious values, and religion mediates social codes of behavior and value. As John Barclay explains,

> Infants learned very early which powers to propitiate in the home, and the demands of *pietas* to one's forebears, living or deceased, made it unthinkable that a child would wish to break the time-honored traditions or show less than full respect for the *paterfamilias*. Family loyalty constituted a cardinal virtue, and the routine domestic ritual, associated with the Genius of the head of the household, served to reinforce that loyalty by the subtle and powerful influence of religion.[25]

Within the domestic cult, the cosmic and human orders meet under the household authority of the *paterfamilias*. From the ancient Mediterranean perspective, people within households and across the *polis* promote social harmony when they worship the same deities. This connection may be seen in the fact that the goddess Vesta has her primary residence in the House of the Vestals in the Roman Forum.[26] Karl Olav Sandnes describes the basic parallel between the *sacra publica* and the *sacra privata*: "The fundamental assumption that the household is a city-state in microcosm means that domestic worship is seen in a political perspective...What happens in the families may safeguard or endanger the harmony and well-being of the wider community."[27] Thus, to differentiate from or challenge the household order undermines the purposes, honor, and prosperity of the *familia* and the *polis*, which becomes evident in the next section concerning Christian conversion and family metaphors.

---

[24]Osiek, 15.

[25]John M. G. Barclay, "The Family as the Bearer of Religion," in *Constructing Early Christian Families*, 68.

[26]Osiek and Balch, 84.

[27]Karl Olav Sandnes, "Equality Within Patriarchal Structures: Some New Testament Perspectives on the Christian Fellowship as a Brother- or Sisterhood and a Family," in *Constructing Early Christian Families*, 155.

Family Metaphors and Early Christian Communities

The first Christian communities emerged within the social context of ancient Mediterranean society with its family values of Aristotelian household management, kinship honor, and domestic religion. Like Greco-Roman society, early Christian communitiess employed household metaphors to structure social practice and derive religious meaning. But a reconstruction of women's traditions in early Christian churches discovers a struggle between two conflicting trends in ecclesiastical household life–family relativization and family re-entrenchment. The following discussion traces the two trends in terms of family metaphors and follows the impact of the latter model on the ministries of women. While questions may be raised about the widespread historical instantiation of the first model, feminist critical scholarship gathers the prophetic traces of egalitarian discipleship in the struggling house-churches.[28] The latter model prevails, yet the former remains a "dangerous memory" embedded from the beginning in Christian praxis.[29]

Family Relativization

In the New Testament, metaphors of kinship and family convey a transformed vision of human association. To varying degrees, the four gospels and Paul's letters share a vision in which the honorable loyalties of family and emperor and the politically correct structures of household become relativized according to the exigencies of discipleship and the radical parenthood of God.[30] The biblical material of family relativization is "primarily a rhetorically powerful metaphorical way of calling for the displacement of every obstacle to true discipleship of Jesus in the light of the imminent coming of the kingdom of God."[31] In this eschatological light, sayings such as "Whoever loves father or mother [or]...son or daughter more than me is not worthy of me" (Mt. 10:37) and "Whoever does the will of God is my brother and sister and mother" (Mk. 3:35) make sense.[32] The call of radical discipleship requires even a separation from blood family as the measure of faithful obedience. Carolyn Osiek claims,

> Jesus' presence will inevitably bring divisiveness that strikes at the heart of household relationships, as he brings not peace but the sword (Matthew), or divisions (Luke)...Not only does his mission pit members of a household against each other but Jesus pits family love and

---

[28]Sandnes is critical of what he terms Schüssler Fiorenza's "theory of decay" from egalitarian to brotherhood households (150–63). He argues that egalitarian relations emerged out of patriarchal house-churches. I am arguing for a more ambiguous relation between the models, an ambiguity filled with tension and struggle.

[29]Sharon D. Welch, *Communities of Resistance and Solidarity: A Feminist Theology of Liberation* (Maryknoll, N.Y.: Orbis Books, 1985), 32–54.

[30]Osiek and Balch, 103–55.

[31]Stephen C. Barton, "The Relativisation of Family Ties in the Jewish and Graeco-Roman Traditions," in *Constructing Early Christian Families*, 81.

[32]Osiek, 2–3.

loyalty against discipleship…The one called to discipleship is not to look back to say good-bye (Luke 9:61) or even to bury a dead father, one of the most sacred duties of a son (Matt. 8:21–22, par. Luke 9:59–60).[33]

Jesus' prophetic summons of radical monotheism, consistent with his Jewish tradition, calls for relativizing family, not as an act of impiety or law-breaking, but toward a greater piety.[34]

Schüssler Fiorenza suggests that Jesus' inclusive praxis overturns the dominant social orders offering people a "solidarity from below."[35] In the new family order, no one but God is called father or master (Mt. 23:9). The divine householder even values those without procreative potential (eunuchs) and puts all members on equal footing (Mt. 19:12, 20:12).[36] McFague calls attention to Jesus' table fellowship, which upsets the conventional practices of family honor and incarnates God's scandalous love for sinners and the poor, those who cannot provide social gain.[37] In the new honor code, children and slaves move up from the lowest places in the household order because they embody the privileged paradigms for true discipleship (Mk. 10:15).[38] The messianic "kingdom" of Jesus, claims Letty Russell, becomes a new household where God welcomes all people with nourishing hospitality.[39]

The exodus from Greco-Roman household piety presents new opportunities for women in particular. Schüssler Fiorenza portrays the Jesus movement as a "discipleship of equals" in which male and female disciples walk in the power of God, present as Spirit, and embody together a "praxis of inclusive wholeness."[40] Jesus' preferential option for the poor and marginalized includes women: "In the Jesus-movements women of all walks of life could become disciples, although they were socially marginal, religiously inferior, and for much of the time cultically unclean."[41] Peter's ill mother receives healing in the touch of Jesus and rises to serve his mission and ministry (Mt. 8:14–15).[42] Martha, Mary, and Lazarus befriend Jesus as his sisters and brother who seek the will of God (Mk. 3:35). Mary of Magdala, Salome, and other women follow Jesus through Galilee, minister to him, and come with him to Jerusalem, eventually not to deny Jesus, but to risk their own lives with him in

---

[33]Ibid., 6.

[34]Barton, 98–99.

[35]Schüssler Fiorenza, *In Memory of Her*, 145–51.

[36]Warren Carter, *Households and Discipleship: A Study of Matthew 19–20*, JSNTSup 103 (Sheffield: JSOT Press, 1994), 17–22, cited in Osiek and Balch, *Families in the New Testament World*, 132.

[37]McFague, 45–52.

[38]Schüssler Fiorenza, *In Memory of Her*, 148.

[39]Letty Russell, *Church in the Round: Feminist Interpretation of the Church* (Louisville, Ky.: Westminster John Knox Press, 1993), 58–60.

[40]Schüssler Fiorenza, *In Memory of Her*, 118–30.

[41]Elisabeth Schüssler Fiorenza, *Discipleship of Equals: A Critical Feminist Ekklesia-logy of Liberation* (New York: Crossroad, 1993), 176.

[42]Elaine Wainwright, "The Gospel of Matthew," in *Searching the Scriptures Vol. 2: A Feminist Commentary*, ed. Elisabeth Schüssler Fiorenza (New York: Crossroad, 1994), 647–49.

his death (Mk. 15:40; Lk. 23:49; Mt. 28:56).[43] Receiving the first appearance of the resurrected Jesus, Mary of Magdala proclaims his abiding presence with all disciples (Jn. 20:11–18).

After Pentecost, the vision of a transformed *familia* continues in the Christian missionary movement. Karen Jo Torjesen claims that the earliest Christians understand themselves explicitly as an alternative family or household:

> The Christian communities of the apostolic period designated themselves a "household church" (*he kat' oikon ekklesia*, literally "coming together at home"; 1 Cor. 16:19, Philemon 2, Col. 4:15). The creation of a new family structure was affirmed in the practice of holding properties in common and in the collective responsibility assumed for the poor, the sick and the widowed.[44]

For first-century women accustomed to identifying their role, status, and power in relation to male authority, the household church offers space for emancipation. "Ecclesial freedom" further means a transformation of value for slaves, whose new identity is based on brotherhood and sisterhood, rather than in relation to masters (Philem. 8–20).[45] But even though the new communities meet in homes, Christian identity does not at first mean the creation of a cultural "Christian family." Conversion addresses individuals as well as households; thus, household churches include

> adult freeborn and freed men and women, single and married, perhaps with their children but without spouses, as well as male and female slaves, perhaps also with children, but without their owners. The idea that everything was done in family or household units is not supported by the evidence.[46]

The "household of freedom" includes members according to God the Spirit, with baptism of male and female replacing male circumcision as the principle of relation for all household members.[47] Each new member, male or female, slave or free, Jew or Gentile (Gal. 3:28) receives charismatic gifts by the Spirit, who freely distributes them not according to gender or social

---

[43]Schüssler Fiorenza, *In Memory of Her*, 320–21.

[44]Torjesen, 126–27.

[45]Peter C. Hodgson, *Revisioning the Church: Ecclesial Freedom in the New Paradigm* (Philadelphia: Fortress Press, 1988), 27. By the term "ecclesial freedom," Hodgson means "the ideal, distinctive, or essential features of the Christian church…which set it apart from other religious communities as a unique form of redemptive existence." On the participation of slaves in early Christian communities, see Osiek and Balch, 174–92. They conclude that Christians owned slaves and continued to do so well into the Constantinian era, but also that slaves were admitted to baptism and full membership in the Christian community. The human dignity of slaves was recognized by their acceptance into the community, without calling into question the institution of slavery itself (188). In light of Philemon, adoption of Aristotelian household management by the early churches represents a re-subordination for slaves as well, even though they receive baptism.

[46]Osiek, 16.

[47]Russell, *Church in the Round*, 61.

status but for the edification of the household.[48] Schüssler Fiorenza describes household members as *"pneumatikoi:* Spirit-filled persons," who teach, lead, preach, baptize, break bread, serve, heal, and prophesy in present awareness and expectant hope of God's *basileia* (kingdom).[49] Peter Hodgson argues that the household churches are a "creation of the Spirit," where "Spirit refers to that modality of divine activity whereby God indwells and empowers not merely human subjectivity but *intersubjectivity.*"[50] As Schüssler Fiorenza interprets Luke 17:21, the *basileia* emerges in the *midst* of people.[51] The presence of God as Spirit breaks down the dividing walls of social status and sustains the egalitarian ethos of the community.

Ancient Mediterranean family values actually create at first a positive effect on women's leadership in the household churches.[52] Since the earliest model of church leadership is the familiar role of household manager, women's leadership is considered acceptable and natural. Torjesen writes, "The early church's specific leadership functions posed no barriers to women, whose skills and experience as managers amply prepared them to assume the duties of teaching, disciplining, nurturing and administrating material resources."[53] Until the third century, wealthy women such as Phoebe (Rom. 16:1–3) serve as benefactors or patrons of churches.[54] The communal gatherings occur in their homes or in urban areas within an apartment room—usually in the dining room—and center around a common meal provided by the benefactor or other leaders.[55] Torjesen claims an analogy exists between women's patronage of house churches and women's patronage of Greco-Roman private banquet associations, political networks, and civic projects.[56] Since the central act of Christian worship moves from the Jewish familial sabbath meal to the eucharist celebration, the status and power of women in these gatherings exist in no ancillary or conciliatory way.[57]

---

[48]Hans von Campenhausen, *Ecclesiastical Authority and Spiritual Power in the Church in the First Three Centuries,* trans. J. A. Baker (London: Adam and Charles Black, 1969). Concerning the charismatic constitution of the church, Von Campenhausen writes, "Even the regular everyday functions and ministries within the Church are seen as the operation of gifts, not of offices and prerogatives, and only as gifts are they known and freely acknowledged by the congregation" (296).

[49]Schüssler Fiorenza, *In Memory of Her,* 296–97. *Basileia* is the Greek word for kingdom or empire. Schüssler Fiorenza uses the term without translation to preserve its nonmasculine sense. Schüssler Fiorenza claims the Jesus movement shared with other Jewish reform movements an anticipation of the coming reign and renewed dwelling space of God. But "the Jesus movement refused to define the holiness of God's elected people in cultic terms, redefining it instead as the wholeness intended for creation" (113). On kingdom as *basileia,* see also Hodgson, 22–23, 35–37.

[50]Hodgson, 33. Emphasis added.

[51]Schüssler Fiorenza, *In Memory of Her,* 119.

[52]Karen Jo Torjesen, "Reconstruction of Women's Early Christian History," in *Searching the Scriptures: A Feminist Introduction,* ed. Elisabeth Schüssler Fiorenza (New York: Crossroad, 1993), 304.

[53]Torjesen, *When Women Were Priests,* 82.

[54]Russell, *Church in the Round,* 61.

[55]Torjesen, "Reconstruction," 304–5. See also idem, *When Women Were Priests,* 88–109.

[56]Torjesen, *When Women Were Priests,* 17–18.

[57]Ibid., 127.

Drawing on New Testament records, noncanonical resources, and inscriptions, scholars Schüssler Fiorenza, Torjesen, and Russell give evidence that early church women served in the roles of minister (*diakonos*), elder (*presbyteros*), prophet, teacher, and bishop (*episcopos*).[58] Scriptural references to women's names, such as Lois and Eunice (1 Tim. 1:5) or Apphia (Philem. 2), suggest the fact of female ecclesiastical leadership. Torjesen cites a painting in the Priscilla catacomb of Rome portraying seven women seated around a semicircular table bearing loaves of bread.[59] The central figure appears to preside over the meal. Torjesen further cites a mosaic dedicated to two women saints, Prudentiana and Praxedis, in a Roman basilica that includes the two saints, Mary, and a woman whom the inscription identifies as "Theodora Episcopa," that is, Bishop Theodora. The *a* on Theodora has been scratched, "leading to the disturbing conclusion that attempts were made to deface the feminine ending, perhaps even in antiquity."[60]

Such attempts to rewrite the realities of an earlier era are not isolated. One of the difficulties with feminist reconstruction of female leadership in the early churches has been the androcentric interpretation of terminology referring to women's ministries. For example, both women and men are called *diakonos* (minister) in the New Testament, but in reference to women, androcentric translators render *diakonos* as servant, helper, or deaconess, minimizing and trivializing women's leadership.[61] Phoebe's title, *prostatis* of the church at Cenchreae, clearly identifies her as the leader of the community, and Paul describes his relationship to her as one of client-patron. Schüssler Fiorenza observes that "such patronage did not consist merely in financial support and hospitality on behalf of clients but also in bringing her influence to bear and in using her connections for them."[62] Typically, androcentric New Testament interpretation downgrades Phoebe's leadership, as well, to the status of helper or sister.

But in early Christianity, female leadership is not confined to the local house churches. Women's charismatic gifts lead them into the public sphere as itinerant evangelists, missionaries (*apostoloi*), preachers, and founders of new communities.[63] Women such as Prisca (Priscilla), Junia, and Mary (Rom. 16:3–7) "labor in the Gospel," not under Paul's authority but either with him and others as coworkers or with independent status.[64] Women travel not only

---

[58]See Schüssler Fiorenza, *In Memory of Her*, 160–84, 246–47; idem, *Discipleship of Equals*, 151–79; idem, "Word, Spirit and Power: Women in Early Christian Communities," in *Women of Spirit: Female Leadership in the Jewish and Christian Traditions*, ed. Rosemary Radford Ruether and Eleanor McLaughlin (New York: Simon and Schuster, 1979), 29–70; Russell, *Church in the Round*, 58–61; Torjesen, *When Women Were Priests*, 5, 9–50, 76–82, 115; and idem, "Reconstruction," 293–94.

[59]Torjesen, "Reconstruction," 293–94; and idem, *When Women Were Priests*, 52.

[60]Torjesen, *When Women Were Priests*, 9–10.

[61]Schüssler Fiorenza, *Discipleship of Equals*, 157.

[62]Schüssler Fiorenza, *In Memory of Her*, 181.

[63]See Schüssler Fiorenza, *In Memory of Her*, 168–75; idem, *Discipleship of Equals*, 104–16; Torjesen, "Reconstruction," 293–97; and Russell, *Church in the Round*, 60–62.

[64]Schüssler Fiorenza, *In Memory of Her*, 169.

as coworkers with men, as Priscilla travels with Aquila, but with one another, such as Tryphaena and Tryphosa (Rom. 16:12) or Euodia and Syntyche (Phil. 4:2–3). The noncanonical text *Acts of Thecla* presents a young woman called to renounce her cultural and family ties and "go preach the gospel and baptize."[65] Thecla's witness joins with stories of women martyrs, Montanists Priscilla and Maximilla, gnostic teacher Philoumeme, and other women leaders who provide evidence that "Christianity has not been patriarchally determined from its very inception and has not been an integrated segment of its dominant patriarchal Jewish or Greco-Roman societies."[66]

Historical reconstructions of women's leadership in early Christianity provide evidence for a tradition of family relativization. Though New Testament texts also portray household churches structured along patriarchal lines, the evidence remains clear that female leadership is a practice in early Christian communities and that, furthermore, attempts to obscure and minimize this reality have been in force for some time. Indeed, these efforts soon gain their full momentum.

Family Re-entrenchment

New Testament texts show that not only egalitarian kinship systems constitute the early churches. In 1 Thessalonians, the patriarchal household model operates in full effect, for Paul here exhorts the community as his sons to honor their brotherhood in Christ, follow his fatherly example, and maintain the right order to their domestic households.[67] Through this letter, the derivative status of women converts within the Thessalonian church prompts the question of whether they are accepted as codisciples. Moxnes claims that while the synoptic family imagery suggests a household of inclusive caring and sharing of resources, in Acts, Paul's letters, and the pastoral epistles, the primary model of household is an association that "follows its head."[68] The familial metaphors of father and sons, inheritance, brotherhood, honor, and obedience to ecclesiastical authority begin taking center stage. No longer an alternative to Greco-Roman models, God's household corresponds to dominant social norms.

Once the churches gain social power and influence, they adopt conventional structures of honor and privilege.[69] While Paul questions the status of marriage and procreation as mediating Christian faith, he does accept patriarchal authority for community life, as evidenced in his argument with the

---

[65]Torjesen, "Reconstruction," 296.

[66]Schüssler Fiorenza, *Discipleship of Equals*, 74. Concerning these women leaders, see Torjesen, "Reconstruction," 298–302.

[67]Lone Fatum, "Brotherhood in Christ: A Gender Hermeneutical Reading of 1 Thessalonians," in *Constructing Early Christian Families*, 190–93.

[68]Moxnes, 36.

[69]Osiek and Balch, 102.

unveiled women prophets in Corinth (1 Cor. 11).[70] But the pastoral epistles most forcefully show "the concern of the 'Great Church' to secure its future, economically and demographically, through the conventional medium of family life and by means of networks of household and 'elders' who were to provide the leadership for the urban churches."[71] The ambiguity of hierarchical gender relations in Paul's letters shifts toward a univocal position on household order and the subordination of slaves, free women, and children. What was first decentered by the radical monotheism of Jesus—kinship and kyriocentric household—eventually re-emerges as the discourse and practice of Christian faith. Carolyn Osiek and David Balch conclude, "The church had the potential through Jesus' disturbing parables and its baptismal ecclesiology for creating a true equality of discipleship under the unique and sole fatherhood of God. Ironically, it did not do so, but chose instead to multiply the human symbols of patriarchal authority in the name of God."[72]

The driving motivation in the re-entrenchment of the traditional *familia* model is Christian apologetics. Within the social and religious cosmos of Mediterranean society, conversion of a slave, child, or wife to the Christian faith constitutes a breach of domestic and civic order. Thus, accusations of sedition, immorality, and impiety plague Christian communities. In order to downplay this subversiveness for missionary purposes and to counter criticism, church leaders of the pastoral epistles adopt an apologetic stance, drawing on Aristotelian political theory to reformulate the "constitution" of God's "large house" (2 Tim. 2:20–21).[73] Through "selective acculturation," Christian churches adopt Aristotelian household codes, thus conforming to the hierarchy of ruling Roman powers and lessening the subversive threat.[74] In Colossians 3:11, the author drops the "no longer male and female" phrase from the Galatians baptismal formula and transforms the image of Christ as exalted slave (Phil. 2:7, 9) into the cosmic Lord, who replaces Caesar as Head of the Body.[75] In 1 Peter 2:18–3:6, Christian wives and slaves remain subordinate, chaste, and obedient in order to maintain harmony and win converts,

---

[70]Ibid., 120. First Corinthians 11:7–10 states, "For a man ought not to have his head veiled, since he is the image and reflection of God; but woman is the reflection of man. Indeed, man was not made from woman, but woman from man. Neither was man created for the sake of woman, but woman for the sake of man. For this reason a woman ought to have a symbol of authority on her head, because of the angels."

[71]Barclay, 78.

[72]Osiek and Balch, 220.

[73]Balch, 28–30. See also Elisabeth Schüssler Fiorenza, *Bread Not Stone: The Challenge of Feminist Biblical Interpretation* (Edinburgh: T & T Clark, 1990), 72–79.

[74]Balch, 33. In *Bread Not Stone*, Schüssler Fiorenza challenges interpreters who construe these church "developments" as a "necessary adaptation," an affirmation of the "goodness of creation," or a "subversive subordination" (79–83). Balch joins Schüssler Fiorenza's position in arguing that the changes further do not represent a "mean" between absolute patriarchy and equality. Even if the adoption of household management codes are interpreted as a "survival strategy for Christian women in pagan households," the codes need not be normed for ecclesiastical and familial social structure (27–29).

[75]Osiek and Balch, 123.

even though they do not have to worship the Roman gods.[76] For apologetic purposes, Christians show that their new religious orientation will not upset the orthopraxis of the city-state.

The pastoral household codes normed by Christian churches prescribe the Aristotelian rules for ecclesiastical ordering: Wives submit to husbands, slaves submit to masters, and sons (children) submit to fathers (Col. 3:18–4:1; Eph. 5:22–6:9). Schüssler Fiorenza claims "the central interest of these texts lies in the enforcement of the submission and obedience of the socially weaker group—wives, slaves and children—on the one hand, and in the authority of the head of the household, the *paterfamilias*, on the other hand."[77] Thus, like his Roman-citizen counterpart, a faithful bishop or deacon of the household of God must provide evidence of being an effective manager of his own personal *oikos*–his household of obedient and submissive slaves, children, and wife (1 Tim. 3:1–15).

By adopting Aristotelian political theory, which at the time, imperial leaders also employ for re-entrenching their own authority in society, church leaders betray a struggling egalitarian ethos for a "patriarchal pattern of submission."[78] The two models become incompatible because, according to Aristotle, an egalitarian constitution presumes equality exists among those who are "by nature" unequal. Thus, egalitarian church households may be judged as inherently seditious, since those by nature unequal (women, children, and slaves) live without the appropriate rule.

The patriarchal pattern of submission twists emerging egalitarian efforts into an economy of domination in which wives, children, and slaves forfeit their identity according to God the Spirit and are marked again with an identity determined by ancient Mediterranean social norms. Through these norms, and as the context of worship shifts from domestic households to public buildings, female ecclesiastical leadership becomes controversial. Church leaders Tertullian and Jerome decry female ministerial activities with men in the public realm as shameful and wanton.[79] Thus, women who baptize and teach are admonished to undertake *oikos*-appropriate roles in keeping with the household trajectory of the pastoral texts. Tertullian's protest against women's entering public debates reveals the re-emerging pattern of patriarchal governance: "It is not permitted to a woman to speak in church, but neither is it permitted her to teach, nor to baptize, nor to offer, nor to claim for herself a lot in any manly function not to say [in any] sacerdotal office."[80]

Even though injunctions against women's public voices arise, Torjesen claims women's leadership is not fully contested until the third and fourth centuries, when the model for the church shifts from household to the empire,

---

[76]David L. Balch, *Let Wives Be Submissive: The Domestic Code in I Peter* (Ann Arbor, Mich.: Scholars Press, 1981), 108–9.

[77]Schüssler Fiorenza, *Bread Not Stone*, 71.

[78]Ibid., 71–73.

[79]Ibid.

[80]Tertullian, *De Virginibus Velandis*, 9.1, quoted in Torjesen, *When Women Were Priests*, 159.

and leadership changes from charismatic ministry to leadership by ruling office.[81] In examining the post-Pauline epistles, the Epistle of Clement, and Ignatius' letters, Schüssler Fiorenza claims church authority shifts from "translocal charismatic authority with its amalgamation of the apostolic and prophetic toward an understanding of authority vested in the local offices, especially the monarchical episcopacy."[82] In other words, Christian churches choose territorial officers, thereby replicating the mechanics of the state. Architecturally, the space of communal worship changes from private homes to public basilicas.[83] Theologically, the changes represent a return to patriarchal order in the struggling households of freedom. As Ignatius of Antioch argues, the great house of God finds its ecclesiastical order in a *pater patriae*, the bishop (recall Caesar's self-designation) who presides in God the Father's place and serves as the primary focal point of church unity.[84]

Hans von Campenhausen suggests that the "trend toward an unbalanced ascendance of office" during the first three centuries of church history occurs in the face of the gnostic crisis:

> The confusion of enthusiastic sects, proliferating and splitting off in all directions during the gnostic crisis, seemed to the Church to be threatening all her links with the past, and consequently to make the safeguarding of her [*sic*] original doctrine and tradition the matter of supreme importance. The result was not merely the formation of the "apostolic" canon, but also the establishment of an apostolic office.[85]

But by setting up an office to preserve an original deposit of faith or identity and guarantee its continuity, the household of God in effect becomes a "house of authority" in which faith is understood more in terms of validity than viability.[86] Authority as office evolves with a legalistic, political, and institutional character. Von Campenhausen criticizes this development because church leadership loses its dialectical relationship to charismatic authority.[87] With the rise of ecclesiastical offices, the gifts "have no further functional part to play in the general scheme of church life, but become the specially cultivated preserve of the more highly 'endowed' Christians and their disciples."[88] The shift from spiritual gifts to ecclesiastical offices reinforces the developing prohibitions against female leadership.

---

[81]Torjesen, *When Women Were Priests*, 155–58; and idem, "Reconstruction," 297.

[82]Schüssler Fiorenza, *In Memory of Her*, 294–95.

[83]Torjesen, "Reconstruction," 304–6.

[84]Fiorenza, *In Memory of Her*, 293–94.

[85]Von Campenhausen, 297–98.

[86]Edward Farley and Peter C. Hodgson, "Scripture and Tradition," in *Christian Theology: An Introduction to Its Traditions and Tasks*, ed. Peter C. Hodgson and Robert H. King (Philadelphia: Fortress Press, 1982), 35–61. According to Farley and Hodgson, the house of authority with its bricks of salvation history, scripture principle of identity, timeless dogma, definitive canon, and uncritical teaching office, is in fact contrary to ecclesial existence.

[87]Von Campenhausen, *Ecclesiastical Authority and Spiritual Power*, 297.

[88]Ibid., 300.

In the early churches, re-entrenching the patriarchal *oikos* formally domesticates free women, slaves, and children. Interests of order and rank override emancipatory hermeneutics and the struggling egalitarian praxis. What begins as a household in which no one but God is to be called father or master (Mt. 23:9–10) eventually gives way to an oppressive, hierarchical institution ruled by clerical authorities, church fathers.[89] To achieve honor within God's household, domesticated members must maintain their ordained place, abide in harmony, and serve the appropriate authorities. Christian apologetics sacrifices the gifts of free women, children, and slaves by creating docile and useful persons in God's expanding empire.

A Docile and Useful Person

Re-entrenchment of the kyriocentric household sunders God as Spirit from freedom and grafts Spirit to authority, while freedom becomes ancillary, if not suspect, just as female leadership eventually becomes suspect. With the locus of female participation shifting from the discipleship of equals to an *oikos*-appropriate economy of domination, pneumatological models shift from Spirit as the liberating source of ecclesial existence to Spirit as the ordering, conforming, and disciplining guarantor of the Father's divine economy. In effect, an "economy of the Same" re-orders the diverse community of *pneumatikoi*, effacing difference and reflecting only the will of the One Head over the Many members.[90] The following studies provide traces of this poisonous pneumatology in action.

Paul and the Galatian Brotherhood

At times in the New Testament, the conflict between the two models of household seems clear, as in the family relativizing synoptic pericopes and the post-Pauline pastoral codes. But in other cases, the use of family metaphors presents an ambiguous situation. In Galatians, according to Esler's study, Paul adopts kinship language to create an alternative Christian identity among Jew and Greek, slave and free, and male and female householders (3:28).[91] Neither bloodlines, the law, nor gender status determine social standing in the community of believers, only their transfigured status as adopted brothers (*adelphoi*, 1:2, 11; 3:15; 4:12, 28, 31; 5:11, 13; 6:1, 18), sons of God the Father (1:1–3; 3:26; 4:1–7), the seed of Abraham and Sarah through Christ (3:7, 16, 29), and Paul's own children in the faith (4:19–20). The Spirit of God's Son has been sent into their hearts so that now, as fellow heirs, they cry "Abba" (4:6). Paul redraws the boundary of identity through a new opposition—those with faith in Christ and those without. For Paul, the new brotherhood "inside"

---

[89]Schüssler Fiorenza, *In Memory of Her*, 151–79, 211–32.

[90]Luce Irigaray characterizes patriarchy as an "economy of the Same," in which female identity signifies only the negatively reflected image of male desire and identity. See *This Sex Which Is Not One*, trans. Catherine Porter (Ithaca, N.Y.: Cornell University Press, 1985), 74. For a more detailed presentation of the feminist maternal analysis reflected here, see chapter 5.

[91]Esler, *Constructing Christian Families*, 121–49.

exists in contrast to the competitive, honor-seeking culture of "outside" society. By reinforcing the faith community's vertical dimension through a common divine parenthood, Paul calls forth a strengthened horizontal loyalty as siblings. Brothers sharing lineage to Abraham and God must now cooperate, rather than argue enviously with one another (5:26). They should bear one another's burdens with tolerance (6:2), in contrast to competitive struggles for honor, and thus derive honor through upbuilding the family. Paul claims that those Galatians contending for circumcision are in fact living by the flesh, rather than by the Spirit, whose fruit is "love, joy, peace, patience, kindness, generosity, faithfulness, gentleness, and self-control" (5:22).

Esler concludes that Paul's letter to the Galatians supports a form of social interconnection and loyalty challenging today's depersonalized, greedy and competitive secularism.[92] But, while Paul crafts positive values of social unity through his kinship metaphors, negative dangers exist as well. As seen in the exploration of ancient Mediterranean family values, when family unity and honor receive the highest value, internal conflict and struggle become threatening; thus, social control is reinforced to the exclusion of working through difficulties or confronting injustice within the community. A feminist maternal perspective warns that shoring up the vertical dimension of the community through an identity of God as *paterfamilias* risks gaining loyalty with a price: conformity and fear. Paul's model, while liberating in terms of equal constitution (neither male nor female...), still perceives conflict or differentiation shamefully as weakness, lack, betrayal, or disobedience. Strong emotion, anger, and conflict number among other deficiencies of virtue and faith (5:19). Paul's metaphorical language of sonship and brotherhood further potentially excludes equal participation of those in other kinship roles. How do daughters, sisters, spouses, and mothers participate in the brotherhood except as mediated through their fathers and brothers? Re-entrenching the ancient Mediterranean honor/shame dynamic directs the functioning of Spirit language toward reinforcing processes of unity based on social accommodation. In the end, Paul's nonconfrontive "fruit of the Spirit" may unintentionally promote poisonous outcomes and limit the possibility for mutuality in community formation.

Clement of Rome and Unity in the Spirit

Moving pastoral texts of early church fathers further display the melding of Aristotelian political theory and ancient Mediterranean family values with ecclesiastical leadership and Spirit language. Barbara Ellen Bowe's study of 1 Clement presents Clement of Rome appealing to God's divine order for the Corinthian church as God's city-state (*politeia*) in the face of challenges directed

---

[92]Ibid. Esler writes, "In an era when an unjust distribution of the world's goods, corrupted political processes, population pressures, bureaucratization and increasing pluralism in moral values contribute to our growing sense of depersonalization and powerlessness, we are capable of being enriched by immersion in the familial intimacy and values advocated by Paul" (144).

against the presbyterial leadership.[93] Unity within the church can only be preserved through harmonizing the cosmic, political, familial, and ecclesiastical orders of the community under the proper authorities. Clement advises the brotherhood of Corinthian citizens:

> Let us respect those who rule us
> let us honor the aged
> let us instruct the young in the fear of God
> let us lead our wives to that which is good.[94]

Regarding the "good" to which wives should be led, Clement writes:

> Let them exhibit the lovely habit of purity
> let them show the innocent will of meekness
> let them make the gentleness of their tongue
> manifest by their silence
> let them give their affection not by factious preference
> but in holiness to all equally who fear God.[95]

Bowe claims that although Clement maintains a patriarchal social order, he advocates "an intensified communal ethic" aimed toward a collective vision of the good over and against the self-seeking interests of individuals (the opponents of the Corinthian presbyters).[96] Clement employs the relational metaphors of fellow citizens, household, brotherhood, flock, and even army to stress the communal, cohesive character of the body of Christ.[97] Each of these images implies a created structure and order required for harmonious life together. Thus, while the Spirit has been poured out upon the whole community, the Spirit manifests holiness, purity, and unity through the community's vertical (institutional) dimension.[98] The communal ethic receives its value in members' voluntary yielding to authority, rather than through explicit domination.[99] According to Bowe, Clement's appeals to order and obedience "stress in a positive sense a voluntary subordination of self-interests to the corporate goals of the community based, above all, on the example of the Lord Jesus (1 Clem. 16:1–2)."[100]

Even though Bowe retrieves the communally based ethic of Clement's appeal, she does not raise the critical question of *how* the ethic creates solidarity. For Clement, order promotes peace and unity, and therefore critical challenges to the existing order constitute an unfaithful breach in the bonds of kinship. Schüssler Fiorenza quotes from 1 Clement 3:3 in making her argument that

---

[93]Barbara Ellen Bowe, *A Church in Crisis: Ecclesiology and Paraenesis in Clement of Rome* (Minneapolis: Fortress Press, 1988).

[94]Ibid., 100. On the metaphors of "citizenry" and "brotherhood," see 86–89.

[95]Ibid.

[96]Ibid., 104.

[97]Ibid., 103.

[98]Ibid., 104–5.

[99]Ibid., 110–11.

[100]Ibid., 121.

order is the author's key theological concept: "And so 'the dishonored' rose up 'against those who were held in honor,' those of no reputation against the notable, the stupid against the wise, 'the young against their elders.'"[101] The poisonous pedagogy of the patriarchal household model interprets challenge or criticism as dishonor, rebellion, disrespect, and disobedience. If harmony in the order stands as the highest social and spiritual good, then in effect the social good becomes the will of the one in authority and discipline the extension of this will. Thus, unity in the Spirit occurs at the expense of difference in the Spirit. Schüssler Fiorenza calls attention to Clement's disciplinary rhetoric:

> God, therefore, is called Father of eternity and Master of the universe "who disciplines us" (56.16). Those Corinthians, therefore, who are "responsible for the revolt must submit to the presbyters,…be disciplined,…learn obedience,…and curb their tongues" (57.1f), so that they can hold a creditable, though insignificant, place in Christ's flock, the church.[102]

Bowe criticizes Clement's legitimation of an oppressive church order that systematically excludes women from leadership and office. But she positively prioritizes the value of voluntary submission to authority for the sake of unity. This move, though, still maintains an inherently hierarchical and conservative social order, for Bowe does not question the terms under which members voluntarily yield. Clement may "reframe" the Corinthian dispute within the ethic of "communal fidelity to God," but Clement grounds his communal ethic on a model of unity as conformity.[103] Spirit's association with egalitarian intersubjectivity has twisted to Spirit guaranteeing order in conformity to the institutionalized Christ-subject, the patriarchal office holder.

Tertullian and the King's Officer

Tertullian presents the next study of the shift in pneumatological functioning. Like the previous authors, Tertullian is not a systematic theologian with a formal doctrine of the Spirit. But in his writings, he uses models and metaphors implying particular assumptions about the Spirit's role and person. Tertullian's pneumatology, which found in the New Prophecy movement (Montanism) "a measure of congeniality," upholds the Spirit or Paraclete as primarily concerned with ensuring ecclesiastical discipline, but also with providing spiritual authenticity and teaching of apostolic doctrine.[104] Von Campenhausen describes Tertullian, the Roman lawyer and first Latin father of the church, as "a man of law, of the divine command, and of unconditional obedience."[105] David Rankin portrays Tertullian as a relentless disciplinarian who never left the Catholic Church but challenged its leaders toward more

---

[101]Schüssler Fiorenza, *In Memory of Her*, 292.

[102]Ibid.

[103]Bowe, 156.

[104]David Rankin, *Tertullian and the Church* (Cambridge: Cambridge University Press, 1995), 43.

[105]Hans von Campenhausen, *The Fathers of the Latin Church* (London: Adam & Charles Black, 1964), 27.

authentic faith and spiritual purity.[106] Tertullian's pneumatology raises concerns about spiritual elitism, but his wedding of military, political, and familial metaphors for the Spirit also reinforces the image of Spirit as guaranteeing church order and discipline.

Tertullian's treatise *Against Praxeas* provides an example of this pedagogical pneumatology in action.[107] Here, Tertullian speaks against Praxeas, a modalist, who has been teaching the *simplices,* the unlettered majority of church members, that Tertullian's theology involves two and three gods, while he, Praxeas, has taught the one, true God.[108] In response, Tertullian argues that distinction within the Trinity need not imply tri-theism or a challenge to the Father's monarchy. For Tertullian, distinction and unity comprise the Trinity's divine character. Yet his understanding of unity draws on the model of royal dominion, which in effect negates the possibility for authentic difference. As a king's "officers" or representatives administer the king's empire on the local level, the Son and the Spirit guarantee the ongoing operations of the Father's monarchy.[109] Having a Son in no way threatens the Father's rule, for the Son, as "deputy," only makes visible what the Father intends.[110] The "third sequence," or Spirit, continues the governance, for "I reckon the Spirit from nowhere else than from the Father through the Son."[111] As in Roman society, with its unifying law and discipline, the Father's single and sovereign rule extends through the Son and the Spirit.[112] The second and third persons work within the rule of the monarchy, for their will is the Father's will. Thus, the Three constitute a One without opposition.

Even though he underscores the relational character of the Trinity, Tertullian maintains the relation as a hierarchical order drawing on the Latin understanding of authority. Letty Russell claims the root meaning of the English word *authority* comes from the Latin word *auctoritas,* derived from the verb *augere,* meaning to augment or increase.[113] She explains:

> As Hannah Arendt reminds us, our concept of authority in Western civilization derives from the Roman idea that those in authority constantly augment the foundation of the ancestors or founders of Rome. In this perspective, authority—as the right to influence because of relationship to the origins of life, faith, and society—forms the Roman patriarchal paradigm. The authority of the founding fathers is understood as the legitimization or authorizing of domination in politics, culture, and household. [114]

---

[106]Rankin, 43.

[107]Tertullian, *Tertullian's Treatise Against Praxeas,* ed. Ernest Evans (London: SPCK, 1948), 130–79.

[108]Ibid., 30.

[109]Ibid., 133–34.

[110]Ibid., 168.

[111]Ibid., 134.

[112]Torjesen, *When Women Were Priests,* 162–63.

[113]Russell, *Household of Freedom,* 24.

[114]Ibid., 24–25.

In Tertullian's theological model, the order of God's great house moves from the patriarchal household to include the political rule of the empire. The language of King and Lord combined with Father replicates the Roman understanding of authority within the increasingly institutionalized church. Authority as an extension of the rule and will of God the Father and King aligns family and church in terms of Aristotle's politics: There are those who rule and those who by nature require rule. The language of Spirit functioning as one of the King's officers ensures proper extension of unity from the authoritative head. But unity without differentiation or the space for conflict and resolution creates a poisonous context for family, church, and societal households.

John of Chrysostom and Order in the Ranks

The theological association of order, unity, and Spirit continues. Bishop of Constantinople John of Chrysostom turns to pastoral household codes for his sermons on marriage and family life.[115] He explains that the Christian household involves an ordering of authorities or "ranks," where "the husband is the head of the wife, and husband and wife together have authority over the children."[116] In marriage, the man and woman become one flesh, with the man fulfilling the position of head, as leader and provider, and the woman providing the body. He explains the spousal relation of head and body:

> The wife is a second authority. She should not demand equality, for she is subject to the head; neither should the husband belittle her subjection, for she is the body. Let the hands, feet, and all the rest of the body's parts be dedicated to the service of the head; but let the head provide for the body, for the head is responsible for all the members. Nothing can be better than a union like this.[117]

Within this natural order, the whole body sustains well-being only when the various body parts (wives, children, and slaves) yield to the head's authority. Thus, Chrysostom promotes obedience as the most important contribution the body can make to the union. Through the obedience of the body parts and loving leadership of the head, peace and harmony prevail not only in the household, but in the state as well.

Pursuing a vision of social harmony, Chrysostom draws an analogy between the family and military unions:

> As with a general whose troops are so well organized on the front that the enemy cannot find a place to penetrate for an attack, so it is with husband and wife: when the concerns of everyone in the house

---

[115]Saint John of Chrysostom, *On Marriage and Family Life*, trans. Catherine P. Roth and David Anderson (Crestwood, N.Y.: St. Vladimir's Seminary Press, 1986).
[116]Ibid., 65.
[117]Ibid., 53.

are the same, harmony reigns in the family, but if not, the entire household is easily broken up and destroyed.[118]

Family (like military) harmony dissolves primarily through insubordination to, rebellion against, and contradiction of the primary authority by those composing the lesser ranks. The concerns of the troop members or body parts must conform to the concerns of the head, since order permits only one will, the will of the head, and therefore precludes mutuality. For Chrysostom, while wives share an "equality of dignity" with husbands, they cannot share an "equality of leadership."[119] Mutuality only exists between those of equal rank and ability to rule. He advises, "The female sex is rather weak and needs a lot of support, a lot of condescension."[120] Thus, the head bears the following responsibility:

> Instruct your wife, and your whole household will be in order and harmony. Listen to what Paul says, "If there is anything they desire to know, let them ask their husbands at home." If we regulate our households in this way, we will also be fit to oversee the Church, for indeed *the household is a little Church.*[121]

Christological assertions of Jesus' headship, lordship, and spousal relation to the church buttress the divine sanctioning of the patriarchal order.[122] We have already seen the subordinating effects of this model in the pastoral codes of household management: "Wives, be subject to your husbands as you are to the Lord. For the husband is the head of the wife just as Christ is the head of the church, the body of which he is the Savior. Just as the church is subject to Christ, so also wives ought to be, in everything, to their husbands" (Eph. 5:22–23). In his homily on this text, Chrysostom endorses the Triune family order and explains that Christ left his Father to marry his bride, the church, and thus became one flesh with her. In the marital union, Christ fulfills the role of head, and the church serves as the body with many members. [123]

Chrysostom claims that since "authority must necessarily rest in one person," Christ is the authoritative leader of the church.[124] But within the whole body is one organizing and ordering principle, the Spirit of Christ:

> Paul places the head in authority and the body in obedience for the sake of peace. Where there is equal authority, there never is peace. A household cannot be a democracy, ruled by everyone, but the

---

[118]Ibid., 57–58.

[119]Ibid., 57.

[120]Ibid., 56.

[121]Ibid., 57. Emphasis added.

[122]See Mary Daly, *Beyond God the Father: Toward a Philosophy of Women's Liberation* (Boston: Beacon Press, 1973), 69–97; and Rosemary Radford Ruether, *Sexism and God-Talk* (Boston: Beacon Press, 1983), 116–38.

[123]Chrysostom, 52–53.

[124]Ibid., 53.

authority must necessarily rest in one person. The same is true for the Church: where men are led by the Spirit of Christ, then there is peace.[125]

For Chrysostom, union with Christ means men submit to the authority of Christ and thus are led by his Spirit, resulting in harmonious order and peace within the community. In the same way as the body of Christ subjects itself to its head, so should wives be obedient to their own heads, their husbands. Through the ranks' submission, harmony prevails, and one spirit animates the marriage and household, just as one Spirit animates the body of the church. In contrast to the household of freedom, where the Spirit animates an intersubjectivity structured as equality and mutuality, in Chrysostom's pastoral order the Spirit functions within the well-ordered body by bringing the ranks into unified action with the dictates of the head.

But Chrysostom takes another theological step in the patriarchal/kyriocentric family model by way of an analogy. Since the husband and wife create one body (with the husband as head), just as Christ and the church create one Body (with Christ as the head), and since Christ and the Father are also one, Chrysostom concludes, "We see that the Father is our head also."[126] In Chrysostom's theological order, God the Father fulfills the ultimate head and authority, united with his obedient Son. Extending the authority of the Father, the Son takes on the role of head and authority in his marriage to the church. The pattern of Father over Son and bridegroom over bride reflects the kinship patterns functioning within patriarchal economies. From Chrysostom's perspective, men, assuming the role of the bridegroom, master, and father, extend the authority of the divine Father and assert their headship in human households through rightly ordering their own domestic *oikos*. Chrysostom's sermons portray a body politic and pneumatology oriented around the concepts of rule, rank, and submission to authority. Throughout the entire economy of salvation, God the Spirit works to bring forth union and appropriate order. Subordinate to the Father and the Son, the Spirit has become domesticated within the household of God, no longer inspiring fiery tongues, but conforming docile and useful persons, just like himself, to the authority of the Father.

Picking Up the Path

For our day, people across academic disciplines seek new models of communal life that celebrate diversity and reflect democratic, inclusive values. Many religious communities also seek these ideals but struggle with the theological frameworks necessary for reconstructing their Christian identities in contemporary contexts. Is it possible to re-imagine God, our world, and God's relation to the world according to the values of mutual recognition, dignity, reconciliation, partnership, and justice? Is it possible to imagine a world and

---

[125]Ibid.
[126]Ibid., 52.

a Trinity where differentiation, conflict, and negotiation are part of the mutual struggle toward shared community? Is it possible to embody a discipleship of equals, a community of multiple heads and multiple wills, rather than One Head and One Will?

Legacies of Aristotelian political theory and the patriarchal household continue providing stumbling blocks to re-figuring the lives of families, churches, and democratic societies. The male- or lord-headed household model remains deeply embedded within Christian liturgies, creeds, institutions, and religious practice. Yet the model lies deeply embedded within Western culture as a whole. Fortunately, when we trace the language of Spirit, we see glimpses of inclusive freedom and egalitarian community. Unfortunately, as the church re-entrenched patriarchal family life through adopting Aristotelian political theory, Spirit language functioned at least in an ambiguous way, in relation to freedom and community, and at the most, as an oppressive authority creating docile and useful persons. Today we can name the subordinating and domesticating functions of Spirit language, a poisonous pneumatology. The challenge is to learn from the Christian churches' historical and theological struggles toward new models of family and church praxis. The following chapter explores several contemporary pneumatologies in light of the concern for social models of diversity-in-unity. In each case, a feminist maternal standpoint strengthens the pneumatologies by pointing out potential poisonous pitfalls and incorporating the aim of mutual recognition. We close with Catherine Keller's hopeful words for the turn to the Spirit in contemporary theology:

> It is as though the Spirit has picked up a path left behind back when Christianity shut down its gender ambiguities, its communalizing complexity, and its perichoretic nuances in order to provide the empire with the kyriarchal service of Oneness.[127]

---

[127]Catherine Keller, "The Theology of Moltmann, Feminism, and the Future," in *The Future of Theology: Essays in Honor of Jürgen Moltmann,* ed. Miroslav Volf, Carmen Krieg, and Thomas Kucharz (Grand Rapids, Mich.: Eerdmans, 1996), 152.

CHAPTER 7

Re-fining Contemporary Options
of the Spirit

Hope is the Spirit energizing our spirits to persevere in the
conviction that human beings can learn to live in unity with one
another and with creation, that truth will prevail in the long-
term, that freedom and justice for all will increase, that beauty
and love can turn aside ugliness and triumph over evil, that
dissent from a partial good can clear the way for a larger good,
and that in the Spirit there is a splendid equality of the many,
each enriching the life of all.[1]

That Love Might Burn in All

The previous chapter demonstrated that when patriarchal family values
prevailed in early Christian household churches, one of the ways Spirit
language functioned was to re-domesticate household members within
hierarchical family and church orders. Representing a paradigm shift from
the language of Spirit enlivening the rich gifts of inclusive disciple communities, re-domestication instilled a poisonous pneumatology primarily concerned
with male authority, proper order, and unilateral power. Theologically the
many conformed to the One, creating, in effect, an economy of the Same. A
fundamental theological model, the patriarchal family (or kyriocentric household) promoted social unity as uniformity, in which personal or ministerial
differentiation was interpreted as a seditious act.

Contemporary Christian theology stands more than fifteen hundred years
away from its early formative period, but without continuous reformation,
oppressive social values and distorted relational models continue uncritically
in theological traditions. While democratic social vision has transformed political, economic, and cultural life for many people, with Christian theology
contributing positively, theology remains accountable for more justly including marginalized voices. The danger of poisonous legacies continues, testified
to by survivors' experiences of family violence and clergy sexual misconduct.

---

[1]Lee E. Snook, *What in the World is God Doing? Re-Imagining Spirit and Power* (Minneapolis:
Fortress Press, 1999), 133.

Introduced in chapters 1 and 2, the turn to the Spirit in contemporary theology provides one area of study motivated by inclusive concerns for liberation, life, and diversity. Theologians today acknowledge previous negative associations of Spirit language with uniformity and subordination. As Jürgen Moltmann reflects on the universal fellowship of the Spirit, "Uniformity and the surrender of individuality in favour of an overriding unity are not the goal of life."[2] Michael Welker claims the invigorating unity of the Spirit "becomes a reality not by imposing an illusory homogeneity, but by cultivating creaturely differences and by removing unrighteous differences."[3] Echoing Moltmann and Welker, Colin Gunton asserts that far from abolishing particularity between people, the Spirit "rather maintains and even strengthens particularity. It is not a spirit of merging or assimilation—of homogenization—but of relation in otherness, relation which does not subvert but establishes the other in its true reality."[4] Recent Spirit explorations recover biblical and doctrinal traditions supporting the Spirit's association with forming and empowering inclusive, diverse communities. In contrast to patriarchal legacies of homogeneity, contemporary pneumatologies interpret unity in the Spirit as relational *diversity-in-unity*.

But a feminist maternal standpoint further refines contemporary works on the Spirit. Moltmann, Welker, and Gunton each make positive moves in reviving the dynamic, intersubjective character of life in the Spirit, but their pneumatologies still maintain vestiges of patriarchal models. This chapter presents their distinctive contributions to contemporary pneumatology and raises questions from a feminist maternal perspective. While each theologian restores the other for relations of recognition, elements of their pneumatologies become obstacles in the shared goal of diversity-in-unity.[5] As argued in previous chapters, making a difference in relation requires both assertion and recognition, thus risking conflict with persons and communities. Contemporary pneumatologies seeking diversity-in-unity must address the pneumatological impetus for struggling beyond relations of nonrecognition. Moltmann, Welker, and Gunton hold forth the vision, but fall short in advocating dynamics of the Spirit for reaching *mutual* recognition. The following tri-part exploration shows how a feminist maternal standpoint refines, and thus strengthens, contemporary projects of the Spirit so "that love might burn in all."[6]

---

[2]Jürgen Moltmann, *The Spirit of Life: A Universal Affirmation* (Minneapolis: Fortress Press, 1992), 226.

[3]Michael Welker, *God the Spirit* (Minneapolis: Fortress Press, 1994), 25.

[4]Colin E. Gunton, *The One, the Three and the Many: God, Creation and the Culture of Modernity* (Cambridge: Cambridge University Press, 1993), 183.

[5]An extensive analysis of each theologian's pneumatology is beyond the scope of this project. My work raises questions about particular elements of their pneumatologies in light of a common pursuit of social diversity-in-unity.

[6]The phrase is from an anonymous eighth-century Latin hymn titled "Joy! because the circling year," *Australian Hymn Book* (Sydney: Wm. Collins Publishers, 1977), 392. I am grateful to John Ward, who shared this hymn as part of a Murdoch University class project.

Jürgen Moltmann's Spirit of the Cross

Freedom as domination destroys life. As domination, freedom is not freedom in its true sense. The truth of human freedom is to be found in the love that longs for life. This leads to unhindered, open community in solidarity. Only this freedom—freedom as community, or sociality—is able to heal the wounds which freedom as domination has inflicted and still inflicts.[7]

According to Lyle Dabney, Jürgen Moltmann unexpectedly turned to the Spirit in his theology when he realized that his *theologia crucis* (theology of the cross) involved the Spirit's passive subordination to the central redemptive activity of the Father and the Son.[8] Christian hope began, for Moltmann, with the sacrifice and abandonment of the Son by the Father in the event of the cross, Good Friday. Yet his Western binitarian lenses excluded the resurrecting Spirit from the "deep conformity of will" between the Father and the Son; thus, Dabney concludes, "the Spirit of God remains a *crossless* Spirit, indeed one who stands finally in contradiction to the God of the cross."[9] Moltmann also realized his eschatology was mired in the reformed legacy of God's utter discontinuity from the world. The Spirit, bound up in eternity, bore no hope of truly transforming a supposedly god-forsaken world. Moltmann's turn to pneumatology thus signifies his theological movement "beyond a 'theology of the Word' to an unfolding 'theology of the world.'"[10]

Since the 1980s the advent of the Spirit has helped Moltmann explore the implications of Trinitarian democratization, narrate the messianic mission of the earthly Jesus, and refigure the doctrine of redemption within the doctrine of creation.[11] By rejecting the Western churches' subordination of the Spirit to the Son (through the *filioque* clause), Moltmann liberates the Spirit for full participation in the divine economy. The Spirit's personhood can now be determined through the mutuality and co-inherence of the Triune partners who together, yet in distinctive ways, serve the aim of New Creation. Enriched by interaction with feminism, ecology, Orthodoxy, liberation politics, and theologies of embodiment, Moltmann presents the fruit of his work in an "unplanned" book devoted entirely to pneumatology.[12] In *The Spirit of Life*,

---

[7]Moltmann, 119.

[8]D. Lyle Dabney, "The Advent of the Spirit: The Turn to Pneumatology in the Theology of Jürgen Moltmann," *Asbury Theological Journal* 48, no. 1 (Spring 1993): 98–99. For Moltmann's text, see *The Crucified God: The Cross of Christ as the Foundation and Criticism of Christian Theology* (New York: Harper & Row, 1974).

[9]Dabney, 98. Dabney's reference to "the deep conformity of will" is from Moltmann, *The Crucified God*, 243.

[10]Dabney, 101.

[11]See Moltmann's *The Trinity and the Kingdom: The Doctrine of God* (New York: Harper & Row, 1981); *The Way of Jesus Christ: Christology in Messianic Dimensions* (London: SCM Press, 1990); and *God in Creation: A New Theology of Creation and the Spirit of God* (San Francisco: HarperSanFrancisco, 1991).

[12]Dabney, 101.

Moltmann renews pneumatology through the biblical tradition of *ruach*, the breath, wind, and dynamic energy of God that creates and recreates space for life:

> We sense in ourselves the personal dynamic given to us, and then perceive it in everything else that lives. The experience of this vital power is as protean as living things themselves; and yet for all that it is a single vital power, which has gathered everything living into a great community of life, and sustains it there.[13]

Moltmann's vision includes the whole of life, "the community of creation," in which the churches dwell and for whom the churches seek receptivity to the wider operation of the Spirit in the world.[14] As introduced in chapter 1, Moltmann's holistic pneumatology celebrates the possibility of experiencing God in all things, and all things in God. The Spirit's *immanental transcendence* thus discloses *love of life* as the core value of Christian spirituality.

A holistic pneumatology, though, does not privilege unity at the expense of difference in relations. Unity in the Spirit for human beings includes the rich, diverse embodiment of life, imaged by Moltmann as an open "cosmic friendship" with others different from oneself. Regarding human others, Moltmann explains:

> The basic law of the community of Christ is acceptance of others in their difference, for it is this experience of our neighbours, and only this, which is in line with Christian experience of God. Here other people's difference is not defined against the yardstick of our own identity, and our prejudice about people who are not like us. The difference is experienced in the practical encounter which mutually reveals what we are and what the other is.[15]

In Christian friendship, the Spirit enlivens unique, personal individuality, seeking at the same time the passionate participation of people in mutual love, shared fellowship, and just relations in the world. Through the Spirit of life, humankind lives in hope of God's new creation, understood not as the dissolution of particularity, but as the fulfillment of creation's great diversity-in-unity. By turning to the Spirit, Moltmann overcomes the great theological gulf between Word and the world.

But what about the crossless Spirit? How does Moltmann incorporate his concern for creation's continuity with God in and through the discontinuity of suffering and death?[16] In *The Spirit of Life*, the *theologia crucis* emerges as a

---

[13]Moltmann, *The Spirit of Life*, 274.

[14]Ibid., 225.

[15]Ibid., 258.

[16]In "The Advent of the Spirit," Dabney explains that Moltmann turned to pneumatology to overcome the discontinuity between God and the world in his early work on eschatology. Pneumatology thus enables "real continuity between the present and the future through the discontinuity of the present's brokenness and failure" (96).

pneumatologia crucis, a Spirit of the cross, through connection with the biblical tradition of *Shekinah*–God's empathetic indwelling of space and time.[17] As God's *Shekinah* descends and accompanies the suffering people of Israel into exile, the Spirit of God accompanies Jesus in his abandonment and sacrificial death on the cross. Jesus does not die alone and rejected by the Father, for the Spirit-*Shekinah* becomes his companion in suffering.

But the Spirit-*Shekinah* accomplishes more than accompanying Jesus through the discontinuity of death. God's Spirit "leads" Jesus into the mutual history between himself and his Father, in which "through obedience" (Heb. 5:8) he will "learn" his role as the messianic Son.[18] Jesus becomes the determining subject of his messianic suffering and death by way of the Spirit: "The Spirit is not something [Jesus] possesses. It is the power that makes him ready to surrender his life, and which itself sustains this surrender."[19] Jesus surrenders his life as God's atoning option for the future. Through the Spirit's leading, Jesus dispenses with economic, political, and religious strategies, so all he can do is suffer the forces that oppose him, and then die in weakness. But the One who has come forth from the Spirit and dies in the Spirit is reunited with the Father in the birth pangs of resurrection. The Spirit's energies for life sustain and transform Jesus' continuity with the Father and creation.

For Moltmann, the cross bears hope for a creation groaning in weakness and in death. The cross further opens up the possibility for humanity's justification in God's economy of reconciliation. Incorporating insight from liberation theology, Moltmann claims the cross justifies all of sinful humanity, but for victims and for perpetrators in two different yet related ways. Granted, complications arise in using simple categories to characterize people, who may be both victims and perpetrators throughout their lives, but for Moltmann, history's different soteriological concerns–victimization and perpetration–must be named as sin and accounted for in reconciliation. First, for people deprived of their human rights, the victims of history, God restores their rights through Jesus' solidarity with them in suffering. Moltmann explains, "The suffering, tormented and murdered Christ is on the side of the victims, not the agents. He himself becomes a victim among other victims. The forsaken Christ is the most beset of all the people who are beset, and who despair of God."[20] But the despairing, surrendering Jesus is not just one more victim. His vindication by the Spirit secures justice for all those living with injustice. Through the Spirit of the cross, God's justice *re-humanizes the de-humanized.*

Yet Jesus' atoning sacrifice also renews justice for the unjust perpetrators. In surrendering, Jesus carries the sin of perpetrators and endures the death of sinners; thus, God *re-humanizes the inhumane* by transmuting human guilt into divine suffering. The divine atonement reveals God's pain, but as Moltmann

---

[17]Moltmann, *The Spirit of Life,* 47–51.
[18]Ibid., 61.
[19]Ibid., 63.
[20]Ibid., 130.

writes, "God's pain reveals God's faithfulness to those he has created and his indestructible love, which endures a world in opposition to him, and overcomes it."[21] The *pneumatologia crucis* establishes righteousness for sinners, making possible forgiveness and liberation from guilt.

With the inclusion of the Spirit on Good Friday and Holy Saturday, the cross now becomes an event in the life of the Trinity.[22] All humanity participates in the new, reconciled life through the Spirit's justice forged in one person, Jesus. As divine Judge, God's Spirit has restored dignity for victims and spoken in the guilty consciences of those who commit violence. Formerly estranged enemies, perpetrators and victims now taste together the shared peace that also means true life—shalom. In the fellowship of the Spirit of the cross, "people accept one another mutually, and reciprocally recognize each other's dignity and rights. Compassion is alive. In that fellowship, human socialities are as good as the fortunes of their weakest members."[23] The Spirit of the cross leads victims and perpetrators through the discontinuity of history toward a new creation in which estrangement no longer defines the parameters of possibility for anyone.

Moltmann clearly incorporates a liberation perspective within a reformed order of salvation, but his Spirit of the cross, despite other holistic attempts to pneumatologically reconnect redemption with creation, continues focusing a reconciliation paradigm away from human history to a God apart from history. Definitely the cross occurs in history, but how does the cross of Jesus relate to the rest of history's crosses?[24] With God as the measure and context of all suffering, *God's* pain and *God's* atonement risk overshadowing the pain of victims/survivors and the accountability of perpetrators.[25] The Spirit as Judge and Reconciler relates to the oppressed and oppressors, but the struggle for justice becomes a work of the cross and not a labor between the estranged themselves.[26] Moltmann highlights the work of transforming unjust structures, such as relieving the international debt crisis and changing ecologically destructive economies, but these practices follow from the just-making of persons in Christ, rather than constituting justification itself. The project of incorporating liberation into a justification paradigm closes unsuccessfully with an unresolved tension between justice and justification.

---

[21]Ibid., 136.

[22]During the proceedings of the Australian Theological Forum's symposium "The Task of Theology Today: Tracking the Spirit in Tradition and Contemporary Thought" (Canberra, April 7–11, 1999), Lyle Dabney, who did his doctoral work with Moltmann, raised the important question for pneumatology, "What happens to the Spirit on Holy Saturday?"

[23]Moltmann, *The Spirit of Life*, 143.

[24]Jon Sobrino refers to the many crosses of history in *Christology at the Crossroads: A Latin American Approach*, trans. John Drury (Maryknoll, N.Y.: Orbis Books, 1978), 179–235.

[25]See Rebecca Chopp's analysis of Moltmann's theology in *The Praxis of Suffering: An Interpretation of Liberation and Political Theologies* (Maryknoll, N.Y.: Orbis Books, 1986), 115–16.

[26]See Nancy M. Victorin-Vangerud, "The Spirit's Struggle: Reconciliation in Moltmann's *Pneumatologia Crucis*," *Colloquium* 29, no. 2 (1997): 95–103.

A telling example of this tension in the Spirit of the cross comes from Moltmann's account of the experience of perpetrators. In a moment of personal disclosure, he shares the feelings of guilt with his fellow Germans when "they remember 'Auschwitz.'"[27] Through the reconciling atonement of the Spirit of the cross, Germans may experience a power that frees them from self-hate and self-destruction for lives of righteousness and justice. But rather than provide examples of reconciliation praxis for Germans, Moltmann closes the section on justification for perpetrators with an Orthodox Easter proclamation of the great reconciliation feast, when we will "speak to those who hate us" and "for the resurrection's sake, we will forgive one another everything."[28] In the face of such overwhelming tragedy and loss, the eschatological perspective addresses destroyed possibilities and the terrible weight of the dead. But by neglecting a praxis of justification in the *pneumatologia crucis*, in spite of other works and personal witness to political, social, and economic transformation, Moltmann's pneumatology risks a loss of connection with the world and history, a connection he adamantly seeks to make from the outset of *The Spirit of Life.*[29]

Originally, Moltmann turned to a *theologia crucis* to more adequately incorporate historical suffering into the reality of God, but the Spirit of the cross too quickly resolves the extent of the negative.[30] Like an enabling, well-meaning parent, God serves as the intermediary, taking care of the situation and then expecting estranged family members to live in peace. From a feminist maternal standpoint, Moltmann's model undercuts the necessary process of assertion, confrontation, and conflict within relations of distorted recognition. In addition to God's speaking privately in the perpetrator's guilty conscience, perpetrators must also face directly the words of their victims (if possible). God may restore the dignity of victims/survivors, but restoration must also come through human responsibility taken for concrete personal and institutional changes. Recognition of the other in reconciliation cannot be applied abstractly or before the fact from outside the disrupted relationship. Justice, forgiveness, love, and reconciliation, comprising the Spirit's recreation of space

---

[27]Moltmann, *The Spirit of Life*, 133.

[28]Ibid., 138.

[29]Clearly, by his written works and collaborations with others, Moltmann seeks to connect theology and social transformation. See Jürgen Moltmann, *On Human Dignity: Political Theology and Ethics* (London: SCM Press, 1984); and *Creating a Just Future: The Politics of Peace and the Ethics of Creation in a Threatened World* (Philadelphia: Trinity Press International, 1989); Johann-Baptist Metz and Jürgen Moltmann, *Faith and the Future: Essays on Theology, Solidarity and Modernity* (Maryknoll, N.Y.: Orbis Books, 1995); and Jürgen Moltmann, Nicholas Wolterstorff, and Ellen T. Charry, *A Passion for God's Reign: Theology, Christian Learning and the Christian Self*, ed. Miroslav Volf (Grand Rapids, Mich.: Eerdmans, 1998). Theologians concerned with historical hope such as Jon Sobrino and Catherine Keller claim their indebtedness to Moltmann's theology in *The Future of Theology: Essays in Honor of Jürgen Moltmann*, ed. Miroslav Volf, Carmen Krieg, and Thomas Kucharz (Grand Rapids, Mich.: Eerdmans, 1996).

[30]Anselm Min questions whether Moltmann loses the negative dialectic of God in his more encompassing aim of a holistic pneumatology. See Min's "Liberation, the Other and Hegel in Recent Pneumatologies," *Religious Studies Review* 22, no. 1 (January 1996): 29.

for life and freedom, all have historical and institutional dimensions incorporating the transformed relations of victims and perpetrators.

From Self-surrender to Self-commitment

Part of the problem is that Moltmann conflates the relation of victim and perpetrator into one person, the Son. Thus, the struggle for recognition in reconciliation becomes a process of identification and conformation with Jesus through what Moltmann terms a "*conformitas* christology."[31] Since the Son is reconciled with the Father through the Spirit, victims and perpetrators theoretically find hope through identification with the Son according to the patterns previously identified. But the model of conformation, complicated by the language of surrender and self-sacrifice, prescribes human passivity rather than the active labor of conflict resolution. As crucial as it is for victims and perpetrators to identify themselves within the domain of God's care, pneumatologies of reconciliation need not foreclose the possibility that divine grace and amnesty may be discovered *within* the process of attaining mutual recognition.[32] Jesus' substitutionary death for both sufferers and sinners too quickly resolves the historical struggle for freedom and peace. The Spirit of the cross, like the prophets and priests in Jeremiah 8:11, risks crying "peace, peace" when there is no peace.

A feminist maternal standpoint raises questions about vestiges of patriarchal family values in Moltmann's pneumatology. Narratives of the perfect, obedient Son who conforms his will to his Father's will and learns total trust through suffering resonates fearfully with survivors' experiences of victimization.[33] The pedagogical, even disciplinary, images of the Spirit leading and teaching Jesus obedience promote a view of Jesus' self-sacrifice and surrender as good ends in themselves. The perfect divine Victim, Jesus freely trusts the Spirit of the Father, even though the Father abandons Jesus to violation, torture, and death. Solidarity for victims may result from identification with Jesus in his abandonment, but what if the identification is pressed further between God and a parent who abandons his (or her) child? A feminist maternal inquiry does not contest Jesus' sense of abandonment, but raises questions about the theo-logic of the family narrative. Since in the logic, Jesus' abandonment by the Father accomplishes a divine purpose, this implies victims/survivors internalize their experiences of abandonment as purposive, necessary, or even

---

[31]Moltmann, *The Spirit of Life*, 131.

[32]On justification as amnesty for humanization, see Elsa Tamez, *The Amnesty of Grace: Justification by Faith from a Latin American Perspective*, trans. Sharon H. Ringe (Maryknoll, N.Y.: Orbis Books, 1993).

[33]See Carol J. Adams and Marie M. Fortune, eds., *Violence Against Women and Children: A Christian Theological Sourcebook* (New York: Continuum, 1995); Joanne Carlson Brown and Carole R. Bohn, eds., *Christianity, Patriarchy and Abuse: A Feminist Critique* (Cleveland: Pilgrim Press, 1989); Donald Capps, *The Child's Song: The Religious Abuse of Children* (Louisville, Ky.: Westminster John Knox Press, 1995); Annie Imbens and Ineke Jonker, *Christianity and Incest*, trans. Patricia McVay (Tunbridge Wells, Kent, U.K.: Burns & Oates, 1991); and Darby Kathleen Ray, *Deceiving the Devil: Atonement, Abuse and Ransom* (Cleveland: Pilgrim Press, 1998).

good. The logic of atonement through abandonment shifts the focus to God and away from the raw, robbing abuse of power in human society. The pedagogical Spirit of the cross, far from liberating persons for freedom from domination, leads to resignation and despair in sufferers who have been co-opted by perpetrators into idealizing powerful persons as worthy of loyalty and trust, like God, the perfect parent, right or wrong.

Besides questioning the normative values of self-surrender and suffering, a feminist maternal standpoint also questions the eschatological dynamics of the Spirit of the cross. Moltmann's pneumatological insight claims the possibilities of the future lie with God in the face of all human attempts to foreclose possibility or leave history to define its own parameters. From an eschatological perspective, the past has no absolute power to imprison human beings within bonds of suffering and victimization. The past further retains no power over guilt for sin or for the perpetuation of oppression, however far one is removed from evil events. Love overcomes all estrangement, even the immense estrangement of victims and perpetrators. Thus, for the Spirit of the cross, love stands in opposition to anger, for anger lives in the past, holding on to the past and making hurt or wrong the defining reality. Moltmann writes,

> Love fulfills the commandment (not to make images), because it does not tie anything down to what was once reality, in the past. It throws open the new free spaces of the future. Anger nails other people down to what they once were or did. But love perceives the other person together with his or her future, and his or her still unawakened potentialities. Anger gives the other person no time and no chance. But love has time and can wait.[34]

Since anger has no purpose except to restrain the present and the future from God's possibilities, the Spirit of the cross privileges love over anger. But from a feminist maternal standpoint, anger may be the only way forward into the future, not as an end in itself, but as the only way through a poisonous past by calling attention to the poison and asserting one's dignity. Anger opens the possibility for mutual recognition, allowing the wounds to receive fresh air for healing. From a feminist maternal standpoint, love and anger can both "breathe...as angels, not polarities," so wrongs can be redressed (since the past is always present still) and new relations ventured.[35]

In this exploration, Moltmann's Spirit of the cross transforms the community of creation in continuity with the divine Triune community through the discontinuity of suffering and death. The strengths of a holistic pneumatology lie in the connections of Spirit with creation (not just

---

[34]Moltmann, *The Spirit of Life*, 263.
[35]In her poem "Integrity," Adrienne Rich writes: "Anger and tenderness: my selves. And now I can believe they breathe in me as angels, not polarities. Anger and tenderness: the spider's genius to spin and weave in the same action from her own body, anywhere–even from a broken web." See *A Wild Patience Has Taken Me This Far: Poems 1978–1981* (New York: W. W. Norton, 1981), 8–9.

sanctification of souls), with the life and death of Jesus (not just resurrection), and with victims (not just forgiven sinners). Motivated by the love of life, the Spirit of the cross reveals God's suffering with creation in order to recreate life through the divine energies. In the eschatological aim of new creation, unity in the Spirit affirms the unique diversity of beings living in love as friends beyond past wrongs. Open friendship, as a spiritual praxis, means valuing the other as a person with dignity and possibilities for relations of freedom, not domination.

But a feminist maternal standpoint claims that both self and other make a difference. Questions are posed for the Spirit of the cross: How do persons in the Spirit move beyond relations of distorted recognition or nonrecognition to relations of mutuality in recognition? What is the pneumatological impetus for change? How adequate is a pneumatology of self-surrender for a praxis of life, liberation, and diversity? By privileging the cross through the lens of self-surrender, Moltmann neglects the wider horizon of Jesus' messianic praxis— "pro-existence."[36] Thus, a feminist maternal perspective shifts the focus on Jesus' *self-surrender* to Jesus' *self-commitment* in the Spirit of God. Jesus' messianic commitment to life entails a richer portrait of his relations with others beyond the idealized value of self-surrender. Led by the Spirit, Jesus risked conflict and placed himself in contexts of struggle for God's identity, his own identity, and others' dignity. Recognizing others, particularly persons not recognized by religious, social, political, and economic powers, Jesus also asserted himself with friends, disciples, antagonists, and institutions. The gospels give witness to a Jesus of protest, prophetic proclamation, and commitment to God's abundant life for all. Interpreting the cross as self-surrender puts at risk the focus of Jesus' life on *life*. Christine Gudorf makes the case:

> We must lift up the goodness of life, that which Jesus attempted to demonstrate; it is good for all to eat and drink together, to bake and fish, to sow and harvest, to celebrate weddings, to cherish children, to pray and to do these things together without judgement or exclusion.[37]

A feminist maternal standpoint claims Jesus committed his life first and foremost to the flourishing of life, God's "kin-dom"; thus, following in his name implies a corresponding self-commitment.[38] Persons struggling for mutual recognition take heart in their commitment to Jesus' inclusive and just vision, in contrast to whether they have surrendered their lives to an idealized, general notion of obedience. At stake is not the issue of being a good child, but the question: To what spiritual vision of abundant life (Jn. 10:10) is one's own life committed?

---

[36]Ray, 138.

[37]Christine E. Gudorf, *Victimization: Examining Christian Complicity* (Philadelphia: Trinity Press International, 1992), 73.

[38]Ada Maria Isasi-Diaz, "Sisterhood: Core of a Liberating Struggle," The Antoinette Brown Lecture (Vanderbilt University, Nashville, March 29, 1982).

In her feminist study of atonement, Darby Ray argues that the theological means of redemption must be consistent with the vision of redemption itself.[39] If liberation and reconciliation hold out a vision of healing, wholeness, and freedom for self and community, then the way of liberation and reconciliation must also reflect these values. Moltmann's holistic pneumatology presents a vision of freedom from domination in a community of diverse friends, but the redemptive means demand of Jesus a self-surrendering way. Thus, Moltmann's means present obstacles for his vision and dangerously undermine his best intentions in the end. A feminist maternal standpoint re-fines the Spirit of the cross through placing it within the larger horizon of Jesus' pro-existence praxis, thus re-figuring the ideal of self-surrender toward an ecumenical value of self-commitment.

Michael Welker's Spirit of Justice and Mercy

> People have emphasized over and over again that God's Spirit works union, unanimity, and unity among human beings, indeed that the Spirit "holds together" all that is created...Less clarity and energy have been devoted to saying that the "unity of the Spirit" not only tolerates differences and differentiation, but that it maintains and cultivates differences, that do not contradict justice, mercy, and knowledge of God.[40]

While they share similar themes, Michael Welker's postmodern, pluralistic pneumatology presents a contrast to Moltmann's holistic and more "systematic" Spirit of the cross.[41] Welker criticizes modern theology's reliance on universals, proposing instead a more modest, realistic approach that values diverse, particular experiences of God. Biblical witnesses to the Spirit reflect great diversity, from early experiences of the Spirit's power in the time of the judges through the prophets and Jesus of Nazareth—the messianic bearer of the Spirit—to the outpouring of the Spirit in Pentecost and the early churches. For Welker, postmodernity's celebration of pluralism helps theology receive anew the Spirit's presence in and through "emergent" processes of cultural, political, and social communication.[42] While pluralism can also be debilitating and destructive, theology's contemporary challenge lies in discerning the invigorating and creative pluralism of God the Spirit.

While Moltmann turns to an ecological *ruach* and empathetic *Shekinah*, Welker draws on the Spirit's prophetic connection with community life

---

[39]Ray, 54–55.

[40]Michael Welker, *God the Spirit* (Minneapolis: Fortress Press, 1994), 22.

[41]Min, 29.

[42]Key to Welker's pneumatology is the sociological work of Nicholas Luhmann, *Ecological Communication* (Chicago: University of Chicago Press, 1989). Welker defines emergent processes as "those constellations, conditions, and structures whose appearance on the scene cannot be derived from preceding constellations, conditions and structures, although diverse elements that define both conditions persist in them...And one must add that there is also nothing at all left over" (28).

according to God's righteous promises of public justice, mercy, and knowledge of God. Righteousness extends beyond morality with its conventional hierarchy of good and bad, insiders and outsiders, and respect and disrepute. Persons upon whom the Spirit rests fulfill the law, which establishes institutional justice for the disadvantaged, resolves conflict between the powerful and powerless, and protects the vulnerable and easily excluded. For communities in the Spirit of God, mercy "must always remain open and sensitive to new groups of weak, afflicted and disadvantaged persons in a community…[that] becomes committed to constant self-change and self-renewal, to self-critical rethinking and reorientation."[43] Reflected in the practices of justice and mercy, knowledge of God secures socially communicable expressions of God's Spirit, not only personal or individual experiences. Ambiguously experienced in the early traditions, God's promises come together in Israel's hope for a messianic bearer of the Spirit who will extend the promises to the nations (Isa. 11:1–5, 9–10; 42:1–4, 6–8; 61:1–11).

Welker characterizes the messianic bearer of the Spirit through the servant song of Isaiah 42, highlighting verse 2, "He will not cry or lift up his voice, or make it heard in the street."[44] Because God's righteousness transcends any one national or cultural frame of reference, the Spirit-bearer faithfully establishes justice by absolutely rejecting all political, military, economic, or social exercises of power "from below." Justice and mercy are public, but in bringing them about, the Spirit-bearer foregoes crying out in the face of oppression, suffering, and death. Instead, the messianic prophet remains silent, gathering up the disrespect, contempt, and rejection from those who benefit through human standards. The powerlessness of the Spirit-bearer precisely renders all ideologies of domination ultimately futile, however politically correct their tone, and thus draws universal attention and loyalty to God's promises. Welker explains:

> In the recognition that a person who was ostracized, despised, even persecuted and executed in the name of the prevailing orders is God's chosen one, people are opened to the recognition of God's righteousness…It becomes possible to recognize that the most well-intended, apparently most proven, well-articulated, recognized forms and practices of righteousness are also corruptible and corrupted.[45]

Within the hopeful presence of the messianic Spirit-bearer, emerging systems of mercy and justice resist simple schemes of identification. God the Spirit creates relations of pluralistic solidarity across nations and challenges groups, persons, or movements that close themselves off from others. No one group, person, movement, or nation can claim justice, mercy, and knowledge

---

[43]Welker, 119.
[44]Ibid., 124–34.
[45]Ibid., 131–32.

of God for themselves, not even Israel. Potentially drawing all people, the silent, powerless servant reveals the ever-open, inclusive, multifaceted domain of God's reign.

Christian biblical faith attests that Jesus of Nazareth fulfilled the hope of God's promises and thus as the Christ embodied the concrete presence of the Spirit.[46] From Welker's perspective, Jesus rejected organized political action, self-promotion, and structural change, entering instead a variety of individual and collective experiences of personal suffering. Encountering the disintegrating, demonic forces of people's lives at the most basic level, Jesus delivered people from distress, healed their powerlessness, and restored them to coherent patterns of living with dignity and hope. He eschewed making his voice heard in the streets and gave his life in total sacrifice, without public means of power. In Jesus' life, death, and resurrection, the Spirit of God is recognized as "the selflessly delivering power of the Crucified One."[47]

But at Pentecost, this power is made available, poured out, to a diverse community of disciples with a universal scope. Welker uses the image of a "force-field" to express his interpretation of the Spirit as the "public person" of Jesus.[48] The Spirit of justice and mercy, concretely present in the person of Jesus, now brings people into the force-field of Jesus' ongoing influence. In one sense, Jesus' public personhood was manifested in his selfless relations with people prior to his death, but in Pentecost the possibility of standing within Jesus' force-field becomes open for many emergent manifestations of selflessness. Welker presses the notion of personhood beyond individualistic, monistic images. Jesus' liberating, healing relations with others–in their own particular embodiments–constitute his spiritual personhood. Pentecost gives Jesus' Spirit-bearing personhood a universal scope–a potentially universal force-field–inclusive of diverse cultures, movements, persons, and institutions, some of whom may actually exist in conflict with one another. Through these different workings of the Spirit, God's promises of justice, mercy, and knowledge of God extend in hope throughout creation.

Welker draws his central image for the Spirit's influence (centered on the personhood of Jesus) from Ezekiel's prophetic texts concerning the change of human hearts from stone to flesh (11:17b, 19–20; 36:26–28). In the prophet's religious imagination, hearts of stone imply invulnerable persons unmoved by their own and others' suffering. They are, in effect, heavy and dead to the world. But the presence of God the Spirit transforms stony individuals into sensitive, empathetic persons alive to the world's frail perishability. Inspirited persons with hearts of flesh become capable of selfless living in a world of debilitating, devouring powers and principalities. Welker claims that "to be alive is to be capable, in diverse frames of reference, of self-withdrawal for the

---

[46]Ibid., 183–227.
[47]Ibid., 222.
[48]Ibid., 239–48, 311–12.

benefit of other living beings."[49] Confronted by Jesus' selflessness, stony-hearted persons encounter the force-field of the Spirit and receive hearts of flesh. Now touched and moved by suffering, they discover the possibility of withdrawing themselves in order to give space to others for life.

Welker links his pneumatological concept of self-withdrawal with Paul's "fruit of the Spirit" (Gal. 5:22–23):

> Free self-withdrawal for the benefit of others gives fellow creatures open space and possibilities of development that surprise and delight them. It does not pin them down, does not make claims on them, but gives them space for their own development. This free self-withdrawal can express itself in strained relations as patience and gentleness. In the act of taking an interest in other people, it can unfold as kindness and generosity. But free self-withdrawal for the benefit of fellow creatures finds its most complete expression in love.[50]

Like Moltmann, Welker sets forth love as the great unifying characteristic of God the Spirit. But unity in the Spirit doesn't mean conforming others to a specific agenda or incorporating them into a preexistent structure. Love means withdrawing one's own claims and opening up free space—socially, psychologically, and ecologically—for others' development and determination as living beings. The Spirit of justice and mercy cultivates differences among people in many interdependent and interrelated communities who receive their dignity, respect, and personhood from God and not any corruptible human measures.

From Self-withdrawal to Self-assertion

By interpreting anew the prophetic and Pentecost texts, Welker formulates a postmodern pneumatology that undercuts simplistic, private, and unidirectional understandings of God the Spirit. Diversity in love emerges as the primary testimony of the Spirit, constituted by relations of self and other in which neither is subordinated. A feminist maternal standpoint, though, questions Welker's pneumatological movement from debilitating, oppressive relations to creative, invigorating pluralism. The goal is vital and necessary, but how do people get there? For mutual recognition, assertion of personhood is crucial in changing or restoring relations; thus, confrontation and conflict become part of the emerging process. What impetus does Welker's Spirit of justice and mercy offer in the struggle for mutual recognition?

Curiously, Welker does frame his project as a liberation pneumatology. He opens his book by identifying feminist and liberation movements as emergent processes of God the Spirit.[51] But throughout his presentation, he adamantly distinguishes the presence of the Spirit from all political or social

---

[49]Ibid., 166.
[50]Ibid., 249.
[51]Ibid., 16–21.

action, which undercuts his initial empathy. Certainly, feminist and liberation movements need to view themselves self-critically in larger processes of struggle and solidarity, even in processes with other groups bearing different agendas. Yet in absolutely distancing the Spirit to avoid arrogant idolatry of practice, Welker risks losing the connection of justice and mercy with any process or action at all. Emergent processes, however complex, dynamic, and interrelated, still require human action, and human action incorporates political, social, and economic dimensions. Welker neglects liberating praxis to the point where we question whether the Spirit of justice and mercy is an "apolitical, even anti-political," pneumatology of liberation.[52]

For Welker, liberation as self-withdrawal for the benefit of others occurs through fleshly human hearts sensitive to greedy, self-full patterns of living. In empathy with suffering others, inspirited persons selflessly withdraw their claims to the social, political, and material resources needed by others for a more equitable flourishing of life together. A feminist maternal standpoint supports this important dimension of self-critical awareness, but the onus of the Spirit's influence is on the overextended self. What is the pneumatological praxis of others in debilitating contexts? Welker uses the language of "waiting" on the action of the Spirit, but is waiting the only faithful prescription?[53] He does connect Spirit and suffering others in his pneumatology, but at the interface of deliverance and healing, which seems to occur in an existential realm, beyond political, social, or economic domains. At the interface of Spirit and person, Spirit is active and humanity passive. While rightfully concerned that people do not think they control or determine the Spirit, Welker neglects the vital intervention of the other. Potentially a paternalistic model of pneumatological relations, the Spirit first opens possibilities for the overextended self; then, through self-withdrawal, possibilities are opened up for cramped and debilitated others.

But the possibility for self-withdrawal may come to the attention of the overextended person, community, or nation through the active assertion of those in need of space, resources, legislation, or other conditions for development and freedom. From a feminist maternal viewpoint, the Spirit's force-field also includes the diverse, multidirectional acts of subordinated people making known their presence and igniting conflict with stony institutions. While there are times to wait with love, joy, peace, patience, kindness, generosity, faithfulness, gentleness, and self-control, God the Spirit of justice and mercy also emerges in assertive processes of conflict and the struggle for recognition. The Spirit's engagement in a feminist maternal model reflects another direction—first, the Spirit opens up possibilities for underdeveloped others; then in the Spirit these persons initiate new possibilities for the privileged and powerful.

In Welker's model, human self-withdrawal is mediated through the force-field of the Spirit centered on the self-withdrawing Jesus, the messianic

---

[52]Min, 30.
[53]Welker, 133.

Spirit-bearer. Concerned with family ideologies of selflessness, a feminist maternal standpoint calls attention to Welker's singular association of Jesus and the suffering servant. A richer, multifaceted portrait of Jesus, including his prophetic self-assertion and confrontive communicative presence, provides greater emergent possibilities for the different soteriological needs of overextended and underdeveloped persons. Stories of Jesus' challenging convention and interacting with his antagonists present a messianic Christ who did not always keep silent in the streets or disassociate himself from political, economic, social, and religious institutions. Even narratives of Jesus' healings, table fellowship, and encounters with women, children, and marginalized persons portray him as asserting himself and recognizing the assertions of others. Jesus' praxis of creating space for others to live required not only times of self-withdrawal, but times of self-assertion in the Spirit of justice and mercy.

Without a more complex portrait of Jesus as the messianic bearer of the Spirit, relational dynamics such as selflessness, powerlessness, or suffering risk at least becoming goods in themselves. If valued as the norms for faithful praxis, these dynamics become poisonous for subordinated persons bound by passivity, silence, and blind trust. Again, the means of redemption (silent self-withdrawal, powerlessness) become obstacles in conflict with the vision of redemption in the Spirit (a free, differentiated community). Victims, survivors, and others in dehumanizing relations know all too well the patronizing personal and institutional strategies of waiting for perpetrators to withdraw or change. At some point, people no longer remain silent; justice and mercy necessitate crying out and the use of systems for accountability and restitution. Relations of proper trust require that both self and other make a difference. From a feminist maternal standpoint, Welker's Spirit of justice and mercy, while offering positive images of diverse, emergent processes inclusive of self and other, neglects the praxis of subordinated others in the work of creating space for life. The emergence of mutual recognition requires not only strategies of self-withdrawal, but strategies of self-assertion, in the Spirit.

Colin Gunton's Spirit of Particularity

> We are accustomed–too accustomed–to speak of the Spirit as the unifier: bringing it about that in Christ we become one with the Father and each other, and so on. But trinitarian love has as much to do with respecting and constituting otherness as with unifying.[54]

Colin Gunton turns to the Spirit in *The One, the Three and the Many* as part of a Trinitarian strategy for reclaiming the created dignity of human beings in the face of modernity's drive for homogeneity, symbolized by the red and white Coca-Cola sign on nearly every corner of the global market. In Gunton's narrative, modernity rightly rebelled against the authoritarian, theological

---

[54]Gunton, 256.

transcendence of God in the Western tradition that pitted God's unchanging, abstract will against human freedom. But the "cure [was] worse than the disease," for with the displacement of God came an influx of "deities of immanence"—social progress, capitalism, socialism, science, and technology—with human individuals taking upon themselves the displaced god's mantle of Creator.[55] Cartesian self-certainty and Kantian moral autonomy disengaged human subjects from the world and fostered instrumental relations between self and others, who, like God, have gradually disappeared in real significance. Now the singular, atomistic subject lives with the tension between utter depersonalization and the myth of fulfillment, both stemming from the new immanental deity, consumerism. Lost is the sense of human beings created mysteriously in the image of God to serve God's praiseworthy ends, not the market.

Gunton levels his criticism at consumer society, but his real target is Western theology's tendency to blame contemporary problems on "secular" modernity alone without seeing the deep-seated difficulties within Western theology itself. Taking up the Parmenidean quest for the timeless, unchanging reality of the One underneath the worldly particulars of the Many, Western theology developed a Trinity of persons united in the uniformity of substance, rather than the particular relations comprising the persons, as in Eastern theology.[56] Western theology subordinated the Many to the One, played out through images of God's unilateral power and invulnerability. In its rejection of this deity, modernity transfigured the notion of person as one into its logic of human autonomy. Modernity's view of human beings, constituted by universal reason or will, continues subordinating the particulars of finite persons in finite time and space.

By returning to the Eastern Trinitarian concept of *perichoresis*, Gunton turns the ontological table and privileges particulars over the universal, not only in human reality, but in divine reality.[57] In fact, the relational constitution of human beings with other humans and with the world as other can only be established through a relational understanding of God's being. In Gunton's project, God's substance or essence is relationality, as played out in the divine dance of *perichoresis* between the Father, Son, and Spirit. "Being is diversity within unity" in the integrated pluralism of God.[58] Thus, the particularity of

---

[55]Ibid., 41, 228.

[56]For a critical analysis of Gunton's dialectical framework and "historical scapegoating" of Parmenides, Heraclitus, and Augustine in this work, see David S. Cunningham, *These Three Are One: The Practice of Trinitarian Theology* (Oxford: Blackwell, 1998), 31–33, 39–41, 94–95.

[57]In *The One, the Three and the Many*, Gunton describes the concept of *perichoresis* as "a way of showing the ontological interdependence and reciprocity of the three persons of the Trinity: how they were only what they were by virtue of their interrelation and interanimation, so that for God to be did not involve an absolute simplicity but a unity deriving from a dynamic plurality of persons" (152). *Perichoresis* refers to a cyclical movement, an encircling of partners with one another. Elizabeth A. Johnson associates *perichoresis* with John Damascene and writes, "There is a clasping of hands, a pervading exchange of life, a genuine circling around together that constitutes the permanent, active, divine *koinonia*" (220). See *She Who Is: The Mystery of God in Feminist Theological Discourse* (New York: Crossroad, 1992).

[58]Gunton, 213.

the divine persons, in relation to one another, is not temporary, to be dissolved toward some higher state of perfect divine being. Trinitarian logic acknowledges others as vital for personhood (*hypostasis*); thus, God's communion of love for the world as other, and God as other for the world, overflows from the giving and receiving of the divine persons.

Gunton turns to the Spirit as the way of rekindling the relational ontology of Western theology. From the Hebrew Bible, *ruach* conveys God's self-giving empowerment of human beings in their particular relations to God and to one another. Likewise in the New Testament, *pneuma* expresses the interpersonal connection between humanity and God, as in Romans 8:15–16, "When we cry, 'Abba! Father!' it is that very Spirit bearing witness with our spirit." For Gunton, God's Spirit brings God and the world into relation. Spirit constitutes the reality in which beings open themselves to one another in their own particularities without abolishing the differences between them. Thus, God is Spirit, but humans have spirit:

> God is Spirit because of the unqualified openness of the triune persons to each other and to God's free and unnecessitated movement outwards to creation and redemption to that which is not God, to the finite and temporal. Humans have spirit because they in their own limited way are open to God and each other and to the world.[59]

In Gunton's pneumatology, that which is or has spirit is able to be open to that which is other than itself and move dynamically into relation with the other. But inspirited beings are not first individuals who then create relations; persons are individuals already in their relations with others. The key for human transformation in the Spirit is the ever-expanding and ever-deepening openness to relations with others.

Gunton's social ontology leads him to make two claims about God the Spirit. First, Spirit has to do with crossing boundaries between different beings. Second, the Spirit's boundary-crossing presence doesn't subordinate particularity; Spirit maintains and even strengthens the differences. Spirit is "the liberating Other," who in God's economy relates Jesus to the Father and to those who follow him.[60] Typically in Western theology, following Augustine, the Spirit has been understood as the unifying bond of love between the Father and the Son.[61] Challenging simple notions of unity, Gunton's liberating Spirit recasts the bonds of love in and through the particularity of each Triune person. The particularizing Spirit respects the otherness of the Father and the Son, yet opens them to communion in each other. Likewise, the Spirit respects

---

[59]Ibid., 188.

[60]Ibid., 183.

[61]See Augustine, *The Trinity*, trans. Stephen McKenna, ed. Charles Dollen (Boston: Daughters of St. Paul, 1965). In Book VII, 3:6, Augustine writes that the Holy Spirit "is that perfect love which joins together the Father and the Son and attaches us to them" (134). Later, in Book VIII, 10:14, he draws on the human analogy of the lover, the beloved, and the love: "What else is love, therefore, except a kind of life which binds or seeks to bind some two together, namely the lover and the beloved" (162).

human otherness yet opens humans to relationship with the Son as the focal point of creation, and then through the Son with the Father as well. Reflecting the communion of the Trinity, the communion of humanity becomes concretely manifest in the church, the network of people freed to share their rich, diverse gifts with the world in participation with the Spirit of particularity. Crossing boundaries and strengthening differences in relationship, God's Spirit "perfects creation" by bringing to completion in time and space that for which each unique creature is created.[62]

But attaining perfection in the Spirit requires, in addition, the Trinitarian ethic of gift and reception. Gunton makes the third claim that human relationality is analogous to the relationality revealed in the self-giving Christ, who is given by the Father for humanity and then gives himself to the Father in return. The Spirit empowers people to give themselves to God and others as "a living sacrifice, holy and acceptable to God" (Rom. 12:1). Gunton re-images sacrificial atonement through the ethic of self-giving, in contrast to notions mandating death and the spilling of blood.[63] Christ's self-giving character establishes a nonreciprocal ethic, since the expectation of others' giving to him does not in any way determine his own act. Gunton privileges giving in his ethic of gift and reception:

> In both the gospels and epistles, the chief ethical emphasis is in contradiction of mere reciprocity. Creative subordination to others in conformation to Christ and replication of his manner of being towards others is the form of humanity that lives out the transcendental (perichoretic) dynamics of things.[64]

In criticism of modernity's egoism, Gunton claims human beings become most truly who they are in the giving of themselves to God. We become God's creatures in our God-given particularities, each one uniquely related to others, as we are conformed to Christ's ethic. Paradoxically, we are most free to give ourselves for others when we become absolutely subordinated to God, not the single dominating will over us, but the relational love of communion.

Gunton's pneumatology challenges modernity's displacement of God and Western theology's displacement of divine diversity in relation. In both modernity and theology, the real particularity of persons has been lost and a rootless, abstract sense of person survives. Postmodernity reclaims the other in its celebration of plurality, but according to Gunton, the relativistic and nihilistic character of postmodernity makes the other irrelevant in the end. The Spirit of particularity, crossing boundaries, strengthening diversity, and perfecting humanity (and thus the world) through an ethic of self-giving, places

---

[62]Gunton, 182, 189–90. Gunton draws on Basil of Caesarea's image of the perfecting Spirit. See "On the Holy Spirit," 15, 36–38 in *Nicene and Post-Nicene Fathers of the Christian Church*, vol. 8, ed. Philip Schaff and Henry Wace (New York: Christian Literature Company, 1895), 22–23.

[63]Gunton, 225.

[64]Ibid., 226.

human others and God as Other at the heart of redemptive possibility. Gunton seeks an ontology of diversity-in-unity, but elements of his pneumatology create obstacles to the goal.

From Self-giving to Self-care

A feminist maternal standpoint supports Gunton's criticism of individualistic, monistic concepts of persons. For human beings closed in on themselves—socially, spiritually, politically, epistemologically—the Spirit appropriately opens them to relations with others without downsizing their unique differences. New relations are fostered in and through the diversity. But what about when relations are fused or distorted? What pneumatological impetus supports particularity when boundaries have been abusively crossed? In poisonous relations, violated persons struggle to set boundaries for themselves, which may necessitate distancing themselves from others, restricting personal access, and even severing relations in regaining a sense of integrity and personhood. Gunton's pneumatological image of connecting people across differences only tells part of the story in boundary negotiation. His concern comes from examining social fragmentation, but a feminist maternal standpoint attends to re-orientating relations of damage. Since maintaining healthy, permeable boundaries in relations requires the fluid interplay of connection and differentiation, the Spirit's association with perfecting particularity must include the relational dynamics that help people resist and struggle against connection with abusive people or institutions.

Gunton's ethic of asymmetrical self-giving also receives refinement through a feminist maternal standpoint. Self-giving assumes persons have something to give. For people surviving abusive relations, clarity about oneself in relation to others may be a difficult, confusing process of discernment and personal change. While Gunton does not advocate selflessness, the ethic of self-giving risks dis-powering persons mired in relations where she or he has been primarily the one giving. Self-giving, as a single priority, neglects an ethic of self-care, which values the reciprocity of giving and receiving in relations. Asymmetrical self-giving leads to depression, burnout, over-functioning, boundary violations, and a host of other dangerous institutional and interpersonal dynamics. A feminist maternal perspective speaks from the experience of patriarchal asymmetry—the mother as primary caregiver and sacrificial icon. But a feminist maternal perspective also speaks from the potential for maternal asymmetry in regard to one's children, who may be expected to continually give of themselves in caring for their mother. While Gunton's reliance on *perichoresis* seeks relational communion, a feminist maternal standpoint questions whether his norm of nonreciprocal self-giving undermines the possibility for attaining his vision. For interpersonal giving and receiving, a pneumatological ethic of symmetrical care is needed to sustain the fullness and richness of relations.[65]

---

[65]For interpretations of mutual participation and reciprocity in *perichoresis*, see Johnson, 216–23; and Cunningham, 165–95.

Like Moltmann and Welker, Gunton bases his pneumatology on a portrait of Jesus through a singular lens. By focusing only on sacrificial self-giving, Gunton reduces the complexity of Jesus' personhood and relations with others. Yet the gospel narratives portray Jesus receiving care from others, tending to his prayer life, returning to the home of friends for safety and support, and traveling in the company of women and men who cared for his needs.[66] As we have seen in the other two sections of this chapter, privileging one aspect of Jesus' life over other characterizations reduces the richness of Jesus' personhood, as well as Christian faith and discipleship. If a pneumatology only highlights sacrificial self-giving in the divine economy, then sacrificial self-giving too easily becomes the sole value for spiritual formation. As a result, talk of creative subordination and conformity to Christ risks reinforcing thoughts, feelings, and behaviors that maintain poisonous dynamics in relationships and institutions.

Gunton claims his ethic of self-giving avoids glorifying suffering and submission to authority.[67] Sacrificial imagery refers to the giving of ourselves to God in praise and not suffering in the first instance, since humans were not created to suffer. But because humans live in a fallen world, for redemption's sake Jesus' self-giving was made perfect through suffering.[68] Still, the pneumatological dynamic of conforming disciples' lives to Jesus' self-giving ethic too closely implies that human life and faith may be made perfect through suffering as well. For a feminist maternal hermeneutic, the sacrificial characterization of self-giving remains a problem. From another angle, why not consider self-assertion, differentiation, or confrontation as forms of self-giving in love for the sake of mutual recognition? Diversity in praise of God would then incorporate multiple ways of praising, even inclusive of the struggle toward human freedom in relation. But do we only praise God when we give of ourselves to others and God? Why not value self-care as one way of giving praise for the gift of life in creation? Refining the Spirit of particularity from a feminist maternal perspective means affirming self-care as one way of valuing self and others in God's economy of praise.

Jesus' Dignity in the Spirit

In her analysis of theological complicity in sexual victimization, Gudorf raises a crucial question, "How powerful can a message of love and trust be when it never addresses principal obstacles to that love and trust?"[69] Gudorf's question echoes Ray's concern that the way of redemption not betray the meaning of redemption itself. In the contemporary pneumatological options of Jürgen Moltmann, Michael Welker, and Colin Gunton, love and trust are mediated within a divine dance of intersubjective communion, yet the sacrificial values of self-surrender, self-withdrawal, and self-giving remain

---

[66]See Rita Nakashima Brock, *Journeys By Heart: A Christology of Erotic Power* (New York: Crossroad, 1988), 50–70.

[67]Gunton, 226.

[68]Ibid., 225.

[69]Gudorf, 92.

unchallenged as obstacles to the full mediation of perichoretic love and trust. Each theologian turns to pneumatology in affirming the relational diversity-in-unity constituting creation's fulfillment within the divine economy. Here, dignity is experienced not in being assimilated into a homogeneous communion (a contradiction in terms!), but in celebration of a unique personal existence lived in relation with others. In refinement of the perichoretic vision, a feminist maternal standpoint challenges the self-sacrificial means of the sanctifying Spirit. For self and other living in mutual recognition, both must make a difference. This insight presses the norm of self-surrender in the direction of self-commitment, the value of self-withdrawal toward the practice of self-assertion, and the ideal of self-giving in the direction of self-care.

The paradigm shift to mutual recognition requires another look at the rich, complex personhood of Jesus of Nazareth. Emerging forth from the Spirit in assertive relations with others, growing in wisdom and compassion through spiritual care and community, and committing himself to God's vast kin-dom, Jesus embodies much more than singular definitions of personhood. From Christian traditions we inherit narratives of Jesus' sacrificial selfhood based on the patriarchal family model, but turning to pneumatology in contemporary theology challenges us to review the relation of Jesus and the Spirit. A feminist maternal perspective retrieves the human dignity of Jesus as a person of spiritual commitment and self-assertion, "worthy" of care and nurture. In refining the pneumatologies of Moltmann, Welker, and Gunton, the dignity of creation's diversity-in-unity must be consonant with the dignity of Jesus in the power of the Spirit. The aim of this chapter has been to refine and strengthen contemporary pneumatological insights so that in the fire of the Spirit, love may burn in all.

CHAPTER 8

Turning to the Spirit in Women's Theologies

I am proposing that Christian idolatry concerning the person of Jesus is not likely to be overcome except through the revolution that is going on in women's consciousness. It will, I think, become increasingly evident that exclusively masculine symbols for the ideal of "incarnation" or for the ideal of the human search for fulfillment will not do. As a uniquely masculine image and language for divinity loses credibility, so also the idea of a single divine incarnation in a human being of the male sex may give way in the religious consciousness to an increased awareness of the power of Being in all persons.[1]

Forgetting the Spirit is not ignoring a faceless, shadowy third hypostasis but the mystery of God closer to us than we are to ourselves, drawing near and passing by in quickening, liberating compassion.[2]

Women's Work

The previous chapter explored the recent turn to the Spirit in the theologies of Jürgen Moltmann, Michael Welker, and Colin Gunton. In each case, a feminist maternal standpoint questioned the connections between Christ and the Spirit toward a more holistic understanding of Jesus' personhood and thus a more holistic pneumatology. But what about women's contributions to the turn to the Spirit? Where do women stand in the renewed vitality of pneumatological inquiry? Chung Hyun Kyung's Seventh Assembly address ignited possibilities for diverse, contextual approaches to the doctrine of the Holy Spirit, yet the majority of works on the Spirit have been produced by male theologians representing a breadth of traditions. Women's *spiritualities*

---

[1]Mary Daly, *Beyond God the Father: Toward a Philosophy of Women's Liberation* (Boston: Beacon Press, 1973), 71.

[2]Elizabeth Johnson, *She Who Is: The Mystery of God in Feminist Theological Discourse* (New York: Crossroad, 1992), 131.

have received much attention, but doctrinal construction on the Spirit of God remains a work-in-process.[3] Have women forgotten the Spirit too?

Despite the paucity of pneumatological focus in women's reconstructive theologies, this chapter suggests women's christological work in the last few decades leads to a strengthened position for exploring new turns to the Spirit.[4] While women from many different social contexts have responded to the gospel question, "Who do you say that I am?" (Mk. 8:29), now pneumatology likewise beckons for creative, inclusive, and liberating responses.[5] With christology, women question the anthropological distortions funding Christian theologies, worship, church institutions, intimate relationships, and ethics. How has the Christ-symbol validated, normed, or idealized certain understandings of what it means to be human, and thus excluded or marginalized other understandings? Christology's potential for oppressive or liberating relations provides the focus for much of women's theological work. But affirmations from women's voices of what it means to be human sparks new directions for Spirit in the household of God.

The theological work of women traced in this chapter leads from women's christologies to women's pneumatologies. The primary question motivating the creative labor along the way is, How do women re-imagine human wholeness? The exploration begins with the radical challenge of Mary Daly, the touchstone for women's christological reflection. Daly clearly identifies the idolatry embedded in christological doctrine and responds with the hope of a world without delimiting models. But from the perspective of women remaining within Christian traditions, Daly's wholesale rejection of christology presents its own limitations for human wholeness. In response, women re-figure christology by drawing on several strategies: first, re-imagining the subjectivity of Jesus; second, re-imagining the subjectivity of Christ; and third, moving to the paradigm of Christic intersubjectivity. But, this chapter argues, the latter

---

[3]Explorations of women's spiritualities include Charlene Spretnak, ed., *The Politics of Women's Spirituality: Essays on the Rise of Spiritual Power within the Feminist Movement* (New York: Anchor Books, 1982); Carol P. Christ, *Diving Deep and Surfacing: Women Writers on Spiritual Quest* (Boston: Beacon Press, 1986); Letty M. Russell, Kwok Pui-lan, Ada Maria Isasi-Diaz, Katie Geneva Cannon, eds., *Inheriting Our Mothers' Gardens: Feminist Theology in Third World Perspective* (Philadelphia: Westminster Press, 1988); Judith Plaskow and Carol P. Christ, eds., *Weaving the Visions: New Patterns in Feminist Spirituality* (San Francisco: HarperCollins, 1989); Deborah Selway, *Women of Spirit: Contemporary Religious Leaders in Australia* (Melbourne: Longman, 1995); Joan D. Chittister, *Heart of Flesh: A Feminist Spirituality for Women and Men* (Grand Rapids, Mich.: Eerdmans, 1998); and David Shallenberger, *Reclaiming the Spirit: Gay Men and Lesbians Come to Terms with Religion* (New Brunswick, N. J.: Rutgers University Press, 1998).

[4]Recent "systematic" works exploring constructive christology, yet needing comparable pneumatological exploration, include Rosemary Radford Ruether, *Sexism and God-Talk: Toward a Feminist Theology* (Boston: Beacon Press, 1983); Susan Brooks Thistlethwaite and Mary Potter Engel, eds., *Lift Every Voice: Constructing Christian Theologies from the Underside* (San Francisco: Harper & Row, 1990); Ann Loades, ed., *Feminist Theology: A Reader* (Louisville, Ky.: Westminster/ John Knox Press, 1990); and Catherine Mowry LaCugna, ed., *Freeing Theology: The Essentials of Theology in Feminist Perspective* (San Francisco: HarperSanFrancisco, 1993).

[5]Elaine Wainwright, "'But Who Do You Say That I Am?'–An Australian Feminist Response," *Pacifica* 10 (June 1997): 156–72.

move in fact introduces a theological shift in women's work from the doctrine of Christ to the doctrine of the Spirit. Providing a fourth response to Daly's initial challenge, turning to the Spirit presents women's theologies with a new horizon for re-imagining human wholeness. Women have not forgotten the Spirit; they have been working hard at forging a place for themselves at the theological hearth.

Beyond Christolatry—A World without Models

Like Chung and her fiery Seventh Assembly address, Mary Daly sparked a religious revolution in 1973 by breaking her silence with *Beyond God the Father*, in which she crossed the threshold from reformer to radical separatist and began "the Be-Dazzling voyage."[6] Reflecting on her new position, this "second Daly" concludes, "a woman struggling for equality in the catholic church or in any christian church, is involved in an inherently contradictory situation. As I now had come to see it, the entire system of myths, symbols, creeds, dogmas of christianity contradicts the idea and the possibility of equality."[7] Within the milieu of women's theological labor, Daly's work presents the pivotal challenge, since for her, feminism and Christianity can only be mutual antagonists.

Un-covering Christianity's patriarchal assumptions, Daly presses the question, How can any Christian vision of salvation be empowering and meaningful for women if Christianity is founded on a dualism of male-as-good and female-as-evil? For Daly, this distorted anthropology first arises when theology casts Eve as the scapegoat for sin and culminates in the symbol of Jesus Christ, the unique God-man who atones for Eve's sin. Embodied exclusively in male form, the doctrine of the Incarnation becomes an ideology that creates false consciousness in women and legitimates the social structures of male power. Daly's simple equation shakes the orthodox house of religious authority—"If God is male, then the male is God."[8]

The equation underwrites Daly's exposure of Orthodox christology as idolatry, or "Christolatry."[9] Idealizing Jesus' maleness over any other attribute of Jesus' personhood—such as his race, his culture, his size and height—enshrines his masculinity within a trinity of male symbolics. Theologies advocating the scandal of particularity, and thus the universalization of human nature in Jesus, refuse to recognize how Jesus' particular sex functions theologically, socially, and ecclesiastically in an entirely different manner than his other particularities. The problem for Christian women "is not that the Jesus of the Gospels was male, young, and a Semite. Rather, the problem lies in the exclusive identification of this person with God, in such a manner that Christian

---

[6]Daly, 71.
[7]Ibid., 173.
[8]Ibid., 19.
[9]Ibid., 69–97.

conceptions of divinity and of the image of God are all objectified in Jesus."[10] The theological outcomes of Christolatry include the repression of female images for divine power of personhood and the distortion of religious under-standings of salvation and human wholeness. Socially, Christolatry legitimizes male dominance and reinforces oppressive structures in family, church, and society.

In the ecclesiastical and liturgical realms, the equation of God and man dictates that only men serve as priests. Any man, regardless of specific qualities, represents the sacrificial body and blood of Jesus in the mass, but no woman can serve. The dividing line is clear. Admonished to imitate the sacrificial love of Jesus—his humility, acceptance of suffering, and obedience—women cannot represent him in the sacramental means of grace. Daly believes this exclusion exists because women's nature is so thoroughly suspect in Christian consciousness. Thus, Daly argues that the victimization of Christian women happens twice—the first way through being made scapegoats for sin, and the second way in constant ritual abnegation, which Daly terms "sado-spirituality."[11] Women need their own flesh and blood in forging new identities and spiritualities.

Ultimately, Jesus fails as a model for women struggling to free themselves from patriarchal structures and false consciousness. Even if women reinter-pret Jesus in feminist terms, his exemplary status continues underwriting both the male monopoly of Christian symbols and the dualistic anthropology. Daly rests her case: A male Savior cannot save women.

> Under the conditions of patriarchy the role of liberating the human race from the original sin of sexism would seem to be precisely the role that a male symbol *cannot* perform. The image itself is one-sided, as far as sexual identity is concerned, and it is precisely on the wrong side, since it fails to counter sexism and functions to glorify maleness.[12]

Yet Daly's charge of Christolatry extends beyond the impossibility of employing the male Christ as a model for women. Criticizing doctrines of incarnation that posit *any* exclusive or complete revelation, Daly believes models for human society, and particularly for women, cannot be drawn from the past or even the present, since women have only begun asking questions and thinking in new ways. Instead, women should create spaces for radical newness and consider this current period a pre-figurative time, in which past models serve only instrumental purposes, not definitive norms.[13] Daly re-minds women that the word *model* derives from the Latin term *modulus,* mean-ing a small measure; that is, "It is necessary to shrink the self in order to imitate a model."[14] In contrast to a shrinking, conformist christology, Daly

---

[10]Ibid., 79.
[11]Mary Daly, *Pure Lust: Elemental Feminist Philosophy* (Boston: Beacon Press, 1984), 33–77.
[12]Daly, *Beyond God the Father*, 72.
[13]Ibid.
[14]Ibid., 75.

envisions a world without models, where women actualize their own full potentials in freedom from past limitations.

The only way Jesus might provide a model for women is in interpreting Jesus as a model-breaker, inviting others not to blind imitation, but to full liberation in their own particular contexts. Daly argues, "The point is not to deny that a revelatory event took place in the encounter with the person Jesus. Rather, it is to affirm that the creative presence of the Verb (Be-ing) can be revealed at every historical moment, in every person and culture."[15] From Daly's radical perspective, true incarnation occurs as the contemporary women's movement moves beyond Christolatry into a greater period of conscious participation in God's living process. Thus, the symbol of the second coming represents not a return of Christ, "but a new arrival of female presence, once strong and powerful, but enchained since the dawn of patriarchy."[16] In this prefigurative stage, women struggle boldly to live in a world without authoritative social and religious models.

Daly's salvific vision entails a separatist women's culture beyond the evil structures of patriarchy, "Be-friending" one another and the natural world.[17] Through Be-friending, women bond across differences, understanding the evils of racism, classism, homophobia, and other social oppressions as fundamental products of the original sin, sexism. Only apart from male culture, the "sado-society," can women spark together toward psychic wholeness.[18]

So what remains of christology after Daly's analysis? For women seeking a nonpatriarchal Christian faith, does Daly's charge of Christolatry mean the end of christology? Is Christian anthropology hopelessly rooted in the original sin of sexism? Must re-imagining human wholeness exclude persons on the basis of the particularity of sex? For many feminists, Daly's critical challenge powerfully presents both liberating and disturbing implications. Her rejection of religious traditions with male-defined deities marks one path of exodus for women seeking nonpatriarchal religious freedom. While some women focus on female images of deity and recover the rituals of ancient Goddess worship or wicca, others respond to Daly's challenge by reinterpreting christology along nonidolatrous lines.[19]

---

[15]Ibid., 71.

[16]Ibid.

[17]Daly, *Pure Lust*, 373–76, 381–86. See also idem, "Be-Friending," in *Weaving the Visions,* 199–207.

[18]Daly, *Pure Lust*, 33.

[19]For resources taking the former path see Starhawk, *The Spiral Dance: A Rebirth of the Ancient Religion of the Great Goddess* (San Francisco: Harper & Row, 1979); Carol P. Christ, *The Laughter of Aphrodite: Reflections on a Journey to the Goddess* (San Francisco: Harper & Row, 1987); Marija Gimbutas, *The Language of the Goddess* (San Francisco: Harper & Row, 1989); Diane Stein, *Casting the Circle: A Woman's Book of Ritual* (Freedom, Calif.: Crossing Press, 1990); and Margot Adler, *Drawing Down the Moon: Witches, Druids, Goddess-worshippers and other Pagans in America Today* (New York: Penguin/Arkana, 1997).

Strategy 1: Re-imaging the Subjectivity of Jesus

The first response to Daly questions her vision of salvation and assumptions about what it means to be human. While many women agree Eve has been scapegoated, they remain unconvinced that women have only been victims and men only perpetrators. This response to Daly grows out of a conviction that the Christian tradition is not a monolithic block of patriarchal thought and practice. Though great predicaments exist, women of faith have not been completely negated or totally distorted within the diversity of church legacies. Claiming a position of prophetic critique found within Christianity, Rosemary Radford Ruether argues, "Our own critique of scripture for failing to live up to its own prophetic promise reflects and is rooted in the self-criticism that goes on in and is basic to biblical faith itself."[20] Thus, regarding the agenda of Christian feminist theology, Anne Carr suggests, "The task is to search for resources within the biblical, theological and intellectual traditions that enable Christian feminist theology to be understood as an intrinsic theological task. The task implies not only a Christian critique of sexist or patriarchal culture but a feminist critique of Christianity."[21]

Responding to Daly's charge, theologians like Ruether and Carr turn women's christological focus from Jesus the unique being—the God-man—to Jesus' own life of action. This move recovers and reinterprets Jesus' life in the world, his relations with other people, and the social structures of his day. Reforming theologians move from doctrine to deeds, from person to praxis. Thus, Christian feminists meet the challenge of doing christology by re-imagining the person and work of Jesus.

For example, Letty Russell reinterprets the biblical language used of Jesus—Lord and Son. Jesus is the Lord, yet he lives out his Lordship as a servant.[22] Jesus is the Son of God, yet Jesus' Father, or *abba*, discloses himself with an entirely different character than patriarchal fathers, and Jesus' kinship with him constitutes a new understanding of family and household.[23] Jesus' personal qualities of mutuality, compassion, and solidarity reflect a model of egalitarian relations; thus, claiming Jesus as Lord means rejecting the model of dominating lordship and following the way of partnership with God and other persons.[24] In this sense, Jesus uniquely embodies true personhood and helps both men and women embrace their full human becoming as partners together in the "household of freedom."[25]

---

[20]Rosemary Radford Ruether, *To Change the World: Christology and Cultural Criticism* (New York: Crossroad, 1983), 5.

[21]Anne Carr, *Transforming Grace: Christian Tradition and Women's Experience* (San Francisco: Harper & Row, 1988), 99.

[22]Letty M. Russell, *Human Liberation in a Feminist Perspective* (Philadelphia: Westminster Press, 1974), 133–42.

[23]Letty M. Russell, *Household of Freedom: Authority in Feminist Theology* (Philadelphia: Westminster Press, 1987), 36–41, 52–54, 82–85.

[24]Russell, *Human Liberation*, 144–45. See also idem, *The Future of Partnership* (Philadelphia: Westminster Press, 1979).

[25]Letty M. Russell, *Becoming Human* (Philadelphia: Westminster Press, 1982), 138. See also idem, *Household of Freedom*, 73–99.

Taking up a similar strategy in re-interpreting the subjectivity of Jesus, Chung Hyun Kyung, Maria Pilar Aquino, and Mercy Amba Oduyoye explore nontraditional metaphors for Jesus–liberator, brother, comrade, shaman, martyr, ancestor, and even grain.[26] In contrast to Daly's rejection, these attempts retain the claim of Jesus as the Christ, yet create new christological meanings reflective of their own cultures and political struggles. Jesus as the Christ no longer excludes, but invites women to join him in the work of partnership, freedom, and human wholeness.

Strategy 2: Re-imaging the Subjectivity of Christ

The second strategy Christian women choose in constructing an inclusive christology distinguishes the person, Jesus, from the Christ-symbol. By focusing on Jesus' praxis, they conclude that anyone following in Jesus' way of life also participates in embodying the Christ. Thus, Jesus becomes necessary to God's divine revelation, but not sufficient or final. Instead, Jesus' praxis sustains the basic paradigm from which a multitude of Christ-subjects ignite. Rosemary Radford Ruether's christology offers a classic example of this second strategy.

In response to the charge of Christolatry, Ruether agrees that christology presents the core problem for women, but she concludes that christology also holds the key to the solution. Rather than reject christological doctrine because of its distorted anthropology, Ruether's reformist plan retrieves christology from patriarchy. She characterizes her aim: "The doctrine of Christ should be the most comprehensive way that Christians express their belief in redemption from all sin and evil in human life, the doctrine that embraces the authentic humanity and fulfilled hopes of all persons."[27]

Liberating the symbol of Christ, Ruether at first highlights the prophetic praxis of Jesus of Nazareth (like the women in the first strategy). Once stripped of masculine divine imagery,

> the Jesus of the synoptic Gospels can be recognized as a figure remarkably compatible with feminism. This is not to say, in an anachronistic sense, that "Jesus was a feminist," but rather that the criticism of religious and social hierarchy characteristic of the early portrait of Jesus is remarkably parallel to feminist criticism.[28]

The particularity of Jesus, as "the embodiment of God's universal new Word," attains significance not because the Word was made flesh in male form, but because this Word concretely lives out a whole new social order not

---

[26]Chung Hyun Kyung, "Who is Jesus for Asian Women?" in *Asian Faces of Jesus*, ed. R. S. Sugirtharajah (Maryknoll, N.Y.: Orbis Books, 1993); Mercy Amba Oduyoye, *Hearing and Knowing: Theological Reflections on Christianity in Africa* (Maryknoll, N.Y.: Orbis Books, 1986), 97–108; Maria Pilar Aquino, *Our Cry for Life: Feminist Theology from Latin America* (Maryknoll, N.Y.: Orbis Books, 1993), 138–49.

[27]Rosemary Radford Ruether, "The Liberation of Christology from Patriarchy," in *Feminist Theology: A Reader*, ed. Ann Loades (Louisville, Ky.: Westminster/John Knox Press, 1990), 138.

[28]Ibid.

founded on gender dualism.[29] In contrast to securing patriarchal Christianity, the symbol of Christ directs theology and Christian communities toward a liberated and liberating humanity.

Thus, in response to the question whether a male Savior saves women, Ruether responds, "Yes!" but with a major clarification. Echoing Daly, Ruether criticizes patriarchal theology's enthronement of the "imperialist Christ" who reigns as *Pantocrator*, Lord of the Cosmos, and secures the reigning status quo of ruling lords over the divinely decreed social order.[30] The imperialist Christ-subject cements sexist society and church institutions by legitimating male power over women and subordinating women's spiritual gifts. But for Ruether, imperialist christology distorts the prophetic biblical tradition. Instead of underwriting male power, Ruether's alternative, the "prophetic-iconoclastic Christ," empties patriarchy of its power.[31] She explains, "In this sense Jesus as the Christ, the representative of liberated humanity and the liberating Word of God, manifests the *kenosis* of patriarchy, the announcement of the new humanity through a lifestyle that discards hierarchical caste privilege and speaks on behalf of the lowly."[32] In solidarity with the marginalized, the prophetic-iconoclastic Christ reverses the social order of privilege—the first shall be last and the last first (Mt. 19:30; 20:16). But more than turning upside-down the present hierarchy, the praxis of the prophetic-iconoclastic Christ manifests a new order "where hierarchy itself is overcome as a principle of rule."[33] Within the new order, Christ liberates women, "the oppressed of the oppressed...for the new humanity of service and mutual empowerment."[34] Once liberated, women in turn freely liberate others, making salvation entail the full, authentic humanity of women. While Daly's vision involves living beyond models, from Ruether's perspective, Jesus can be a Savior for women because he models the prophetic way of being in the world.

Women who challenge social privilege and identify with the marginalized extend the embodiment of Jesus' liberating praxis. In Ruether's christological reconstruction, Christ includes Jesus, but "is not...encapsulated 'once-for-all' in the historical Jesus."[35] Contrary to the first strategy, Christ may be represented or modeled by persons other than Jesus, for "each Christian must take up this same way, and in so doing, become Christ to one another."[36] Ruether's Christ becomes a universal symbol, inclusive of women and men embodying "Christic personhood" and contributing to the needs of human and cosmic

---

[29]Ruether, "The Liberation of Christology from Patriarchy," 147.

[30]Ruether, *To Change the World*, 48–49.

[31]Ibid., 53–56.

[32]Ruether, *Sexism and God-Talk*, 137.

[33]Ruether, *To Change the World*, 53.

[34]Ibid., 55, 56.

[35]Ruether, *Sexism and God-Talk*, 138.

[36]Rosemary Radford Ruether, "Can Christology Be Liberated from Patriarchy?" in *Reconstructing the Christ Symbol: Essays in Feminist Christology*, ed. Maryanne Stevens (New York: Paulist Press, 1993), 24.

liberation.[37] While not necessarily male, Christ may be encountered "in the form of our sister," as the martyr Blandina in the *Acts of the Martyrs of Lyons and Vienne*.[38] In place of patriarchal Christianity's imperialist and exclusively male Christ, Ruether envisions a "WomanChrist," present through the herstory of Christian sisters, but also "ever projected on the new horizon of history that appears before us, leading us on to our yet unrealized potential."[39]

By distinguishing between Jesus the Christ and Christ the new redeemed humanity historically present in Jesus and others, Ruether opens the door for creative feminist thinking. But women have also challenged Ruether's anthropological assumptions, leading to questions about her own vision of salvation. How can feminist theology speak of a universal sisterhood without acknowledging women's differences and the historical alienation between women?[40] Does the WomanChrist represent an essentialist norm for female humanity that includes some and excludes others? Ruether anticipates this criticism. Her reformist methodology clears the way for a continuation of re-imagined Christ-subjects drawn from the diversity of women's contexts.

> As our perception of our incompleteness changes with new sensitivities to racism, sexism and European chauvinisms, must not the image of Christ take ever new forms: as woman, as Black and Brown woman, as impoverished and despised woman of those peoples who are the underside of Christian imperialism?[41]

Retrieving the biblical prophetic tradition enables Ruether to criticize exclusive, imperialist interpretations of Christ and redirect christology toward the humanity of marginalized persons.

The Christological Challenges of Darker Sisters

Women of color challenge white feminism's generalizing language concerning women's experience and God-talk. According to classic feminist analysis, women share the common problem of sexism in churches and other social institutions. Jacquelyn Grant counters that feminism, originally a constructive enterprise of white, middle-class women, naively assumes a sisterhood in which black women supposedly have more in common with white women than with black men. From a womanist standpoint, feminism's singular concern with gender overlooks the problems of racism and classism within black women's "tri-dimensional experience."[42] Grant's North American

---

[37]Ibid.

[38]Ruether, "The Liberation of Christology from Patriarchy," 148. See also idem, *Sexism and God-Talk*, 131–38.

[39]Rosemary Radford Ruether, *Womanguides: Readings Toward a Feminist Theology* (Boston: Beacon Press, 1985), 112.

[40]See Ellen Armour, *Deconstruction, Feminist Theology and the Problem of Difference* (Chicago: University of Chicago Press, 1999).

[41]Ruether, *Womanguides*, 112–13.

[42]Jacquelyn Grant, *White Women's Christ and Black Women's Jesus: Feminist Christology and Womanist Response* (Atlanta: Scholars Press, 1989), 209.

analysis parallels Anne Pattel-Gray's critique of the Australian feminist movement that Aboriginal and Western women are "not yet *Tiddas*" (sisters).[43] Grant raises her vital challenge to feminists such as Daly and Ruether:

> To misname themselves as "feminists" who appeal to "women's experience" is to do what oppressors always do; it is to define the rules and then solicit others to play the game. It is to presume a commonality with oppressed women that oppressed women themselves do not share. They have simply accepted and participated in the racism of the larger American society when they have done so.[44]

Thus Grant offers "the challenge of the darker sister" and asks whether Ruether's Christ in the form of one's sister obscures and distorts the oppressive realities of feminism's darker sisters.[45]

Grant contends that white women's preoccupation with Christ as distinct from Jesus too easily lets white women abstract from Jesus' praxis and focus exclusively on their own needs and sufferings. Feminist christologies preoccupy themselves with how women have been classified *other* to the exclusion of feminists' comparable participation in the oppression of other women.[46] In constructing a womanist christology, Grant turns from the potentially abstract Christ symbol back to Jesus of Nazareth and his radical identification with the least of these (Mt. 25:31–46) and the poorest of the poor (Lk. 6:20). Just as the spiritual cries "nobody knows but Jesus," so within the context of black women's history, Jesus stands as "the divine co-sufferer" empowering black women in situations of oppression. Grant sets forth womanist solidarity with Jesus, "As Jesus was persecuted and made to suffer undeservedly, so were they. His suffering culminated in the crucifixion. Their crucifixion included rape, and babies being sold."[47] Resurrected from death, Jesus affirms the humanity and struggles of the very least of black women creating hope that their tri-dimensional suffering (race, class, and gender) is not the last word.

Just as womanist foremothers Jarena Lee and Sojourner Truth knew they imaged the whole redemptive humanity of Jesus Christ, black women today find in Jesus an affirming and empowering humanity for their own liberating praxis. Grant draws on James Cone's "Black Christ" in situating Jesus' relation with African Americans as a particular oppressed people.[48] But while Grant shares Cone's belief that the particularity of the black Christ validates

---

[43]Anne Pattel-Gray, "Not Yet Tiddas: An Aboriginal Womanist Critique of Australian Church Feminism," in *Freedom and Entrapment: Women Thinking Theology,* ed. Maryanne Confoy, Dorothy A. Lee, and Joan Nowotny (Melbourne: Dove, 1995), 165–92.

[44]Grant, 200.

[45]Ibid., 177–230.

[46]For a self-critical analysis of feminist theology and the difference race makes see Susan Thistlethwaite, *Sex, Race and God: Christian Feminism in Black and White* (New York: Crossroad, 1989), particularly her critical christological reflections on Jesus and Christa, 92–108.

[47]Grant, 212.

[48]James H. Cone, *God of the Oppressed* (San Francisco: Harper & Row, 1975).

its universal inclusion of oppression, she critically extends black liberation theology in identifying Jesus with black women, "the particular within the particular."[49]

> God becomes concrete not only in the man Jesus, for he was cruci-fied, but in the lives of those who will accept the challenges of the risen Savior–the Christ. For Lee, this meant that women could preach; for Sojourner Truth, it meant that women could possibly save the world; for me, it means that today, this Christ found in the experi-ence of Black women, is a Black woman.[50]

Jesus' experience so completely identifies with black women's cruciform ex-periences that Jesus Christ is in fact today a black woman.

Womanist Kelly Brown Douglas affirms Grant's starting point of black women's experience for christology, but questions Brown's shift from the black Christ to the black woman Christ. Instead of a tri-dimensional analysis (race, class, and gender) of black women's oppression, Brown argues for a "multi-dimensional and bi-focal analysis that confronts all that oppresses the Black community as it impinges upon the community or is harbored within."[51] Brown includes the ways black women contribute to death and destruction through their own oppressiveness, for example, in relation to black gays and lesbians. For Brown, a womanist black Christ may be seen in the faces of both black women and men who struggle for wholeness of the entire black community.

Together, Grant and Brown raise the challenge of dark sisters in con-fronting the abstractions of patriarchal and feminist christologies. The whole-ness of redemptive humanity incarnated in Jesus Christ and those with whom he identifies demands that contemporary christology include the subjectification of people most dehumanized by white domination. Grant explains:

> At last! Black women are indeed becoming subjects. More and more they are resisting the objectification by those whose histories and herstories continue to render them invisible. And so to the question, "Who do you say that I am?" Black women say that you are the one who is with us and among us in our community as we struggle for survival. You are the one who not only is with us, but you are one of us.[52]

Grant's christological methodology encourages the constructive efforts of women from diverse cultural contexts. As dark sisters voice their own

---

[49]Grant, 216.

[50]Ibid., 220.

[51]Kelly Brown Douglas, *The Black Christ* (Maryknoll, N.Y.: Orbis Books, 1994), 109.

[52]Jacquelyn Grant, "Subjectification as a Requirement for Christological Construction," in *Lift Every Voice*, 213. See also Delores S. Williams, "Black Women's Surrogacy Experience and the Christian Notion of Redemption," in *After Patriarchy: Feminist Transformations of the World Reli-gions*, ed. Paula M. Cooey et al. (Maryknoll, N.Y.: Orbis Books, 1991), 1–14.

subjectification from quite different social locations, a multiplicity of re-imagined Christ-subjects emerges. Speaking from her African Akan culture, Mercy Amba Oduyoye narrates the story of Christ in the form of her foremother, Eku, who found water, drank deeply, and saved her people during the drought.[53] The experiences of African women in birth, motherhood, and the struggle for life reflect Jesus' own ministry in birthing new communities of faith, mothering those without hope, and sacrificing for the wholeness of all people.[54] From the context of Chinese women, Kwok Pui-Lan finds an identity between her context and the suffering of Jesus:

> It is the very person on the cross that suffers like us, was rendered a no-body, who illuminates our tragic human existence and speaks to countless women in Asia. We are not looking to Jesus as a mere example to follow, neither shall we try to idolize him. We see Jesus as the God who takes human form and suffers and weeps with us.[55]

Centering on God's empathetic relation to humanity in Jesus, Kwok re-imagines Jesus as "the suffering, struggling people of Asia" and in particular "the broken body of women who refuse principalities and powers."[56] Likewise speaking from "an epistemology of the broken body," Korean theologian Chung Hyun Kyung re-imagines Jesus as a weeping Asian mother.[57] Joining these images, Nellie Ritchie writes from the perspective of Latin American women, "We meet Jesus in the midst of pain, the struggle, the strength and the hope of those—victims of injustice—who devote themselves to the cause of justice."[58]

Through the hermeneutical privilege of the least of these, Grant's black woman Christ sparks together for social transformation with the Christ-figures of dark sisters from other cultural contexts of oppression. While Jesus remains normative, each Christ-subject represents "a local theology" in which women's experiences and cultures contribute to the re-imagining process.[59]

---

[53]Mercy Amba Oduyoye, "The Christ for African Women," in *With Passion and Compassion: Third World Women Doing Theology*, ed. Virginia Fabella and Mercy Amba Oduyoye (Maryknoll, N.Y.: Orbis Books, 1988), 35–36.

[54]Mercy Amba Oduyoye, "Birth," in *New Eyes for Reading: Biblical and Theological Reflections by Women from the Third World*, ed. John S. Pobee and Barbel von Wartenberg-Potter (Geneva: World Council of Churches, 1986), 41–44.

[55]Kwok Pui-Lan, "God Weeps with Our Pain," in *New Eyes for Reading*, 92.

[56]Kwok Pui-Lan, "Re-imaging Jesus," paper presented at RE-Imagining: Ecumenical Decade–Churches in Solidarity with Women Conference (Minneapolis, Minn., November 4–7, 1993).

[57]Chung Hyun Kyung, *Struggle to Be the Sun Again: Introducing Asian Women's Theology* (Maryknoll, N.Y.: Orbis Books, 1990), 104.

[58]Nellie Ritchie, "Women and Christology," in *Through Her Eyes: Women's Theology from Latin America*, ed. Elsa Tamez (Maryknoll, N.Y.: Orbis Books, 1989), 94.

[59]Robert J. Schreiter, *Constructing Local Theologies* (Maryknoll, N.Y.: Orbis Books, 1986), 1–20. See also Ada Maria Isasi-Diaz and Yolanda Tarango, *Hispanic Women: Prophetic Voice in the Church* (San Francisco: Harper & Row, 1988), 60–76, 94–113; and *The Will to Arise: Women, Tradition, and the Church in Africa*, ed. Mercy Amba Oduyoye and Musimbi R. A. Kanyoro (Maryknoll, N.Y.: Orbis Books, 1992).

In response to Daly's challenge of Christolatry, Christian women from diverse cultural contexts conceive anew the subjectivity of Christ in ways significant for their own religious subjectification. Created in the image of God, the least of these assert their own inclusion in the redeemed humanity of Jesus Christ. For today, the experiences of feminists, womanists, and other dark sisters constitute analogies between Jesus' struggle for abundant life and their own, so much so that the second strategy of constructing a viable christology re-centers Christ in the subjectivity of one's sisters.

Strategy 3: An Intersubjective Christa/Community

A third position emerges in response to Daly's original challenge providing a generous, yet critical, view of the preceding christologies of subjectivity. In her book *Journeys by Heart*, Rita Nakashima Brock takes up the common question, How should Christian theology image human wholeness?[60] What are the assumptions about humanity underlying our christologies and soteriologies? By focusing on Jesus as an individual (in fact, on any particular Christ-subject), Brock claims christology loses sight of the relational constitution of human beings. Therefore, Brock responds to Daly by shifting christological frameworks from a *subjective* view of human beings to an *intersubjective* portrait. In Brock's estimation, christology, both feminist and otherwise, has not seriously considered the relational humanity of Jesus, for if Jesus was truly a human being, then Jesus too was a self-in-relation.

The previous christologies of subjectivity would claim they take into account, even radically affirm, Jesus as a relational person. Jesus' theo-ethic incorporates relating to others in mutual, nonoppressive patterns. But Brock counters that the theological focus of feminist and womanist christologies still centers on *Jesus* as a *relational person*, not on the *relationships* themselves, inclusive of the persons. Forging her christology on relationality as the site of divine presence and power, Brock argues that no single person reveals the Christ. Instead, the symbol of Christa/Community conveys an alternative to the individualistic and inevitably masculine symbol, Christ.

Reclaiming *eros*, the relationship-seeking desire in the heart of persons, Brock contrasts her "christology of erotic power" with Ruether's prophetic-iconoclastic Christ.[61] Ruether's Christ presents a heroic individual, involving others in a liberating praxis, but still as a singularly redemptive individual who maintains a privileged relationship with God. As the Christ, Jesus initiates the liberating engagement, which inspires others and invites them to participate. But Brock explains the problem with positing Jesus as sole Liberator:

---

[60]Rita Nakashima Brock, *Journeys by Heart: A Christology of Erotic Power* (New York: Crossroad, 1988).
[61]Ibid.

As liberated man, [Jesus] liberates and empowers others. The oppressed function in Ruether's scheme as victims to be acted upon. The world is not described as constitutive of Jesus' personal awareness of God or as a source of his power. Jesus is the hero and liberator. While Ruether claims the redeemer is also redeemed, she gives no evidence for how, since only the liberated can liberate.[62]

Though not imperialistic, the linear flow of power through Jesus is insufficient for collective human healing. Ruether's christology still languishes in a "heroic, unilateral model," which perpetrates patriarchal values such as hierarchy, superiority, and passive dependency.[63] The iconoclastic Christ confronts patriarchal valuation and structures, but

> missing from Ruether's position is the crucial presence of members of Jesus' community as embodying God/dess and having a transforming impact on him. Without alternative relationships, the iconoclastic shattering of power-over is also the fragmentation of self. We require relationships that support us to develop the play space that can see through destructive powers, even our own.[64]

Transformation of self and other occurs through a community of mutual support, according to Brock. The model of the prophetic-iconoclastic Christ leaves Jesus at the center and privileges individualistic selfhood over the profound reality of relationality.

If Christianity offers an effective vision of salvation for women and men, relationship and community must become "the whole-making, healing center of Christianity."[65] Inevitably, in shifting from Christ to Christa/Community, Brock re-imagines Jesus as a participant in community, since "Jesus was cocreated by his world, as we are by ours."[66] Jesus grew up in relation, intimately involved with others in his culture, with a mother, father, siblings, extended family, and friends. Seeing through the heroics of Jesus' human development, Brock explains, "If Jesus was reported to have been capable of profound love and concern for others, he was first loved and respected by the concrete persons of his life. If he was liberated, he was involved in a community of mutual liberation."[67] Jesus' return to Capernaum for support, his visits in the homes of friends, and the stories of women traveling with Jesus in ministry and standing by him in his death provide clues for Christa/Community and its heart of erotic power. For Brock, Jesus participates centrally in the Christa/Community, but he neither brings erotic power into being nor controls it:

---

[62]Ibid., 65.
[63]Ibid.
[64]Ibid., 66.
[65]Ibid., 52.
[66]Ibid., 63.
[67]Ibid., 66.

Christa/Community is a lived reality expressed in relational images. Hence Christa/Community is described in the images of events in which erotic power is made manifest. The reality of erotic power within connectedness means it cannot be located in a single individual. *Hence what is truly christological, that is, truly revealing of divine incarnation and salvific power in human life, must reside in connectedness and not in a single individual.* The relational nature of erotic power is as true during Jesus' life as it is after his death. He neither reveals it nor embodies it, but he participates in its revelation and embodiment.[68]

Through the symbol of Christa/Community, Brock takes seriously the humanity of Jesus as a self-in-relation. Heroic, unilateral models present divine presence and power in one privileged subject who then becomes universal and representative for all. But universalization renders the diverse and fleshly embodiments of human beings as inessential and secondary to their abstract inclusion in Jesus as the Christ. Ruether's concept of Christic personhood draws on abstract notions of unity and wholeness. While the symbol of Christ extends to include sisters (and brothers) beyond Jesus, Jesus' new humanity arises from a non(human)relational paradigm. Jesus receives his liberated humanity in relation to God and then shares it with others. With heroic christologies, incarnational unity becomes detached from an understanding of wholeness in relation, where each person influences and affects the others. Brock's vision of human wholeness seeks greater and greater interconnections between people by claiming as essential the embodied particulars of human diversity.

From Brock's point of view, marginalization, subordination, and abuse of the other results from the absence of an embodied, intersubjective understanding of wholeness. Thus, women's christologies receive the responses of WomanChrist, Christ in the form of one's sister, black woman Christ, Mother Eku, weeping Asian woman Christ, and others as efforts to remember the overlooked dignity of women and value people in the image of God. These responses, born of suffering, must not be trivialized or passed through quickly on the way to new theologies. Brock claims her feminist work in fact depends on the dislocation of androcentric and Euro-centric incarnational symbols accomplished by the interplay of Christ-subjects. But Brock makes a decisive challenge: "I believe the individualizing of Christ misplaces the locus of incarnation and redemption. We must find the revelatory and saving events of Christianity in a larger reality than Jesus and his relationship to God/dess or any subsequent individual Christ."[69] Any image of healing or salvation must be communal, for wholeness involves the irreducible, overflowing lives of selves-in-relation. Christa/Community incorporates the connectedness of particulars, not the eradication of difference in the march toward an abstract, universal essence. Brock moves the center of Christian faith from unity in

---

[68]Ibid., 52. Emphasis added.
[69]Ibid., 68.

Christ to unity in Christa/Community. The revelatory and redemptive witness of God's work in history lies not with the individual, but within the relational ebb and flow of community life.

Strategy 4: From Women's Christologies to Women's Pneumatologies

In light of the trajectory from subjectivity to intersubjectivity in women's christologies, a fourth response meets Daly's challenge. Reviewing women's work, specific categories stoke the fire of transformation–relation, mutuality, dignity, embodiment, *eros*, diversity, interconnection, justice, compassion, healing, and community. Taken together, these qualities comprise unique features of intersubjective life and thus lead us in a *pneumatological* direction. Within women's contextual christologies lies a trajectory moving from the second Person of the Trinity to the third Person. The movement does not mean forgetting, marginalizing, or negating Jesus, but instead focuses women's imagination and passion in a direction that situates Jesus within the paradigm of intersubjectivity, or what Carter Heyward classically asserts, "mutual relation."[70] While not separate from individuality, the character of relationality sublates heroic, singular notions of incarnation and presses theology for an incarnational doctrine of the Spirit. Heyward describes the spiritual interconnectedness between our selves and others:

> Relation is where it all begins, life and love and work and pleasure and pain–our selves. As Buber wrote, "In the beginning is the relation." We come into this world connected, related, to one another–by blood and tissue, history, memory, culture, faith, joy, passion, violence, pain and struggle. The lines of continuity between and among us are visible/invisible, sturdy/fragile, inviting/frightening, delightful/sad, occasions for celebration/remorse, depending on which connections we know best, or seek, or acknowledge or explore.[71]

From this relational context of human genesis-in-the-world, Heyward goes on to identify the Spirit of God as "creative womanpower," present and passionate in relations of self and other.[72] Mutuality, interdependency, personhood-in-process, co-redemption, freedom in community–these relational qualities of life prompt turning to the Spirit in women's theologies. A fourth response to Daly involves moving from women's christologies to women's pneumatologies.

---

[70]Carter Heyward, *The Redemption of God: A Theology of Mutual Relation* (Washington, D.C.: University Press of America, 1982).

[71]Carter Heyward, *Touching Our Strength: The Erotic as Power and the Love of God* (San Francisco: Harper & Row, 1989), 192. Martin Buber's quote is from *I and Thou*, trans. Walter Kaufman (New York: Charles Scribner's Sons, 1970), 69. For Heyward's christological reflections, see *Speaking of Christ: A Lesbian Feminist Voice*, ed. Ellen C. Davis (New York: Pilgrim Press, 1989).

[72]Heyward, *Touching Our Strength*, 103.

Yet because of her primary interest in de-centering the individualistic and sexist foundations of the Christ-symbol, Brock retains christological language in her new symbol, Christa/Community. The argument of this chapter, though, claims Brock's work can also be interpreted as an *erotic pneumatology*. The profound relational sensibility in her theology (thealogy?) implies a doctrine of the Spirit, which from the beginning (as we have seen in previous chapters) developed within a social framework of Christian theology. Brock, however, draws on Daly's language of the "Unholy Trinity" to criticize the traditional familial metaphors for the divine persons.[73] In *Beyond God the Father*, Daly links together the Unholy Trinity of "Rape, Genocide, and War" with the "Unwhole Trinitarian symbol of Christianity," which Daly names the "Father, Son, and *Unholy* Ghost."[74] Both Trinities are "demonic," for they generate a "circle of destruction" and alienation for women.[75] While Daly concedes that the Spirit presents a potentially liberating symbol, the third Person of the Trinity in general receives her criticism as a violent and oppressive ghost.

Daly's attitude toward the Spirit continues in Brock's assessment of patriarchal Trinitarian relations. But while both feminists name appropriate theological limitations, neither recognizes the doctrine of Spirit as a positive inspiration for theological reconstruction. Daly and Brock agree that the Spirit represents the patriarchal extension of the Father and the Son. For Brock, this ghost perpetuates women's silence and maintains belief in the polluted, inferior nature of women's bodies. The dualism of spirit and body in Christian legacies further reinforces an anti-incarnational bias in the symbol of Spirit. She concludes, "This ghost has been used to protect the past at the expense of the liberation of real people in the present."[76] Joining Daly, Brock decides the symbol of Spirit conjures a disembodied ghost who haunts women's struggles for freedom by illegitimatizing their experiences and gifts. Brock opts for re-imagining christology instead.

But Spirit needs re-imagining as well. The symbol of Spirit holds forth a rich legacy from Christian tradition. Translated as masculine (Latin, *spiritus*), feminine (Hebrew, *ruach*), and neuter (Greek, *pneuma*) in different languages, Spirit enables theology to move beyond one exclusive gender for God. The connection with *ruach* reclaims creation, breath, and embodied spirit-traditions, as Rebecca Button Prichard discovers in a feminist pneumatology of the senses.[77] But Spirit also incorporates the transformed life symbolized by fire. A social reality of diversity-in-unity, Spirit moves and dances, sings, celebrates, and struggles unlike any fixed or static essence. From a womanist perspective of loving the Spirit, Karen Baker-Fletcher reminds us that we, like Jesus, are

---

[73]Brock, xii–xiii.

[74]Daly, *Beyond God the Father*, 114–22.

[75]Ibid., 122.

[76]Brock, xiii.

[77]Rebecca Button Prichard, *Sensing the Spirit: The Holy Spirit in Feminist Perspective* (St. Louis: Chalice Press, 1999).

people of "dust and Spirit," who may be moved, touched, invigorated, and filled by the Spirit in and through our hopeful, ordinary, life-sustaining relations with one another and the world around us.[78] Daly and Brock point out theological errors past and present, using Spirit to justify the discipline, dismissal, and silence of others.[79] But as women have applied their reconstructive labors to christology, so should they take up the work of re-imagining Spirit. The unholy ghost needs the breath and sparks of new inspirations.

Up to this point, a trajectory of responses to Daly's initial separatist challenge can be seen in women's christologies moving from subjective to intersubjective paradigms. From a breadth of diverse contexts, women challenge incarnational symbols toward encompassing their particular struggles and identities. Feminist, womanist, Asian, African, Latin American (and more) women no longer take for granted the assumptions of inclusion in a universalized Christ. But must contextual women theologians remain in the discourse of christology for incarnational symbols of human dignity, right-relation, and transformation? The priority of relation in women's theologies suggests that the move from women's christologies to women's pneumatologies offers rich and vital opportunities for re-imagining the entire Triune project. Women have not forgotten the Spirit; they have been taking care of the business that any turn to the Spirit in contemporary theology now must address.

We Who Are in the Midst of Struggle

As already intimated, women are turning to the Spirit for innovative spiritual and doctrinal expression. This final section examines the work of Elizabeth Johnson, whose pneumatological turn resources an entire Trinitarian formulation. But before she turns to the Spirit in *She Who Is,* Johnson reclaims the wisdom tradition of Hebrew and Christian scriptures (and their trajectories) as a biblical context for speaking of female images for God.[80] The underlying premise of Johnson's work assumes that women are created in the image of God, thus necessitating female metaphors and symbols for the full disclosure of God's mystery. In the Hebrew Scriptures, *Sophia,* or personified Wisdom in female form, accomplishes the same deeds as the God of Moses, Yahweh. Because of this "functional equivalence," Sophia personifies God's own being in creative and saving involvement with the world.[81] The image and economy of Sophia provides the key hermeneutic for re-figuring the Christian Trinity. She explains the connection: "To say that Sophia is the fashioner of all things,

---

[78]Karen Baker-Fletcher, *Sisters of Dust, Sisters of Spirit: Womanist Wordings on God and Creation* (Minneapolis: Fortress Press, 1998), 15–20.

[79]Consider the controversy surrounding Chung Hyun Kyung in regard to pneumatological authority, chapter 1. We can also remember the controversy surrounding the November 1993 RE-Imagining Conference in Minneapolis. Some women who attended the conference were later harassed and had their jobs threatened. One conference organizer and Presbyterian church leader, Mary Ann Lundy, was forced to resign her position after the outrage in her denomination.

[80]Johnson, 76–103.

[81]Ibid., 91.

that she delivered Israel from a nation of oppressors, or that her gifts are justice and life is to speak of the transcendent God's relation to the world, of God's nearness, activity and summons."[82]

Johnson then turns to the Spirit, like Moltmann, in challenging Christian theology's pneumatological forgetfulness. She makes the astute observation that perhaps theology has easily forgotten the Spirit because of the connection between the idea of the Spirit and the roles and persons of women in church and society:

> We realize that in the Bible the Spirit's work includes bringing forth and nurturing life, holding all things together, and constantly renewing what the ravages of time and sin break down. This is surely analogous to traditional "women's work," which goes on continuously in home, church, and countless social groupings, holding all things together, cleaning what has been messed up, while seldom if ever noticed and hence anonymous. Neglect of the Spirit and the marginalizing of women have a symbolic affinity and may well go hand in hand.[83]

In overcoming theology's forgetfulness, Johnson turns to the Spirit, but her feminist standpoint begins with reflection of Spirit-Sophia and the transfigured women's work of creating, fashioning, delivering, and sanctifying a world. Initially, the association of Spirit with Sophia helps Johnson overcome problems other pneumatologies encounter when importing a female element into the Godhead through the figure of the Spirit. When Trinitarian theology retains the traditional language and order of Father and Son, the Spirit alone as Mother (or other female personification) reinforces gender dualisms and maintains the subordination of the Spirit to the other two male figures.[84] But as Spirit-Sophia joins Jesus-Sophia and Mother-Sophia, Johnson re-figures a gestalt of the Trinity in full female form.

For Johnson, Spirit-Sophia is the creator and giver of life; thus, "life itself with all its complexities, abundance, threat, misery, and joy becomes a primary mediation of the dialectic of presence and absence of divine mystery. The historical world becomes a sacrament of divine presence and activity."[85] Thus, Spirit-Sophia functions as the primary figure of God's "creating, indwelling, sustaining, resisting, recreating, challenging, guiding, liberating,

---

[82]Ibid.

[83]Ibid., 130–31.

[84]In introducing female imagery for God, some theologians re-figure the Holy Spirit as Mother. See Jürgen Moltmann, *The Spirit of Life: A Universal Affirmation* (Minneapolis: Fortress Press, 1992), 157–60; and Donald Gelpi, *The Divine Mother: A Trinitarian Theology of the Holy Spirit* (Lanham, Md.: University Press of America, 1984). But Johnson contends that with a feminized Holy Spirit, "we end up with two clear masculine images and an amorphous feminine third…The equation is thus set up: male is to female as transcendence is to immanence, with the feminine Spirit restricted to the role of bearing the presence of God to our interiority…There is real danger that simply identifying the Spirit with 'feminine' reality leaves the overall symbol of God fundamentally unreformed and boxes actual women into a stereotypical ideal" (50–51).

[85]Johnson, 124.

[and] completing" presence experienced by humans in relation to the natural world, each other, and the complex social systems we live within.[86] From the Western theological tradition, Johnson retrieves the image of Spirit as "the power of mutual love proceeding."[87] But she redirects this tradition through the feminist metaphor of friendship experienced in women's relations with friends, sisters, mothers, and grandmothers. Through these relational analogies Johnson suggests,

> Spirit-Sophia is the living God at her closest to the world, pervading the whole and each creature to awaken life and mutual kinship. Not existence over and against but with and for, not domination but mutual love emerges as the highest value as the Spirit of God dwells within and around the world with all its fragility, chaos, tragedy, fertility, and beauty.[88]

For Johnson, the turn to pneumatology in connection with the Wisdom tradition provides the opportunity to speak of God's freeing and individualizing, yet whole-making and connecting love through female imagery. Retrieving Spirit language, with its norm of mutual love, lifts up the intrinsically relational nature of God. Spirit-Sophia relates to all of life's diverse beings in a worldly shape of kinship.

In her Trinitarian reconstruction, Johnson moves from Spirit-Sophia to the figures of Jesus-Sophia (the incarnate Christ or Wisdom) and Mother-Sophia (unoriginate source of the universe). Together, these three figures present the mystery of divine relation known collectively as mutuality, radical equality, and community in diversity.[89] Johnson argues that the Eastern and Western traditions stressed these relational qualities for the Triune God, but patriarchal models undermined them. Leaders in social and ecclesiastical structures also rejected these qualities as their own norms. Again, like Moltmann, Johnson seeks a direct connection between re-figured Trinitarian symbols and social, political, and ecclesiastical structures. Yet these figures do not represent persons as such, but "the religious experience of being met in this diversity of saving ways."[90] Johnson explains what begins to sound like a modalistic view of God:

> As we trace the vivifying ways of the Spirit, the compassionate, liberating story of Jesus-Sophia, and the generative mystery of the Creator Mother, it becomes clear that the Christian experience of the one God is multifaceted…Sophia-God is beyond, with, and within the world; behind, with and ahead of us; above, alongside, and around us…Shaped by this encounter, thought discerns a distinct kind of monotheism: the one God enjoys a trinitarian existence.[91]

---

[86]Ibid., 133.
[87]Ibid., 143.
[88]Ibid., 147.
[89]Ibid., 216–22.
[90]Ibid., 191.
[91]Ibid.

Because the social analogy of the Trinity provides human beings with the "highest ideal" for humanity, female form can represent the Triune community and women finally claim their full places as *imago Dei* within Sophia-God's economy.[92] Ultimately, Sophia-God is "SHE WHO IS," disclosed as "sheer, exuberant, relational aliveness in the midst of the history of suffering."[93]

Johnson's turn to pneumatology as the starting point for Trinitarian reflection de-centers the rigid and hierarchical ordering of the traditional line-up, Father, Son, and Holy Spirit, which ultimately results in a domesticated and subordinated third place for God the Spirit. Spirit-Sophia further de-centers the exclusive masculine imagery normed for the third Person and, as in Heyward's theology, moves feminist theological discourse in the direction of mutual and equal relations. But Johnson's association of Spirit with Sophia shifts pneumatological discourse from an intersubjective paradigm back to a subjective one. Sophia represents personified Wisdom in female form—an individual woman form. Thus, the We of relationality, which we saw as the telos of mutual recognition and of women's christological labor, becomes reduced to a divine being, She. The multi-gifted gestalt of communal presence, which Johnson originally affirms, becomes unfortunately undermined by the individual symbol, Sophia, even though construed in three different ways of divine encounter. Brock's criticism of liberal feminism applies here—Johnson focuses on Spirit, Jesus, and Mother as relational persons, rather than on relationships themselves, inclusive of the persons.

For new paradigms in women's pneumatologies (and women's Trinitarian theologies), we can value Johnson's turn to the Spirit but retain the social sensibility discovered in *We who are*. Primacy of the intersubjective We does not represent a move to polytheism or a form of New Age gnosticism, but more firmly roots communities in the heart of relational Trinitarian process. Pneumatology becomes the key for sustaining the mystery of the Triune community within the social, interdependent life of this world. Women are created in the image of God, not individually as an image of *She who is*, but collectively as a *We* who together participate in divine creativity and sanctifying labor. For new pneumatologies, the diverse wholeness of the human community serves to image the divine We.

But Johnson's work highlights a further need in women's (and men's) pneumatologies. The mutuality, equality, and diversity of the Sophia-God presents a prophetic ideal in criticism of any human economy of domination, but the question surfaces about how we move toward the ideal from where we stand today. Can this ideal become actual, or is it just an eschatological hope? Can human beings, mired in complex relations of power, struggle toward relations of mutual power and recognition from their asymmetric relations of power-over and distorted recognition? As long as theology merely idealizes

---

[92]Ibid., 208.

[93]Ibid., 241–43. Johnson plays on Exodus 3:14, where Moses receives the sacred and mysterious name of God, "I am who I am," or "I will be who I will be," preserved in the unspeakable tetragrammaton, YHWH.

the telos of struggle, and not the struggle itself, we undermine our efforts toward the ideal. New paradigms in pneumatology must affirm and incorporate the hard work of struggle against domination and toward mutuality. Expressing not only mutuality, equality, and diversity, feminist pneumatological discourse presents additional "fruit of the Spirit" (Gal. 5:22–23) necessary for our diverse struggles. The presence and power of God the Spirit requires re-imagining for *We who are in the midst of struggle.*

From subjective to intersubjective strategies, women's christologies have responded to Mary Daly's critical equation–if God is male, then male is God. Christian women distinguish between the inclusive, liberating humanity of Jesus with others and the imperialistic, oppressive and heroic Christ of patriarchal and kyriocentric constructions. Identifying with the brokenhearted least of these, Christ becomes transfigured into the Christa/Community, incarnated in healing and whole-making relationships. But the move to intersubjectivity sparks the way for inspiration of new pneumatologies. In women's contextual theologies, Spirit needs remembering as well. Associated with the embodied breath and the transforming fire, Spirit incorporates "all flesh" in the dance of divine participation.[94] But is this too unattainable an ideal? What about the hard struggle for mutual recognition within distorted relations of power? In the next chapter, returning to a feminist maternal standpoint provides insight into the two concerns raised in connection with Johnson's pneumatology–Spirit as an intersubjective reality of mutual recognition and Spirit as the sustenance of the struggle for life.

---

[94]Dorothy Lee, "Women, the Flesh and the Johannine Jesus," unpublished paper used with permission. Lee claims the prologue in John does not support the concept of a God-man. The focus of the text is on the Word becoming flesh, inclusive of Jesus, women, and men, and arguably with all created beings. She writes, "In the end, 'flesh' signifies far more than the male bodily existence of the historical Jesus. It points to the ongoing presence of the risen Christ with the community in its sacramental life, through the life-giving work of the Spirit-Paraclete" (11).

CHAPTER 9

A Feminist Maternal Spirit
of Mutual Recognition

The right to a life of dignity belongs to all.[1]

Perichoresis begins at home.[2]

I would never choose to live under attack, but I will never regret
living in ways which sometimes make it almost inevitable.[3]

A New Poetics

The turn to pneumatology in women's theologies provides a strategic
affirmation of contextual difference and solidarity within and across human
communities. Christological discourse, as explored in the previous chapter
and in chapter 5 on early church households, tends to reinforce the subjectivity of an individual One. Pneumatological discourse, based on the relational
paradigm of intersubjectivity, offers an ever-widening horizon of household
participants. Turning to the Spirit as the social presence of God incarnate
overcomes the polarization between the One and others toward a re-centering
of the Many. In contrast to kyriocentric household management, which
domesticates and subordinates the differences of household members, a
feminist maternal economy of mutual recognition seeks a "new poetics of
community" where differentiation becomes the key to justice, love, and global
flourishing.[4] Remembering the Spirit offers women's theologies a theological
alternative to the con-fusing tendencies of oppressive relations.

---

[1]Elsa Tamez, *The Amnesty of Grace: Justification from a Latin American Perspective*, trans. Sharon
Ringe (Maryknoll, N.Y.: Orbis Books, 1993), 43.
[2]Catherine Keller, "The Theology of Moltmann, Feminism, and the Future," in *The Future of
Theology: Essays in Honor of Jürgen Moltmann*, ed. Miroslav Volf, Carmen Krieg, and Thomas Kucharz
(Grand Rapids, Mich.: Eerdmans, 1996), 147.
[3]Dorothy McRae-McMahon, *Everyday Passions: A Conversation on Living* (Sydney: ABC Books,
1998), 83.
[4]Rebecca S. Chopp, *The Power to Speak: Feminism, Language, God* (New York: Crossroad,
1991), 85. "By a poetics I mean not a mere continuation of older images, ways of speaking, or
metaphors for community, but new forms, pictures, images, and sounds of community...A poetics of community will not replace other modes of discourses in community, but it will fund their
richness and fullness in a communion of words which is multivocal and multiform, dense and
rich, imagistic and creative" (85).

This chapter concludes the exploration of Spirit language and its relation to models of family life. With the patriarchal, kyriocentric household providing past funding for Christian theology, spirituality, social life, and church practice, new models of families spark the possibilities for transformation. While poisonous pneumatologies, based on the subordination of the Many to the One, create docile and useful persons, a feminist maternal Spirit of mutual recognition values models of democratic diversity-in-unity. This chapter sets forth the vision of a Spirit for new households, including the "great world house."[5] Along the way we revisit the household of Cornelius and the Gentile Pentecost in Acts 10–11:18, where we discover mutual recognition at the heart of the New Testament witness. Yet in order to work toward mutual recognition in the Spirit, we need to revisit possibilities of conflict and face family fears, out of which grows new "fruit of the Spirit" (Gal. 5:22) for entering and sustaining the struggle. Bearing implications for Trinitarian construction, a feminist maternal Spirit of mutual recognition reveals the *cunning of diversity* in the household of God.

The Spirit of New Households

A feminist maternal pneumatology of mutual recognition situates its voice within the great world house of God's *oikoumene*. Retrieving the biblical connection of Spirit and breath (Gen. 2:7; Ps. 104:29; Job 34:14–5; Jn. 20:22), a feminist maternal Spirit incorporates the vast, interconnected, and interdependent whole of life in creation. Inspirited beings are living beings, struggling to survive, breathe, grow, and connect with others, and thus with God as Other. This organic, holistic pneumatology acknowledges a panentheistic model of the relation between the world and God. The world lives in God, by the Spirit, yet God, the compassionate householder of rich abundance and inclusive generosity, remains unlimited, yet affected, by the world's possibilities.[6] Inspiring a new cosmology of interdependent relations, God the Spirit may be imaged as the hearth of God's *oikoumene*–invigorating, sustaining, transforming, and sanctifying life's incredibly diverse economy.

The interwoven language of ecumenics, ecology, and economics reflects the root word *oikos*, or household, which earns its currency through our human experience of family life. Typically relegated to the private human domain, the metaphors of household and family raise questions about what it means to live together with others and how the sustenance of daily life can be shared justly by all. But what if the private becomes public? Not to rehash the first-wave feminist argument for making the world into a pious, genteel, Victorian home, but the argument of this book takes seriously the possibility that

---

[5]See chapter 1. The reference is from Martin Luther King, Jr., *Where Do We Go From Here: Chaos or Community?* (Boston: Beacon Press, 1967), 167.

[6]On God as householder or economist, see M. Douglas Meeks, *God the Economist: The Doctrine of God and Political Economy* (Minneapolis: Fortress Press, 1989), 75–98.

postmodern feminist family life contributes new values to the larger conversation of public life today.

As Catherine Keller suggests, what if *perichoresis* begins at home and extends out into our global society? Elizabeth Johnson interprets the Greek term *perichoresis*, used in reference to Triune relations by the Cappadocian Fathers, as the

> idea that each person encompasses the others, is coinherent with the others in a joyous movement of shared life. Divine life circulates without any anteriority or posteriority, without any superiority or inferiority of one to the other. Instead there is a clasping of hands, a pervading exchange of life, a genuine circling around together that constitutes the permanent, active, divine *koinonia*.[7]

What if perichoretic mutuality constituted the relations of families and set forth new expectations for relations in the great world house? Thus, claiming a cosmic connection for Spirit and household, a feminist maternal pneumatology further situates itself within the ordinary household lives of families struggling for democratic values such as equal regard, proper trust, diversity, and shared authority, which together make possible the goal of mutual recognition. Valuing *families*, instead of the singular norm of the hierarchical, two-spheres, male-headed family, forges the bricks for a new hearth in today's contemporary households. Standing on the "common ground" of commitment to family life, postmodern feminists "return to the mother's house," but with new maternal identities that care for both self and other, seek justice for all family members, and participate in private and public life.[8]

This is not to say that postmodern feminist families completely embody their new family values in perfect ways. Postmodern feminist families have embarked on a journey to an unknown place, a place beyond patriarchy and its "poisonous pedagogy."[9] They travel a pre-figurative journey in which diverse models are being forged day by day in the hearth of cultural transformation. Yet families struggling today for recognition and dignity face many difficulties, enhanced by the rise of reformist family advocates such as Promise Keepers reclaiming male headship and authority, church judicial decisions against women's ministries and holy unions, economic rationalization of social support programs, and the backlash of violence against gays, lesbians, feminists, and other transformers. While the common ground of critical familism retains the value of self-sacrifice for attaining mutuality in relations,

---

[7]Elizabeth A. Johnson, *She Who Is: The Mystery of God in Feminist Theological Discourse* (New York: Crossroad, 1992), 220.

[8]See chapter 5. The reference to "common ground" is from Don Browning, Bonnie J. Miller-McLemore, Pamela D. Couture, K. Brynolf Lyon, and Robert M. Franklin, *From Culture Wars to Common Ground: Religion and the American Family Debate* (Louisville, Ky.: Westminster John Knox Press, 1997). On feminism's return to maternal identity see Bonnie J. Miller-McLemore, *Also a Mother: Work and Family as Theological Dilemma* (Nashville: Abingdon Press, 1994).

[9]See chapter 5. The reference is from Alice Miller, *For Your Own Good: Hidden Cruelty in Child-Rearing and the Roots of Violence* (New York: Noonday Press, 1983), 3–91.

a feminist maternal standpoint advances a new value in forging the We–self-assertion. For recognition to become mutual, both self and other must make a difference, in contrast to the twisted distortion of the One asserting selfhood and the Many (others) recognizing the One. Thus, a feminist maternal standpoint fans the flames of Spirit in its assertive struggle for dignity, justice, identity, and liberation. The hearth of new households may inspire a new world.

The Gentile Pentecost

But the Spirit of new households represents more than theological contextualization within the experience of postmodern feminist families. The connection of Spirit and mutual recognition lies at the heart of the New Testament witness. Consider the Gentile Pentecost of Acts 10–11:18, easily overlooked by the conventional privileging of the Jerusalem Pentecost in Acts 2.[10] While the Spirit's person and work in the narrative have been interpreted in terms of "forgiveness, cleansing and salvation," further exploration uncovers the Spirit's blessing of dignity and the liberating and inclusive dimensions of the Spirit's dignifying power.[11] The text indicates that mutual recognition becomes possible when human dignity is restored in the Spirit.

In the blessing of dignity, God the Spirit constitutes human meaning, cultural value, and communal energy for the struggle to attain recognition of this dignity within public spaces. But dignity, from the Latin word *dignus*, meaning worthy, must not be identified with any *one* particular culture, community, or attribute.[12] Human beings bear dignity because, from a Christian perspective, God creates human beings as part of the creation in the image of God and claims them with hope through the incarnation.[13] Douglas Meeks suggests, "Human dignity is grounded in God's creativity, that is God's power to call everything that is out of the power of the *nihil*."[14] But human beings do not exist in the abstract, apart from culture, race, sexuality, and gender. The blessing of dignity constitutes an embodied worth and value in human specificity as created by God, yet this blessing extends to all people in all their diversity.

The Gentile Pentecost begins in Caesarea with Cornelius, a Roman military leader and pious Gentile who has a sacred vision in which he learns God

---

[10]Robert P. Menzies in *The Development of Early Church Pneumatology with Special Reference to Luke-Acts* (Sheffield: Sheffield Academic Press, 1991), 264–67. The following discussion is based on earlier work presented in my article "Turning to the Spirit–Retrieving Dignity in the Household of God," *Colloquium* 30, no. 2 (1998): 181–84.

[11]Menzies cites James D. G. Dunn's association of the Gentile Pentecost with forgiveness, cleansing, and salvation in *Baptism in the Holy Spirit* (London: SCM Press, 1970), 82. Menzies claims Dunn's pneumatological rendering of Acts 10–11:15 narrowly focuses on gifts given in response to repentance, instead of communal inclusion and prophetic inspiration.

[12]Ron DiSanto, "The Threat of Commodity-Consciousness to Human Dignity," in *Made in God's Image: The Catholic Vision of Human Dignity*, ed. Regis Duffy and Angelus Gambatese (New York: Paulist Press, 1999), 57.

[13]Jürgen Moltmann, *On Human Dignity: Political Theology and Ethics* (London: SCM Press, 1984), 3–35; and James P. Scullion, "Creation-Incarnation: God's Affirmation of Human Worth," in *Made in God's Image*, 7–28.

[14]M. Douglas Meeks, Introduction, in *On Human Dignity*, xi.

has noticed his devotion and loyalty. In response, Cornelius sends several soldiers to find Simon Peter, who is lodging with a tanner, also named Simon. Cornelius' men set out, and a day later, as they near the city, Peter goes up on the roof to pray. Hungry, he too has a puzzling vision. Something large and white, like a sheet, lowers to the ground by its four corners, displaying formerly unclean creatures. Peter protests, but what God transforms, he must not now reject. Two more times and then the sheet disappears. Suddenly, there's a knock on the door and the Spirit shakes Peter to get up and open the door, for the Spirit has sent these men! The next day he journeys with them back to Cornelius' home in Caesarea. After some bumbling introductions, Peter realizes that even though his religious practice forbids him to enter a Gentile dwelling, he can do so because Cornelius is no longer unclean or profane. As a result, a transformed Cornelius shares his dream with Peter.

Amazed, Peter wonders what he should do. On new common ground, Peter affirms God's nonpartiality and shares the good news of Jesus, anointed by God with the Holy Spirit to do good works, heal, and free people from spiritual bondage. In this light, Peter speaks of Jesus' cross and resurrection. Those who believe in the mission receive forgiveness and new life through Christ's name. Then, just as on the day of Pentecost, the people gathered in Cornelius' home praise God with inspired speech. The Jews with Peter stand amazed. What else can Peter do but baptize them into the new people of God!

The narrative of the Gentile Pentecost conveys the vital connection between God the Spirit and mutual recognition. At the start, Peter stays in the home of a Jewish believer, but the tanner maintains an unclean profession—in other words, his person and profession lack dignity. Peter's presence with him signals the transformation of a "politics of purity" into a "politics of compassion."[15] But little does Peter comprehend how far the Spirit's inclusive compassion reaches! He eventually realizes that the promises and hopes of God's people extend beyond the particular to the universal, including persons of the dominant society. First, a Jewish tanner, then the group of Gentiles receive dignity in the fire of the Spirit. Once unrecognized by the Jews, these Gentiles become gifted partners with God.

Luke associates the Spirit in the Gentile Pentecost with the work of confronting particular cultural values and practices toward "retrieving" a new inclusive humanity.[16] From the perspective of the narrative, what happens between Peter and Cornelius is not a random or casual event, secondary to the apostles' ministries. God the Spirit communicates a new orientation creating a universal identity for the Jesus movement. This world-encompassing horizon presents the Spirit as a personal agent with motivation, intelligence, desire, will, and direction.[17] But Luke also presents the Spirit as a dynamic

---

[15]Marcus J. Borg, *Meeting Jesus Again for the First Time* (San Francisco: HarperSanFrancisco, 1994), 46–68.

[16]José Comblin, *Retrieving the Human: A Christian Anthropology* (Maryknoll, N.Y.: Orbis Books, 1990), 13–14.

[17]William H. Shepherd, Jr., *The Narrative Function of the Holy Spirit as a Character in Luke–Acts* (Atlanta: Scholars Press, 1994), 3–8.

force and prophetic power energizing not only Jesus' mission, but the Gentiles' mission to the world. In the Gentile Pentecost we see the Spirit manifest in the gifted, assertive community, now open in the directions of all cultures and people.

Contemporary pneumatologists provide insight into the blessing of the Spirit appropriate for reflection on the Gentile Pentecost. In the transforming experience of the Spirit's blessing, people formerly without dignity discover they can raise their heads, discern a mission, freely act, and speak in the face of the gravest threat, claiming for themselves the space for abundant life. From his context of Brazilian base communities, José Comblin describes the blessing of the Spirit:

> It is a matter of experience undergone by a community of people who feel that something new is coming about in their midst. This experience has the effect of completely reversing their situation, of changing them from mere passivity to activity: it is like the experience of being born. It is the experience of re-birth. This is the experience that has to be attributed to the Spirit.[18]

Jürgen Moltmann also interprets the work of the Spirit from this liberating and communal perspective when he claims that the experience of God's Spirit involves more than the being-revealed of God's self-revelation and more than finding faith in the heart through proclamation:

> For the Spirit actually brings men and women to the beginning of a new life and makes them the determining subjects of that new life in the fellowship of Christ…Many people express this personal experience of the Spirit in the simple words: "God loves me." In this experience of God they also experience their own indestructible and inalienable dignity, so that they can get up out of the dust.[19]

The Spirit's blessing of dignity means getting up from the dust and claiming one's place in the goodness of creation. But dignity does not mean leaving the dust behind. Human beings, created in the image of God, embody both dust and Spirit, leading Karen Baker Fletcher to claim,

> Jesus reminds us of God's intimate love of creation, which is so deep that God, who is Spirit chooses to be one with creation, transcending it yet permeating it even as it moves out and beyond into all that is unknown to human beings. God as Spirit is the lovingness in creation, which empowers life and aims for balance or justice.[20]

---

[18]José Comblin, *The Holy Spirit and Liberation* (Maryknoll, N.Y.: Orbis Books, 1989), 21.

[19]Jürgen Moltmann, *The Spirit of Life: A Universal Affirmation* (Minneapolis: Fortress Press, 1992), 3.

[20]Karen Baker Fletcher, *Sisters of Dust, Sisters of Spirit: Womanist Wordings on God and Creation* (Minneapolis: Fortress Press, 1998), 19.

The dignity of humanity, the dignity of God's creation, this is what the blessing of the Spirit means for those formerly without recognition.

But there is more to the Gentile Pentecost narrative than retrieving dignity. The affirmation of inclusive dignity leads to conflict within the Jerusalem Jesus movement.[21]   When the leaders of this community hear that Peter baptized Gentiles, at first they are upset and critical of Peter, who returns to clarify the whole series of events. He tells the leaders that the Spirit told him not to make a distinction between Jews and Gentiles as common heirs of God's hopes and promises. If the Spirit gave the Gentiles the same prophetic gift given to them, who was he to hinder the Spirit's inclusive purposes? According to the narrative, the Jerusalem leaders remain silent, then break out in praise, exclaiming, "Then God has given even to the Gentiles the repentance that leads to life" (Acts 11:18).

Recognition through inclusive dignity in God's household necessarily entails conflict as persons formerly without dignity encounter persons accorded dignity by the prevailing social structures. But then, Jesus' own praxis of recognizing people without dignity brought him into conflict with powers dependent on maintaining exclusive privilege. The household of mutual recognition always risks conflict with systems and persons of power whose identity is based (implicitly and explicitly) on the nonrecognition of others. In the narrative, the mission of God the Spirit challenges the formative members of the Jesus movement. The Jerusalem leaders reconsider their own identity in recognition of the dignity of those formerly considered outsiders or others. But while conflict ensues in the Spirit, the Jerusalem/Gentile mission moves forward with God's Spirit. In the Gentile Pentecost, the Spirit empowers both conflict and resolution. A new household forms, without assimilation or subordination of either group's particularity. In the heart of the New Testament, the Gentile Pentecost leads to a deeper understanding of the Spirit's diversity-in-unity.

The Cunning of Diversity

Through reading Acts 10–11:18 with new eyes, the person of the Spirit retrieves dignity, instigates conflict, and empowers communities of differentiated, yet united, participants. The social ontology of the Spirit's presence and work presents a positive valuation of the new household's diversity-in-unity. Often, religious communities pray for the Spirit in situations where unity is desired. Benedictions conclude with persons going forth "in the unity of the Holy Spirit." Popular religious language connects the power and presence of the Spirit with oneness, harmony, and commonality. As youth groups sing, "We are one in the Spirit"; but does oneness in the Spirit imply a relation

---

[21]On Spirit and conflict, see Shepherd, 94–95, 197–202; and Comblin, *Retrieving the Human*, 164.

without difference or a community without conflict?[22] Is life in the Spirit an "economy of the Same," where members reflect to one another a homogenous identity?[23] How can our pneumatologies move beyond "a unitarian concept of community" in which the bonds of spiritual love constitute a simple union of substance or essence?[24]

In response, we can turn from the biblical text to a philosophical resource. For G. W. F. Hegel, Spirit as *Geist* incorporates a complex but creative movement of social freedom for God and God's world.[25] It may seem strange to turn to Hegel at this point, since deconstructive, postmodern critiques usually assess Hegel's philosophical theology as a metaphysical totality or onto-theology.[26] But in recent years, Hegel has re-emerged as a "theologian of Spirit" and thus contributes to recent pneumatological inspirations.[27] In *The Phenomenology of Spirit*, Hegel imaginatively struggles with the intersubjective dynamics of social groups seeking freedom without authoritarianism or fragmentation.[28] The key concept of recognition (*Anerkennung*) enables Hegel to explore theoretical and empirical processes of social diversity-in-unity. Recognition funds a "triadic social holism" in which the structures of human consciousness, being-with-self (*Fürsichsein*) and being-with-other (*Füreinandersein*) are engaged, sublated, and released into a third structure, being-with-self-in-and-through-another, in attaining true freedom.[29] Thus, conflict forms one

---

[22]I am grateful for conversation with Gerard Kelly regarding recognition as an "emerging ecumenical term." See his book *Recognition: Advancing Ecumenical Thinking* (New York: Peter Lang, 1996). For Kelly, recognition involves "seeing one's own faith in the other...prior to and more significantly than simply recognising the other" (16). While seeking a common understanding of Christian unity remains vital for ecumenical relations, my narrative of recognition addresses relations immersed in ideological distortion and disparities of power. I argue we need to recognize both difference and commonality, but this book privileges the former so commonality can be openly and mutually explored.

[23]Luce Irigaray, *This Sex Which is Not One*, trans. Catherine Porter (Ithaca, N.Y.: Cornell University Press, 1985), 23–33, 68–85, 170–91.

[24]Moltmann criticizes the unitarian concept in *The Spirit of Life*, 223.

[25]In German, *Geist* has connections with mind or mental life, but for Hegel, the term implies much more than abstract, individual reason. Peter Hodgson explains the meaning of Hegel's Spirit as *Geist* in *G. W. F. Hegel: Theologian of the Spirit* (Minneapolis: Fortress Press, 1997): "The being of God (the *ontos* of *theos*) discloses itself to be not pure immediacy or abstract substance or 'supreme being' (*das höchste Wesen*) but rather 'spirit' (*Geist*) in the sense of energy, movement, life, revelation, differentiation and reconciliation. Spirit designates a God who is intrinsically self-revelatory, self-manifesting; God is not locked up within Godself but is knowable and related to the world" (7).

[26]For example, see Emmanuel Levinas, *Totality and Infinity*, trans. Alphonso Lingis (Pittsburgh: Dusquesne University Press, 1969), 13, 36–37; and Jacques Derrida, "Violence and Metaphysics," in *Writing and Difference*, trans. Alan Bass (Chicago: University of Chicago Press, 1978), 118–21, 320.

[27]Hodgson, 1–38. See also Hodgson's retrieval of Hegel in *Winds of Spirit: A Constructive Christian Theology* (Louisville, Ky.: Westminster John Knox Press, 1994).

[28]G. W. F. Hegel, *The Phenomenology of Spirit*, trans. A. V. Miller (New York: Oxford University Press, 1977).

[29]Robert R. Williams, *Recognition: Fichte and Hegel on the Other* (Albany, N.Y.: SUNY Press, 1992). A condensed exploration can be found in Williams' "Hegel's Concept of *Geist*," in *Hegel's Philosophy of Spirit*, ed. Peter Stillman (Albany, N.Y.: SUNY Press, 1987), 1–10.

dimension of freedom, particularly when the relations between people or groups involve disparities of power (as in the relation of master and slave). The struggle for recognition achieves freedom when subordination gives way to assertion of being-for-self and mastery gives way to releasing the other by acknowledging the dependence of self on being-for-other. For Hegel, mutual recognition incorporates a mutual process of transformation in which the "'I' that is 'We' and 'We' that is 'I'" forge a shared identity inclusive of difference.[30] Hegel's intersubjective process shares the impetus of Desmond Tutu's *ubuntu* theology—that "a person depends on other people to be a person."[31] Mutual recognition requires the co-transformation of subjects, including God, via social, historical, and interpersonal dimensions of human existence.

Hegel describes Spirit (*Geist*) as the "cunning of reason" in God's economy of historical liberation.[32] But by accentuating the dimensions of differentiation, conflict, and community, a feminist maternal standpoint plays with Hegel's phrase to characterize Spirit as *the cunning of diversity*. In the interest of recognition, the Spirit's dignity finds its telos not in an individual, private, or exclusive identity, but in the desire and need for *mutual* recognition of dignity. Thus, the cunning of diversity employs the vitality of the Many against the One's poisonous order. Within communities, God the Spirit fosters the variety of gifts necessary for the vitality, hospitality, and mission of the community. Without diversity, communities stagnate, die, or turn poisonous; but sustaining dignity in diversity presents a difficult challenge.

Yet from another angle, pneumatological dignity experienced in the community may stand in tension with other communities and social structures that do not acknowledge or may even actively efface that dignity. For example, the ministries of heterosexual women, gays, and lesbians in their own spiritual communities struggle for recognition in larger households of faith. Thus, conflict and struggle in the dignity of the Spirit constitutes the work for social justice.[33] In the Gentile Pentecost, the inclusive dignity of others and strangers (even transformed Roman military oppressors like Cornelius) entailed conflict and struggle with the formative community in Jerusalem. But recognition between the households of Caesarea and Jerusalem further represented a spiritual dignity in tension with the imperialist dignity of Rome. Turning to today, the Spirit's cunning of diversity continues making struggle and conflict with effacing powers a crucial dimension of spiritual life. In fact, in order to survive and challenge oppressive economies of domination as diverse, embodied voices, marginalized people call on and create theological

---

[30]Hegel, *The Phenomenology of Spirit*, 146.

[31]Michael Battle, *Reconciliation: The Ubuntu Theology of Desmond Tutu* (Cleveland: Pilgrim Press, 1997), 39.

[32]Hegel, *The Phenomenology of Spirit*, 33, 502.

[33]On the relation of social justice, Spirit, and dignity see Nancy M. Victorin-Vangerud, "The Spirit's Dignity: Recognition for the Work of Justice," in *Starting with the Spirit: The Task of Theology Today, Vol. II*, ed. Stephen Pickard and Gordon Preece (Adelaide, Australia: The Australian Theological Forum, 2000).

poetics empowering the life-staking struggle for transformation. How does pneumatology sustain people's walking in the way of dignity?

The Realm of Sparks

Through the concepts of dignity and the cunning of diversity, a feminist maternal standpoint brings new meaning to the Jerusalem Pentecost's "tongues of fire" (Acts 2:2–4). Calling into question the household rules, people whose dignity has been retrieved in and through the Spirit speak with inspired speech. Like Chung Hyun Kyung evoking the tongues of the *han*-ridden spirits, God the Spirit stirs up controversy, chaos, and confusion. Yet from the perspective of nonrecognized household members, chaos and confusion already haunt their lives (as in the unholy ghost of poisonous pneumatology). They testify that speaking forth with one's own voice does not "cause" the problem, for the problem of household injustice already exists in modes of twisted recognition. Thus, could the Seventh Assembly hear the voice(s) of the Spirit? Do today's churches connect their theologies of the Spirit with the dimensions of struggle in reclaiming one's voice with dignity?

While the cunning of diversity in its biblical and philosophical presentations incorporates conflict and struggle, the image still seems pristine, even heroic, and from a feminist maternal standpoint, needs immersion in the groaning context (Rom. 8:23) of the Spirit. For a new poetics, the struggle for mutual recognition begins within what Cherríe Moraga names "the realm of sparks," where nonrecognized household members become "welders" for change.[34] Transforming household relations of domination begins in groaning heat, taking deep breaths for the energy to risk oneself or differentiate oneself from the conventional order. Often this can only happen with supportive communities and solidarity from persons who walk alongside and provide an alternative *oikos* of dignity. Advocacy of the Spirit (Jn. 15:26) through the community ignites the possibility for change, even though chaos and lack of control also inhabit the realm of sparks. Similarly, Mary Daly draws on the images of fire and heat to describe the new space women move into after realizing the confining and numbing character of patriarchy. The "Pyrosphere" constitutes "a spiraling zone of molten Passions that permits passage between the surfaces of Elemental female be-ing and the inner cauldron/core, and that supplies E-motional energy to Brewsters."[35] Identifying with conflict, a feminist maternal pneumatology admits the only way to the *perichoresis* of mutual recognition is through the hearth of risky transformation.

While the ideal of mutual recognition involves right relations between all household members, acknowledging the realm of sparks enables a feminist maternal pneumatology to name the inequities of power in poisonous relations. The struggle for recognition does not begin from a level dancing floor,

---

[34]Cherríe Moraga, "The Welder," in *This Bridge Called My Back: Writings by Radical Women of Color*, ed. Cherríe Moraga and Gloria Anzaldúa (New York: Kitchen Table–Women of Color Press, 1983), 219–20.

[35]Mary Daly, *Pure Lust: Elemental Feminist Philosophy* (Boston: Beacon Press, 1984), 197.

where all partners find safe, free space to negotiate reconciliation, share hurtful stories honestly, or confront the past. Spirit images of oneness, harmony, or unity too quickly pressure members into conforming or re-submitting to broken relations without restoring justice and equity. In contexts of family abuse, clergy sexual misconduct, homophobic backlash, or other economies of domination, forging the We of mutual recognition necessitates re-claiming boundaries, separating oneself from fusion with the other, and strengthening modes of self-care and self-assertion. In the Spirit's cunning of diversity, caring for one's own boundaries in defense or survival constitutes an energy of the Spirit, imaged not as unity, but as resistance or separation. When the bonds of love become bondage, spiritual discernment may call for the breaking of those bonds as a pneumatological act, since unity at the expense of justice perverts the Spirit's *koinonia*.

In his pneumatology, Miroslav Volf uses the metaphor of an embrace to characterize the process of reconciliation.[36] In the "drama of embrace," the movement first involves opening one's arms to create space for the other, then waiting and closing one's arms together with the other's arms, and finally opening both partners' arms in free release.[37] In order to have justice, persons must evidence the will to embrace, for Christian faith entails the end of vengeance and the possibility of forgiveness. But from a feminist maternal standpoint, reconciliation as mutual recognition must incorporate, where necessary, the space for "a time to refrain from embracing" (Eccl. 3:5). There are times of saying no to the abusive embrace, the oppressive dance, or the distorted relationship. *No.* You no longer have access to my physical and emotional personhood. No longer will you define me as unclean, aberrant, or sinful. No longer will I collaborate in this deception. No longer do I trust you. No longer will you have boundary-transgressing power, for no longer will I be a victim. While the language of God the Spirit functions in reconciling, restoring, and uniting contexts, a feminist maternal standpoint claims Spirit must be further understood as the energy for life-inspiring fiery tongues in confrontation and calling for recognition in the first place. Incorporating both movements of differentiation and embrace remains the gift of a feminist maternal pneumatology of mutual recognition.

In Moraga's poem, there comes a time when the welder decides to pick up her torch. Life in the realm of sparks means asserting power to make a difference. But the way is not easy, certainly not heroic for most people. When Dorothy McRae-McMahon decided to come out with her truth of living as an Australian Uniting Church pastor, lesbian mother, and partner, she found the struggle for recognition a fiery hearth.[38] The struggle could have made her

---

[36]I am appreciative of Volf's questions and comments regarding a feminist maternal standpoint on reconciliation at Marquette University's 1998 symposium, "Advent of the Spirit: Orientations in Pneumatology."

[37]Miroslav Volf, *Exclusion and Embrace: A Theological Exploration of Identity, Otherness and Reconciliation* (Nashville: Abingdon Press, 1996), 140–47.

[38]McRae-McMahon, 88, 113.

tough, defensive, or vengeful. But she discovered living out her truth in the realm of sparks made her, in fact, more vulnerable. Vulnerability makes the struggle for recognition so difficult that, as in Catherine Foote's poem "Talking to God about Abuse," some days, welders in the realm of sparks struggle just for the will to go on struggling:

> Do you want to hear about the pain of his assault?
> May I tell you about the blood and the brokenness?
> Do you care about the nights I can't sleep?
> Do you care about the days
>   when I struggle for the will to go on struggling?[39]

A feminist maternal pneumatology argues that not only does God's Spirit inspire the beautiful perichoretic dance, God's Spirit inhabits the realm of sparks, where the groans for life and freedom first arise.

Household Fears

Situating pneumatology in the heated crucible of self-assertion, a feminist maternal standpoint revisits "traditional" family values. Whether patriarchal or matriarchal, in families of unilateral power, blind obedience, and subordination, two household fears surface that shape behavior—fear of parental anger and fear of one's own anger, creating together a vicious cycle. A feminist maternal Spirit seeks to break the cycle of this poisonous space.

In poisonous pedagogy, physical and emotional forms of retaliation reinforce compliance and conformity with the will of the head of household. Disruptive family members who differentiate or assert themselves become problems in need of correction, discipline, or control. As Alice Miller demonstrates, poisonous pedagogy creates a system that relieves authorities of responsibility and places blame for punitive adult actions on children.[40] "Don't make him angry," Dorothy Allison's mother repeatedly warned Dorothy about her abusive stepfather.[41] In economies of domination, fear provides the strongest and most pervasive shaping force of the household. Audre Lorde describes the household fears of patriarchy:

> For women raised to fear, too often anger threatens annihilation. In the male construct of brute force, we were taught that our lives depended upon the good will of patriarchal power. The anger of others was to be avoided at all costs because there was nothing to be learned from it but pain, a judgment that we had been bad girls, come up lacking, not done what we were supposed to do.[42]

---

[39]Catherine J. Foote, "Talking to God about Abuse," in *Survivor Prayers: Talking With God about Childhood Sexual Abuse* (Louisville, Ky.: WestminsterJohn Knox Press, 1994), 5.

[40]See chapter 5.

[41]Dorothy Allison, *Trash* (Ithaca, N.Y.: Firebrand Books, 1988), 37.

[42]Audre Lorde, *Sister Outsider: Essays and Speeches* (Freedom, Calif.: Crossing Press, 1984), 131.

In avoiding authorities' punitive anger, children and other vulnerable persons fearfully suppress challenging behavior. Like the children of Lukas Carlé in Isabel Allende's novel *Eva Luna*, who "developed such skill for passing unnoticed that sometimes their mother thought she could see through them," subordinate household members, in particular female children, learn to live with a sense of powerless transparency.[43]   From her context as an Asian American woman, Mitsuye Yamada describes the self-less invisibility of people who do not make a difference to anyone or anything:

> The poor know it only too well, and we women have known it since we were little girls. The most insidious part of this conditioning process, I realize now, was that we have been trained not to expect a response in ways that mattered. We may be listened to and responded to with placating words and gestures, but our psychological mind set has already told us time and again that we were born into a ready-made world into which we must fit ourselves, and that many of us do it very well.[44]

Within economies of domination, subordinates discover that their voices, opinions, needs, and goals do not really matter to authorities, only their conformation to rigid roles that benefit authorities at the expense of the rightful recognition of family members. From her painful childhood memories, bell hooks remembers, "I was never taught absolute silence, I was taught that it was important to speak but to talk a talk that was in itself a silence."[45]

Asserting a stance of difference within an economy of domination becomes fearful for subordinates, who at one level may risk losing their lives and/or the lives of their children.[46] At other levels, subordinates fear losing the relationship, even an abusive one, or the authorities' good esteem. For many women (and marginalized men), assertion of difference or challenge risks losing a position of relative privilege within the economy. Because of the fear of shame, losing control, and hurting or disappointing others, many women avoid conflict at all costs: "Having been brought up to be 'nice girls,' they have learned to avoid differences by suppressing their own identity, interests, and agency. 'Nice girls don't fight' rules their hearts and heads."[47] As a survival strategy, subordinates accommodate and please authorities, rather than "evoke" authorities' anger and enter into conflict.

---

[43]Isabel Allende, *Eva Luna*, trans. Margaret Sayers Peden (New York: Alfred A. Knopf, 1988), 27.

[44]Mitsuye Yamada, "Invisibility Is an Unnatural Disaster: Reflections of an Asian American Woman," in *This Bridge Called My Back*, 39.

[45]bell hooks, *talking back: thinking feminist, thinking black* (Boston: South End Press, 1989), 7.

[46]In "Letter from a Battered Wife," a woman writes: "I could have been dead a long time ago had I been hit the wrong way. My baby could have been killed or deformed had I been kicked the wrong way. What saved me? I don't know. I only know that it has happened and that each night I dread the final blow that will kill me and leave my children motherless." See Joy M. K. Bussert, *Battered Women: From a Theology of Suffering to an Ethic of Empowerment* (New York: Division for Mission in North America, Lutheran Church in America, 1986), 85.

[47]Donna Bivens, Elizabeth Bettenhausen, and Nancy Richardson, "Struggling through Injury in the Work of Love," *Journal of Feminist Studies in Religion* 9 (Spring-Fall 1993): 220.

Household fears of authorities' anger haunt churches as well. In congregations struggling with sexual misconduct, people coming forth with allegations against priests and clergy do so at great risk. Church families and denominational systems often retaliate in punitive ways, ultimately protecting the "father" and silencing, blaming, or rendering invisible the cries and groans of "bad children." The feelings, reputations, and needs of clerical authorities may receive more concern within the church family than the persons making allegations and suffering violation. Nice girls (and boys) are not supposed to fight and should obediently trust church authorities to take care of the problem. Out of fear of further upsetting the ecclesiastical household, nice parishioners and nice fellow clergy avoid conflict by distancing themselves and attending to other family business. The traditional church family continues its complicity with patriarchal domination—clerical authorities assert themselves, and others only recognize that authority.

But the struggle for recognition brings household members face-to-face with their own anger, not only the anger of authorities. Yet admitting personal anger can be dangerous, even potentially annihilating. Ann Kirkus Wetherilt writes concerning white Christian women, "Anger has long been an emotion fraught with fear and tension. They have learned that anger is not acceptable and that it is a fearful thing that, once unleashed, may be totally uncontrollable."[48] Since authorities interpret anger as threatening the house rules, subordinates internalize their anger as a moral wrong, shameful weakness, sin, or even madness. hooks recounts growing up with her family repeatedly telling her that bold questions and poetry would cause her to end up in a mental institution.[49] McRae-McMahon shares, "I was taught as a child that anger is rarely an appropriate response to things relating to myself, although it was all right to become angry in a controlled fashion about the pain of others."[50] In the realm of sparks, facing personal anger that has been delegitimated and repressed makes the struggle for recognition an even more difficult journey.

This is true of congregations struggling through experiences of clergy sexual misconduct. In church families, the anger of parishioners who have experienced violation personally or indirectly may be labeled trivial, unproductive, divisive, and even unfaithful by clerical authorities and other parishioners seeking a quick way beyond the crisis. Thus, unrecognized and unexpressed anger creates false selves in the face of church loyalty or becomes misdirected into destructive personal and congregational dynamics. But in the ecclesiastical realm of sparks, violated persons further find a struggle in acknowledging their anger before a patriarchal God. As Foote testifies,

What do I dare to tell you, God?
What do I dare to talk to you about?

---

[48]Ann Kirkus Wetherilt, *That They May Be Many: Voices of Women, Echoes of God* (New York: Continuum, 1994), 135.

[49]hooks, 6–7.

[50]McRae-McMahon, 62.

May I speak of my anger?
May I tell you of my shame?[51]

In churches and in families, the expression or even acknowledgment of violated persons' anger remains a grave household fear and thus thwarts the possibility for healing and mutual recognition.

New Gifts of the Spirit

In contrast, a feminist maternal standpoint re-names anger as a positive force for household transformation. While poisonous pedagogy asserts that love for family authorities should be expressed in terms of obedience, blind trust, and suppression of anger, a feminist maternal standpoint suggests that anger is necessary for truly loving relations. According to Sara Ruddick, expressing anger enables family members to address betrayals and lack of recognition in order to establish proper trust between themselves and others.[52] Thus, expressing anger actually represents a mode of love and caring. Beverly Wildung Harrison makes the case:

> Anger denied subverts community. Anger expressed directly is a mode of taking the other seriously, of caring. The important point is that where feeling is evaded, where anger is hidden or goes unattended, masking itself, there the power of love, the power to act, to deepen relation, atrophies and dies.[53]

Essential to the restoration of proper trust, anger signifies a distorted relation, and because it is a mode of caring, helps restore the relationship to right-relation. Carter Heyward suggests "rage and compassion, far from being mutually exclusive, belong together."[54] In economies of domination, the "love" enforced by poisonous pedagogy exists as a shallow facade between false selves. Anger provides the energy to take some form of action, which of course calls for discernment in determining wise and unwise forms of action. McRae-McMahon advises:

> Even if our action is part of a larger picture of oppression and we can see no real and immediate results of our efforts, it is still surprisingly helpful to have acted in some small way. It is about a sense of having made our point, of honouring the significance of our life, and of the reclaiming the ground of justice for our life by occupying it and raising our little flag of protest.[55]

---

[51]Foote, 5.

[52]See chapter 5.

[53]Beverly Wildung Harrison, "The Power of Anger in the Work of Love," in *Weaving the Visions: New Patterns in Feminist Spirituality*, ed. Judith Plaskow and Carol P. Christ (New York: HarperCollins, 1989), 220.

[54]Carter Heyward, *The Redemption of God: A Theology of Mutual Relation* (Washington, D.C.: University Press of America, 1982), 221.

[55]McRae-McMahon, 66.

Taking action, even in a small way, creates energy for entering and sustaining the struggle for recognition. Anger initiates differentiation and provides power or energy in service of this work of love. Again McRae-McMahon helps shift the perspective on anger: "To be angry is to lift up an energy and self-respect which is often the beginning of rebuilding our lives."[56]

From a feminist maternal standpoint, re-claiming and re-naming anger allows all family members to be taken seriously and ensures the potential for mutual recognition. In striving to build their bonds of love on honest communication and proper trust, postmodern feminist families value the assertion of difference; thus, anger finds its ongoing role in empowering loving relations. Reclaiming anger as a source of energy for love and right relation, a feminist maternal pneumatology explores the need for new fruit of the Spirit, as Allende's character Eva Luna discovers.

> "That's good, little bird," Elvira would say approvingly. "You have to fight back. No one tries anything with mad dogs, but tame dogs they kick. Life's a dogfight."
>
> It was the best advice I ever received. Elvira used to roast lemons in the coals, then quarter and boil them, and give me a drink of the mixture to make me more courageous.[57]

What new fruit feeds a feminist maternal pneumatology? Paul's list of the "fruit of the Spirit" includes the following: "love, joy, peace, patience, kindness, generosity, faithfulness, gentleness, and self-control" (Gal. 5:22–23). But poisonous pneumatologies invoke these to diffuse the energy of anger and foster an accommodating and conflict-free unity. Even contemporary women's pneumatologies run a similar risk of calling on Paul's fruit of the Spirit in characterizing the Christian life as "docility to the Spirit."[58] While Paul's understandings of the fruit need not exclude anger to achieve their goals, a feminist maternal pneumatology seeks a more open and direct affirmation of anger in sustaining the struggle for inclusive households.

With anger serving the work of love and right relation, new fruit of the Spirit from a feminist maternal perspective includes self-determination, risk, resistance, willfulness, defiance, courage, confrontation, conflict, and voice. In no way a definitive list, these fruit share the common affirmation of a dignified selfhood that breaks through the distorting and "specular" tendencies in patriarchal economies, which order the Many to reflect the will of the head of household.[59] The fruit of anger stands out in contrast to abnegating qualities fostered by pneumatologies of self-sacrifice, surrender, conformation, and withdrawal. Without the new fruit, the vulnerable tension between assertion and recognition too easily breaks down (for the sake of unity!) into relations

---

[56]Ibid., 63.
[57]Allende, 67.
[58]Mary Ann Fatula, *The Holy Spirit: Unbounded Gift of Joy* (Collegeville, Minn.: Liturgical Press, 1998), 153–54.
[59]Irigaray, 170–91. In patriarchal discourse as a specular economy, the other functions merely as a mirror for the authorizing self. Specular discourse reduces the other's difference to the Same.

of twisted recognition and unilateral power. Transforming economies of domination into economies of mutual recognition makes human action in terms of these qualities necessary on the part of subordinate household members. But people need not act alone; human action finds energetic solidarity in the Spirit's empowerment, now interpreted along nonpoisonous lines.

The Spirit's new fruit leads to creative strategies for sustenance and struggle. For example, in contrast to the constant accommodation to prescribed roles and orders required by patriarchy, Dorothee Sölle suggests the strategy of "creative disobedience," in which persons and communities act out of their own internalized authority.[60] Not just a retaliatory reaction, creative disobedience manifests the "liberated spontaneity" of individuals and communities who accept responsibility for engaging the de-humanizing orders of the world with a practice of freedom and resistance.[61]

Joining Harrison and Sölle, Mary Daly reclaims household anger by contrasting it with the docility fostered by patriarchy's "Severed State of Domestication."[62] Her perspective supports new fruit of a feminist maternal Spirit and suggests the strategy of "Righteous Rage":

> As long as women accept the appeasing pay-offs from the Paymasters we stay in the cycle of depression, of severance from Self. Only a change in the situation, a refusal of Severance Pay and a drastic declaration of independency can stop the depressing cycle. The key to the Power of Refusal is the passion of Rage.[63]

Without the energy of anger for resistance, vulnerable household members struggling for the will to go on struggling can easily return to co-opted states of "potted" passion, accommodating themselves to the small spaces for the merely ornamental fruit made available by patriarchy.[64]

Offering a third strategy, bell hooks suggests "talking back" in contrast to the empty speech cultivated for female children.[65] Growing up, hooks remembers severe punishment and verbal abuse designed to break her spirit, resulting from voicing her opinions and writing poetry. Thus, in order to survive and resist, hooks "learned to be vigilant in the nourishment of my spirit, to be tough, to courageously protect that spirit from forces that would break it."[66] She took the name of her maternal great-grandmother, a woman who spoke her mind, and thus claimed a legacy "of defiance, of will, of courage, affirming my link to female ancestors who were bold and daring in their speech."[67] As she grew older, hooks learned that racism and classism further

---

[60]Dorothee Sölle, *Creative Disobedience*, trans. Lawrence W. Denef (Cleveland: Pilgrim Press, 1995), 23–40.

[61]Ibid., 23–29.

[62]Daly, 257.

[63]Ibid.

[64]Ibid., 206–14.

[65]hooks, 5–9.

[66]Ibid., 7.

[67]Ibid., 9.

served to marginalize and trivialize her voice and literary contributions. Thus, the strategy of talking back took on more complex social implications:

> Moving from silence into speech is for the oppressed, the colonized, the exploited, and those who stand and struggle side by side a gesture of defiance that heals, that makes new life and new growth possible. It is that act of speech, of "talking back," that is no mere gesture of empty words, that is the expression of our movement from object to subject—the liberated voice.[68]

hooks's strategy presents a legacy of self-assertion in solidarity with others who struggle together for recognition and dignity. But talking back is more than speaking per se; it is the re-positioning of voices in the direction of change by unrecognized people refusing to be only talked to or talked at. In contrast to the patriarchal fruit of docility and usefulness, talking back provides a strategy for moving in the direction of mutual recognition.

Strategies for struggling toward new households in the Spirit raise the question of the Spirit's own anger. A feminist maternal pneumatology not only claims the Spirit empowers persons for the struggle toward mutual recognition, but the Spirit shares in the experience of anger as well. In her Canberra address, Chung used the image of restless, angry *han*-spirits seeking accountability and restitution for unjust relations. She challenged the Seventh Assembly to hear in the cries of the vulnerable and violated the voice of God the Spirit. Chung's contextual poetics refocused God's anger at the distorted relations *between* members of God's great world house, rather than at the relation between God and the sinner alone. In the dance of life, people stand before God not only as disobedient sinners, but as sufferers who have suffered the sins of dancing partners. Spirit's divine anger joins with the human outrage of Chung, Foote, McRae-McMahon, and others who speak and stand out against oppression and abuse. God the Spirit is not the power that disciplines and distorts the disobedient children of human and heavenly fathers, but the communal holy and whole-making presence of God, who shares in the anger and empowers the will to go on struggling for survival, dignity, and mutual recognition.

From a feminist maternal standpoint, re-claiming and re-naming anger deemed intolerable in patriarchal and kyriocentric households leads to new fruit of the Spirit that funds a variety of communal strategies, such as creative disobedience, righteous rage, and talking back. According to the model of mutual recognition, the Spirit's presence may be affirmed in the related movements of self-care *and* other-care, differentiation *and* unity, resistance *and* connection, disorder *and* order, separation *and* coalition. For right relation and proper trust, the work of the Spirit must be claimed in the "unruly" (differentiating) household members who disrupt dominating households and uncover the twisted conformity, false unity, and unilateral modes of power constituting these relations. Where poisonous pneumatologies focus only on

---

[68]Ibid.

the relation of the disobedient sinner and God, new fruit of the Spirit inspires theologies of accountability, social justice, and recognition *between* members of the household. A feminist maternal pneumatology of mutual recognition struggles for the right of differentiation, acknowledging that just power and sacred presence may be known when neither self nor other is negated.

Spirit, Dignity, and Diversity

The struggle for recognition entails entering the realm of sparks, facing household fears, and envisioning new fruit of the Spirit for communities of diversity-in-dignity. But in a postmodern world, re-claiming the concept of dignity for a pneumatology of mutual recognition raises questions concerning the basis of dignity. Marginalized people question whether dignity should be based on a universal human identity that all people share equally or on distinct, particular identities. Iris Marion Young presents this question as the struggle between an "ideal of assimilation," which transcends group differences for a goal of equal treatment, or an "ideal of diversity," which values positive self-definition of group differences.[69] Can equality be reconceived to incorporate and positively affirm group differences?

In "the politics of recognition," philosopher Charles Taylor contrasts what he terms a "politics of equal dignity" with a "politics of identity" (or difference).[70] The former, fostered by Kant and Rousseau, rose in rejection of social orders structured by the competitive logic of social privilege and preference. Instead, Rousseau proposed the dignity of equal citizenship founded in freedom as nondiscrimination, the absence of differentiated roles, and a tight common purpose. The perspective of valuation was neutral—all human beings were equally worthy of respect. For Kant, dignity was based on the rational autonomy of human agents who could direct their own lives through universal principles. While the politics of equality did not set out to be inhospitable to human needs, Taylor thinks the assumptions of a preference-blind society—neutrality, objectivity, and universality—in fact impose a false homogeneity that inevitably privileges some (the dominant) over others. According to Taylor, the modern notion of selfhood is monological because the autonomous subject generates her or his own authentic truth and value. Thus, equal dignity typically turns out to be what is commonly reflected among those considered peers.

But the politics of difference recognizes the cultural identities of people as valuable and bearing distinct needs. Particular social collectives may hold different cultural aims than other groups in maintaining their distinctive identities. Taylor claims that in our time, a politics of difference is necessary to challenge the damaging, deadly legacies of cultural *misrecognition*:

---

[69]Iris M. Young, *Justice and the Politics of Difference* (Princeton, N. J.: Princeton University Press, 1990), 156–91. Making a similar case for group identity (difference) within democracy, see Ann Phillips, *Democracy and Difference* (Oxford: Polity Press, 1993), 90–102.

[70]Charles Taylor, *Multiculturalism and "The Politics of Recognition"* (Princeton, N.J.: Princeton University Press, 1992), 25–73.

The thesis is that our identity is partly shaped by recognition or its absence, often by the misrecognition of others, and so a person or group of people can suffer real damage, real distortion, if the people or society around them mirror back to them a confining or demeaning or contemptible picture of themselves. Nonrecognition or misrecognition can inflict harm, can be a form of oppression, imprisoning someone in a false, distorted and reduced mode of being.[71]

In contrast to the effacing ideals of assimilation and homogeneity, a politics of difference acknowledges and encourages particular cultural identities. This is not to claim that identity is a given, essentialist reality, but to *recognize* the value, the creative potential of diversity, pluralism, and multicultural learning. For Young, today's struggle is about the *meaning* of difference, whether difference implies total deviance or positive identity. In Young's vision of democratic cultural pluralism, differences between people need not lead to absolutes that justify exclusionary practices; differences compose human relations in which people also share similarities and common aims. Thus, all people have affinity with various and different groups, making accessible participation in social processes a necessity. Likewise, Taylor advocates for a new form of liberal democracy including substantive aspects that affirm specific cultural visions of integrity and survival. For him, the danger lies in associating freedom and dignity with nondifferentiation. Dignity as *mutual recognition* values differences and takes others seriously with openness to understanding self and other anew, while creating more encompassing cultural horizons.

For the interests of pneumatology, Young and Taylor acknowledge the limitations of dignity as merely a universal value. With theological concepts associated with dignity, such as *imago Dei*, body, soul, and, in particular, Spirit, can we appreciate their embodied, contextual, and particular dimensions? Can we value the dignity of self and others without resorting to zero-sum theologies? How can we avoid pneumatologies that lead to economies of the Same? By affirming diversity-in-dignity, we run the risk of justifying anew separate-but-(un)equal treatment for marginalized people who have struggled long and hard for equality.[72] Thus, inclusion in the full life of the household based on the theological affirmation of being created in the image of God or inspired by the Spirit (a theological universal) must further recognize that one is created in the image of God as a particular person—white lesbian mother, black heterosexual othermother, or single father with three children. This exploration suggests moving beyond concepts of dignity based merely on neutral universals toward concepts of dignity as mutual recognition.

---

[71]Ibid., 25.

[72]I am grateful for Mary Louise Uhr's questions at the Canberra ATF conference regarding the dangers of a politics or theo-logic of difference in light of women's struggles for religious equality and open participation in ministries. See *Changing Women, Changing Church: Festschrift to Patricia Brennan, M.D., B.S., Foundation President of the Movement for the Organization of Women,* ed. Mary Louise Uhr (Newton, N.S.W., Australia: Millennium Books, 1992).

Bodies of the Spirit

Incorporating diversity-in-dignity into the very heart of created life and divine life frees the Spirit for a relationship of mutuality between christology and pneumatology. Women's christologies challenge atomistic, heroic views of human beings and point in the direction of interpreting Jesus in relation to the people around him, thus prioritizing relationality and extending the incarnational symbol Christ to include the subjectivities of nonrecognized household members.[73] Women's christologies further reject the model of patriarchal headship and affirm models of mutuality, partnership, and right relation. A feminist maternal standpoint joins in de-centering the patriarchal family model from theological poetics and offers a different vision of wholeness from what is expressed metaphorically in the Body of Christ and the corresponding "christification" of the cosmos.[74]

While the Body of Christ expresses the "classic organic model" for church and cosmic life, the model represents a single, male body in which the head is privileged over the members of the body, as One over the Many.[75] In turning to Aristotelian body politics, the early Christian churches adopted the model to express the relation of the church to Christ and wife to husband in the ordering power of the Holy Spirit.[76] Overseeing the proper functioning of the many subordinate body members, the Head represents the reason or logos of the Body, whose purpose is to follow the will of the Head, making the thoughts, feelings, and will of the Many marginal, invisible, and even subversive. Sallie McFague explains,

> The organic model is a unitary notion that subordinates the members of the body as parts to the whole; it is concerned principally with human and especially male forms of community and organization; and it supports essentialist thinking, for if there is only one body with one head, there can be only one point of view.[77]

McFague suggests that besides norming an androcentric vision, the classic model further reflects anthropocentric, otherworldly, and dualistic (spirit versus flesh) valuations. She explains,

> The great fault with the Christian form of the organic model is its spiritualized, narrow focus: the image it calls up is of Christians (minus bodies) as members of the spiritualized, resurrected body of Christ. What it neglects is the rich, diverse, physical plentitude of creation—in other words, it neglects just about everything.[78]

---

[73]See chapter 8.

[74]For example, see Pierre Teilhard de Chardin, *The Divine Milieu* (New York: Harper & Row, 1960).

[75]Sallie McFague, *The Body of God: An Ecological Theology* (Minneapolis: Fortress Press, 1993), 30–38.

[76]See chapter 6.

[77]McFague 36.

[78]Ibid.

In the end, subordinating the Many to a spiritualized One in effect loses not only the heads of the members, but their bodies as well! By privileging the hierarchical model, Christian pneumatology made a poisonous turn in ordering the Body at the expense of the ministries, voices, and dignity of diverse church members. But the model also cut the connection between Spirit, life, and breath, privileging reasonable humanity over the rest of the inspired beings of the creation. As McFague claims, this kind of pneumatology forgets about nearly everything!

But by re-connecting the relation of Spirit and life, body and breath, and male and female, a feminist maternal pneumatology highlights the cunning of diversity and re-claims dignity in the particular bodies of the Many. The paradigm of mutual recognition infinitizes the Trinity, widening the Spirit's We to its most inclusive status, God related to the world. While a father and son may feast and dance together, without the other many partners, as *many other partners*, the feast remains rather stunted and lonely. The Spirit's We invites a feminist maternal pneumatology to remember not only one body, but many *Bodies of the Spirit*. Mutual recognition necessitates multiple bodies (with their own heads) differentiated from one another, yet constituting a relation and struggling together as speaking, feeling, and willing participants. The image, Bodies of the Spirit, may at first seem to affirm the kind of rampant individualism eroding societies and the ecological household today. But in the face of such rampant abuse of bodies due to the nonrecognition of difference, images that bring clarity to both boundaries and interconnection are compelling for our time. Children are not extensions of their fathers, or parents. Spouses are not extensions of their partners. Laity are not extensions of a pastoral Head. Two-thirds world peoples are not extensions of first world people and powers. The image Bodies of the Spirit shifts pneumatological thinking from hierarchical ordering to mutual recognition. Within this image, the many household members retain their differentiated subjectivities, yet constitute an intersubjective reality as well.

A feminist maternal pneumatology of mutual recognition seeks new poetics of community life drawing on social images of wholeness–the Many being sanctified. These social images can be as inclusive as our artistry will allow. Chung envisions the inclusion of mountains, trees, and birds joining in with Jesus and other human creatures for the Spirit's struggle of life. Anna Raimondi's banner, "And It Filled All the House," painted on a Hawaiian grass mat, images the Spirit flaming forth from mountains surrounded by intermingling faces of racially diverse women and men.[79] From the Australian Aboriginal context, multicolored, multidirectional, and multisymbolic painting expresses the rich relation of land, beings, and Spirit.[80] Instead of the

---

[79]Susan A. Blain, ed., *Imaging the Word: An Arts and Lectionary Resource*, vol. 3 (Cleveland: United Church Press, 1996), 199.

[80]Rosemary Crumlin, ed., *Aboriginal Art and Spirituality* (Melbourne: Collins Dove, 1991).

lone, imperial Jesus looking down from stained-glass windows or above in cathedral ceilings attended by courtly saints and angels, today we need additional images of diverse kin-dom communities and multi-face(te)d symbols of love and action. Our focus turns from the communion of the saints in heaven to the fulfillment of cosmic life, the many breathing Bodies of the Spirit. The embodied norm is not an individual by him- or herself, but the quality of right relation, presented here as the Spirit of mutual recognition.

Trinitarian Implications of Mutual Recognition

Language about God is not without social contextualization, which provides both possibilities and limitations for theological reflection. If Trinitarian language expresses what is most true and profound about God's relation to the world, then that language must be at least congruous with what human beings have come to understand as characterizing right relation. A feminist maternal standpoint claims that Trinitarian language is textured not only by our understandings of maleness and femaleness, but by our assumptions regarding family relations. Doctrinal language regarding God's household, or economy, places the metaphor of family at the heart of Christian theology. Thus, changes in family praxis provide important social contexts from which emerge re-textured Trinitarian thinking. While a full exploration of the Trinitarian implications of mutual recognition exceeds the bounds of this book, several summarizing and closing comments need clarification and point in future directions.

Trinitarian language in Christian theology of the East and West affirms relation (in different ways) as the heart of the divine economy.[81] But what kinds of relations are enshrined around the Trinitarian hearth? From the evidence of women's subordination in the church's historical practice, the Trinity of Father, Son, and Holy Spirit, contrary to theological affirmations of equality and mutuality, idealizes a patriarchal family model, with its broken-hearted norm of love as obedience and subordination. Within this family, the Son manifests his divine Sonship in perfect love for the Father and his will. Adopted sons and daughters become included in the divine economy through the con-fusing and con-forming power of the Father's Spirit, which orders the many household members under his one divine will. These children comprise the Body of Christ, who, in specular communion with the Father, rules as Head over those in the Body. While many gifts exist throughout the members, they are useful only in terms of building up the Body of the One. Through the discipline of the Holy Spirit, docility and usefulness are sustained throughout time, except when dissenting members break this perfect union. In this way, the authority of the Father extends into the world through his representative, the incarnate Son/Word, and thenceforth in continuity with the Son's Body. Supposedly a perichoretic community forms within the bonds of

---

[81]See Catherine Mowry LaCugna, *God for Us: The Trinity and Christian Life* (New York: HarperSanFrancisco, 1991), 53–80, 143–80 .

love, but ultimately, there appears only a family of One, for the specular relation between Son and Father resists the possibility for difference. The continual re-inscription of the economy of Father, Son, and Holy Spirit (as a patriarchal and monarchical household/kingdom) creates, in the end, an economy of the Same.

A feminist maternal pneumatology of mutual recognition, structured as an intersubjective relation of self and other in which neither is negated, provides an alternative model for Trinitarian reflection. Within this economy, both differentiation and mutuality constitute the ongoing struggle of relation and therefore press our pneumatologies beyond paradigms of self-sacrifice to models of self-commitment. Within God's compassionate household, times arise when people need to self-withdraw in commitment to the interests of others. Self-sacrifice understood in this way challenges poisonous notions valorizing sacrifice and self-abnegation merely for the sake of these values. But from the perspective of mutual recognition, self-commitment to God's compassionate household further requires the practices of self-care and self-assertion in order to restore right relation, not only in relation to others but to God as well. A feminist maternal pneumatology challenges Trinitarian theology to recover the image or poetics of Jesus' self-commitment to God's household, which he embodied in forms of self-assertion and self-care, including the willful fruit of the Spirit. The shift to mutual recognition displaces the heroic construal of Jesus' life with others as a morality parable of good and disobedient sons. A feminist maternal pneumatology re-figures the relations of Jesus, other people, and God the Spirit along the lines of proper trust, not self-emptying, blind obedience. Both self and other must make a difference in the cunning of diversity.

In a divine economy of mutual recognition, the dignifying, transforming, and sanctifying presence of God the Spirit may be imaged not as conforming the Many to the One, but as fulfilling the Many in solidarity with God and one another. The ecumenical basis of unity, "that they may be one," shifts away from oneness as sameness, to the hope "that they may be many" in a differentiated sense of wholeness including ecological and economic dimensions.[82] Pneumatological language fits this intersubjective shift, for Spirit-language moves beyond masculine, feminine, and neuter categories. Spirit's sanctifying power and presence contrasts with emanationist modes of return to a primal unity and struggles for the irreducible, mysterious uniqueness of all beings. A divine economy of mutual recognition displaces the Father's consuming ego, however framed as benevolent and self-donating, with the Spirit's erotic We of the whole creation.

Christian theology's disclosure about Spirit articulates the character of this whole-making and holy-making common life. The power of a holistic pneumatology is created in connection with others, not the scarce commodity of the unilateral "I" on whom all others depend to share in the crumbs, but

---

[82]Wetherilt, 146.

the whole and holy-making We of mutual recognition. Thus, from a feminist maternal standpoint, it is inadequate to speak of spirit or Spirit in terms of an individual person. The traditional Trinity portrays God the Spirit as a he, but feminist and feminist-sympathetic attempts to change this identity through female images fall short of the more profound reality of intersubjective life. Spirit constitutes a We, a social infinite composing the textured and complex whole of relational life. Postmodern feminist families challenge the illusory and distorted he-roics of autonomous individuality underlying the patriarchal family and provide instead the model of freedom in egalitarian relationship. The Spirit of new households is not the Spirit of the Father, or the Spirit of the Son, but the liberating bonds of life inclusive of all members of the household. In Trinitarian terms, the Spirit supersedes the Father and the Son toward an incarnate whole appropriately named Spirit.[83] Thus, to invoke the language of Spirit is to invoke an interpersonal, multifaceted life of dignity-in-diversity, a life of both struggle and reconciliation—a transformed shape of solidarity in which family members are freed for love as mutual recognition. The danger in a feminist maternal pneumatology is the reactionary shift from Christocentrism to pneumatocentrism, but the hermeneutical key of mutual recognition between God and creation keeps a pneumatological Trinity from conflating into pneumatological monism. Still, for our time, the theological privilege of pneumatology needs to burn with all its intensity.

Conclusion

We live today within a diverse and interdependent world household. Yet as beautiful and profound as our world can be, from within this house emerge the groans of fear, unrecognized loss, and suffering. Dignity, as the blessing of God the Spirit, provides a pneumatological concept with connections to social movements within and beyond the Christian churches that struggle for justice in our shared household. Through the blessing of the Spirit, persons experience the retrieval of their humanity and intrinsic value as part of God's creation, and are sustained in their struggle for the mutual recognition of their dignity. The struggle entails hopeful conflict and transformation toward the We of a shared humanity without neutralizing differences, but respecting and encouraging the many gifts of all God's people.

Focusing on the pneumatological concept of dignity, Christian theology plays a vital role, not only in the midst of the very public reconciliation struggles of South Africa, Australia, East Timor, and the Balkans, but in the private, anguished struggles of people facing indignities day-to-day. Pneumatology resists accommodating and endorsing the political regimes and market societies of our world that endanger the dignity of humankind and all creation. In re-claiming the Spirit's dignity, can we affirm a reverence for life, a reverence that is not naive, but as profound as it is complex? Can we attune ourselves to the cries and the sighs from within the household walls of families, churches,

---

[83]Hodgson, *Winds of the Spirit*, 276–92.

communities, and nations? How are our theologies helping gifted people walk in the Spirit with dignity through the inevitable conflict that living with dignity entails?

A feminist maternal pneumatology of mutual recognition situates itself not in the doxological mystery of the immanent Trinitarian model, but in the groans and gasps, joys and anguish of postmodern feminist families struggling day-to-day beyond economies of unilateral power, coercion, and subordination. Reflection on the praxis of postmodern feminist families and their new family values contributes to a new poetics in our theologies. In the past lies a brokenhearted, patriarchal model of family life–an economy of domination–that advances the will of the One while subordinating and twisting the wills of others in conformity to the One. In the brave future lies the model of mutual recognition based on values of shared authority, equal regard, proper trust, and diversity-in-dignity.

I have argued that as a result of the re-entrenchment of the patriarchal family ideal, Christian pneumatologies based on this model support a poisonous logic of social relations. Yet by recovering the Spirit's connection with the "household of freedom" and the ecstatic, multigifted "discipleship of equals," a feminist maternal pneumatology of mutual recognition de-centers the patriarchal family model and inspires alternative pneumatological orientations based on democratic, egalitarian ideals.[84] As fiery tongues, voices calling for recognition, dignity, and inclusion, constitute a new hearth in the household of God. Will the raging hearth burn in vain? Or will the Spirit be quenched? Turning toward a new millennium, God the Spirit's multifaceted, emergent struggle for liberated life brings new energy for our interdependent projects of social transformation. May we walk through fire in the Spirit's blessing.

---

[84]See chapter 4. The references are from Letty M. Russell, *Household of Freedom: Authority in Feminist Theology* (Philadelphia: Westminster Press, 1987); and Elisabeth Schüssler Fiorenza, *Discipleship of Equals: A Critical Feminist Ekklesia-logy of Liberation* (New York: Crossroad, 1993).

Author Index

Subject Index